ALONE

ALONE

*A Fascinating Study of
Those Who Have Survived Long,
Solitary Ordeals*

Richard D. Logan, Ph.D.

STACKPOLE
BOOKS

Published by
STACKPOLE BOOKS
5067 Ritter Road
Mechanicsburg, PA 17055

Printed in the United States of America

First Edition

10 9 8 7 6 5 4 3 2 1

Cover design by Mark Olszewski with Christine Mercer

Library of Congress Cataloging-in-Publication Data

Logan, Richard D., 1942–
    Alone : a fascinating study of those who have survived long, solitary
ordeals / Richard D. Logan.
        p.   cm.
    Includes bibliographical references.
    ISBN 0-8117-2500-6
    1. Adaptability (Psychology)   2. Adjustment (Psychology)
3. Survival skills—Case studies.   I. Title.
BF335.L64   1993   92-44228
155.9'35—dc20   CIP

Dedicated to
the memory of my mother, who could have written her own survival story because she lived one; and to the memory of Charles A. Lindbergh, who flew, Sir Francis Chichester, who sailed, Admiral Richard E. Byrd, who endured, and Carl Gustav Jung, who inspired; and to all of the other survivors who, in surviving, became better people.

Contents

Acknowledgments

Many thanks to Hope Mercier, Carol Logan, David Logan, my editors Judith Schnell, David Uhler, and Mary McGinnis, Tere Locke, John Giefer, Jean Broeren, Mary Berken, Michael Collins, Col. Ray Fredette, Reeve Lindbergh, Lady Sheila Chichester, and the staff at the Social Psychology Research Unit.

Foreword

In some ways we are all survivors, as each of us faces ordeals at times. Yet few of us are forced to endure these ordeals truly alone. I was one of those few.

I survived the murder of my family aboard the yacht *Bluebelle* when I was eleven years old. After I escaped by jumping overboard, I spent the next four days adrift on the ocean in a tiny cork raft, a solitary ordeal outlined in Chapter One.

In a way, I am still surviving my ordeal alone. No other person has been through my ordeal so I have felt that it would be difficult for most to understand or relate to my experience. But I have been aware that I harbor many complex feelings deep within me—like many other survivors, I controlled my feelings and memories by hiding them. Until I read Richard Logan's manuscript, I hadn't even allowed myself the freedom of telling my story.

At times I have been troubled by "survivor guilt": Could I have done something to save my family? Why was I the one who survived? Does God have some special mission for me? While I have tried not to dwell on these questions or spend my life searching for the answers, the guilt surfaces often enough.

After I survived my uniquely horrific experience, I discovered a strength in myself that I didn't know I had. As a result, I have always felt obligated to be strong of character, courageous, and a noble example of someone who is supposedly stronger than most people. Consequently, I have sometimes had to be someone I am not, when indeed, all I have wanted is to be left alone and unnoticed. On the other hand, I do realize that in some ways I *am* stronger than most. While I remain an ordinary person in most ways, I have had a lesson in self-reliance to last a lifetime. I proved to myself how much it is possible to take and still survive.

Since my ordeal, I have had a hunger for knowledge of others who have been through solitary ordeals. Reading about others who have struggled to survive similar experiences takes me away from my own situation and gives me support and the realization that I am no longer alone. Thus, I have gradually become more able to deal with my own feelings of sorrow and guilt.

Regardless of the circumstances, all of us who have survived solitary ordeals share a common bond. We all know the true meaning of "alone." My hope for this book is not just that it will help other survivors feel less alone, but that it will help all who read it find the courage to face whatever difficulties may come along in their lives.

Tere Locke

Preface

This book is partly the product of one of those happy accidents that occur too rarely in life. A few years ago I was asked to develop a course at the University of Wisconsin-Green Bay—a school that prides itself on its innovative approaches to education—on the psychology of human adaptability to stress. It just happened that at the time I was reading *Alive*,[1] the story of the Uruguayan rugby team that crashed in the Andes. While I was casting around for ways to make a course on psychological adaptation interesting, it occurred to me that such real-life stories of people struggling to cope with ordeals—those voluntarily chosen as well as those unwillingly endured—might have strong human interest value while also being vivid object lessons in coping and adaptation. As I read more and more of these books and began to realize the treasure of psychological insights that they contained, both on and beneath the surface, I began outlining and collecting excerpts for a book.

My original purpose in writing this book was to use the real-life experiences of survivors to illustrate the psychological effects of solitary hardship and to exemplify mechanisms ordinary people use for coping with that kind of stress—to write, in other words, a book on "how to cope" with extreme ordeals based on accounts by people who knew firsthand. Although many books on survival have been written, and there are many first-person accounts of survival ordeals, no one has yet to my knowledge tried to use the writings of actual survivors as illustrations of the many dimensions of coping. Fortunately, many survivors of ordeals have written remarkably insightful accounts of their experiences that are far more enlightening than accounts written by "experts." It seemed to me that such an approach to the "psychology of coping" would have far more real-world meaning and would be far more compelling to readers than relating dry experimental studies on the effects of stress, sensory deprivation, and so on. Besides, it was more enjoyable to search for apt illustrations by reading gripping first-person accounts. Shortly after beginning this project, however, it became clear that I would have to address more than my original goal. I soon felt I had to try to communicate something of the extent of the hardships faced by various survivors and of the frequently dramatic and moving nature of their ordeals, and I have therefore begun the book in this vein.

Other ideas as well soon began to take on a life of their own. As I began to search for clues as to *why* certain people coped successfully, and why they sometimes even actively sought solitary adversity, the personalities and backgrounds of survivors and adventurers emerged as an important topic. The book at this point becomes more a study of the "psychology of adventure" and a character study of the solitary adventurers Charles Lindbergh, Francis Chichester, and Richard Byrd. The focus here becomes one of trying to answer the question: What is "the Right Stuff"?

Several insights into "human nature" have emerged from this exercise. One concerns the "sense of self" of successful copers. They seem to be more "I" than "me." (This enigmatic point will be elaborated later, but basically I mean that even though they are utterly alone, they are less self-conscious than some of the rest of us—they manage not to dwell on themselves.) Another concerns the fact that even extreme solitary ordeals are not always just devastating; they sometimes yield growth, suggesting a human "need" to tackle and overcome challenge and adversity—a need that perhaps reflects our evolutionary heritage of struggling to survive. But challenge and adversity also provide a perhaps needed and healthy balance to the extreme introspection, self-analysis, and passive consumption that come with modern life. The solitary ordeal can be one way to get "out" of oneself. Paradoxically, however, the experience of real adversity may be a modern form of the ancient "spirit quest" that eventually turns the individual back "inward" again toward self-knowledge—though in a way radically different from passive introspection—and toward the eventual achievement of balance between inward-looking and outward-looking tendencies. It may in fact be the goal to achieve this different kind of self-discovery that motivates both solitary adventurers and some of the survivors of involuntary ordeals. There do appear to be significant instances of such "self-discovery" (admittedly a term whose meaning is not at all clear and that gets tossed around far too much) in the survivors of ordeals, especially those who sought voluntary quests, and some do seem to emerge as more balanced, complex, and "whole" individuals. This latter phenomenon emerges as a major theme of the book.

Why look at *solitary* ordeals? Besides having to start somewhere and with a manageable topic, I was struck by the fact that the solitary ordeal is a powerful metaphor for modern individualism, with its emphasis on finding one's own way in life. Indeed, when Thoreau commented that we all tend to live "lives of quiet desperation," he seemed to be saying that life itself is, or can be, a solitary ordeal. And I think in a way he was right, except I would argue that we have made ordinary life into far more of an ordeal than it needs to be, and that we have in our self-conscious awareness of ourselves become far too ready to see ourselves as victims of any number of annoying and irritating things. I think our nation of complainers—or at least those of us who are truly *privileged* complainers—could benefit from looking at the experiences of some people who really had something to complain about, but who complained so little.

Notes

[1] Read, Pears P. *Alive: The Story of the Andes Plane Crash Survivors.* New York: Lippincott, 1974.

CHAPTER ONE

Staying Alive

"... so long as the mind says 'Yes,' the wretched
worn-out human body cannot say 'No.'"
————Herbert Best, *Parachute to Survival*

"Black coffee, please. And a couple of doughnuts."
————First words of a rescued life raft survivor

Survival stories are many things: tales of high adventure, derring-do, courage, humanity, and tragedy; testimonials to the "indomitability of the human spirit" and a message of hope that the human race will continue to endure; compelling object lessons in the extraordinary ability of humans to adapt to all kinds of adversity—to take far more than we might ever imagine; escapist reading for those who, suffering the vague stresses of a humdrum existence, yearn for more dramatic and invigorating challenges, even if experienced only vicariously; goads to overcome one's personal demons (if others can survive torture, starvation, isolation, freezing, imprisonment, degradation, and so on, then one surely can overcome his or her own comparatively puny neuroses); outlets for the morbidly curious who relish tales of starving, broken, tortured, and even cannibalistic human beings; vicarious encounters with pain and suffering that make one's own present condition seem even more secure and comfortable by comparison. Finally, survival stories are allegories for the human condition, for although some may feel far removed from the day-to-day struggle to survive, there is no escaping the issue of life and death for anyone.

The *solitary* protagonist especially captures the popular imagination in our individualistic society, ever since a newspaper cartoonist during Charles Lindbergh's flight drew a simple picture of a tiny plane winging alone against a backdrop of looming clouds over the ocean— and an entire nation identified with the lone figure who was its pilot. A nation built on "individualism" can much more readily identify with the "lonely survivor" than with a group undergoing an ordeal. The solitary ordeal also is a more obvious vehicle for talking about psychological issues than is a group ordeal. We have of course long revered the solitary hero who seems to belong to no place and no person other than himself (Daniel Boone, the Lone Ranger, Charles Lindbergh, the hardboiled detective, Rambo, Dirty Harry, etc.). This reflects our culture's distrust of people acting collectively and our fear of the submersion of the individual ego into the faceless mass. Our reverence of the "individual" leads us to see the town, city, or society as somehow corrupting the individual self. It is as if we believe that only the truly solitary person can be a truly moral person— one who can ride off into the sunset and be free of the corruption that will inevitably seep back into the town that he (usually "he" in our mythology) has just "cleaned up." Indeed, many survival stories are also, in their way, morality plays: The individual of principle is victimized by the forces of evil, or sometimes by the forces of nature. Simply consider the survival stories that came out of the concentration camps and POW camps of World War II, for example. Or the story of a courageous Papillon struggling to maintain his dignity in the ignominy of a filthy solitary confinement. And, in fact, by a great many of the standards we would ordinarily apply, many survivors do become significantly better people morally—more forgiving, more compassionate, more patient, more balanced in their sense of the right and the wrong.

People seem to be especially drawn to stories of heroic individual adventure and the struggle to survive during challenging eras in history. During forward-looking, outward-looking periods when adversity is faced with optimism, a society favors stories of individuals who successfully overcome impossible odds, like a Teddy Roosevelt, a Lindbergh, a Ricken- backer, or the heroes of Horatio Alger earlier in the century. Such heroes seem always to refuse to sense themselves as victims, even if they are placed in that role. (Conversely, some people today seem only too willing to see themselves as victims even though they are placed in comparative comfort and security, troubled mostly by the neuroses that come with a lack of meaning in one's life.) During pessimistic, inward-looking times, on the other hand, stories become popular in which people struggle hope- lessly against immeasurable horrors and succumb to monsters, natural cataclysms, and bizarre creations of science. Examples of this are the science fiction monster movies of the Depression Thirties and, to a degree, the recent films of shake-and-bake disasters, high-technology catastrophes, and demonic space aliens against which humans are nearly helpless. Such dramas seem to represent a widespread tendency today for people to see themselves as victims, even if they are not necessarily placed in that role. It is almost as if suppressing the need to tackle real, concrete challenges causes it to come back to haunt us in bizarre forms—for instance, in the "thrills" derived from drugs, sky diving, or bungee jumping, or in the craze for finding ever more daunting roller coaster rides in amusement parks.

Survival tales fascinate for many other reasons as well, and one is their dramatic power. Some of the most moving episodes in the human experience can be found in such real-life scenes as the following:

Plane crash survivor Nando Parrado, half-starved, freezing, and exhausted from two days of climbing (and previous weeks of surviving a snow-bound hell with his starving companions high in the Andes), finally struggles to a snow-covered summit from which he believes he will see the green Andean foothills and a path to help and safety for him and his stranded comrades. He sees instead, extending to the far horizon, still more snow-capped mountains and is overwhelmed, for a moment, by helpless rage. He weeps in angry frustration and almost gives up, but he looks around, realizing how much he has accomplished, and pride and determination replace his rage and despair. He has achieved a personal summit, a moment of triumph and self-revelation. He will survive. He will walk out of the mountains to find help for his dying comrades—and be a genuine hero.

In 1936 Admiral Richard Byrd lived for nearly five months alone in a tiny, isolated weather hut buried in the ancient ice during the antarctic night, tortured by the endless darkness, the utter stillness, and his "immense" (his word) isolation, all the while slowly dying from the rigors of starvation, 60-below-zero temperatures, carbon monoxide poisoning from a faulty stove, and exhaustion. Unwilling to radio for help for fear of endangering a rescue party, somehow he endures and plods through his daily routine. But his increasingly erratic radio telegraph transmissions betray his precarious condition to his home base, and successive rescue parties push out to reach him, only to fall back each time because of blizzards and equipment failures. Byrd meanwhile seems to agonize more about the safety of the rescue parties (who, in an unspoken old-fashioned gentleman's agreement, never acknowledge that they are in fact coming to rescue him, but say instead that they are coming to observe meteor showers) than he does about his own situation, but his need for help is nonetheless desperate and his longing for companionship equally strong. For days he forces his weakening body out of his ice-bound hut to stare into the deep black polar night for signs of the rescue party, and to set off flares to guide them toward him. At long last, he sees one day in the far blackness the glow of snow tractor headlights that mean that other human beings are coming to join him in the void. Ever the stoic, and the gentleman, his first gesture is to invite them in for food. They in turn try to hide their horror at finding him an emaciated and scabby skeleton.

Eleven-year-old Terry Jo Duperrault, daughter of an American family on their dream cruise in the Caribbean, goes to sleep after an idyllic day of sailing through the Bahamas and is jolted awake to the sudden horror of her family being murdered around her by the berserk charter skipper. As she struggles to gain and keep her senses in the nightmare into which she has abruptly awakened, she cowers below in her bunk until she realizes the cabin is filling with water and the boat sinking. In an extra-ordinary exercise in self-discipline, she flashes back to the pretend jungle survival games she used to play as a little girl alone in the woods and, in that mode, remembers a life raft lashed to the deck topside. In the dark of night she sneaks up on deck, manages to avoid the charter skipper, unties the raft, throws it overboard, and jumps in after it. As the ship sinks, a line from the raft remains snagged on it, and Terry Jo and the raft begin to be pulled under, but the rope slips free and the raft bobs back up to the surface.

A few moments after sleeping snugly with her family around her, Terry Jo is drifting alone at night on the vast sea, facing her second sur-vival ordeal and trying to comprehend what has just happened to her. As she begins this second ordeal, a brief shower surrounds her with eerily beautiful sparks as the drops of rain set off the phosphorus in the water. She drifts for days, slowly dying from thirst, hearing her father's voice, being kept company by a pod of pilot whales, and seeing islands that aren't there. Four days later a Greek freighter diverts by chance from its usual course and steams through Providence Channel in the Bahamas. A lookout spots a white object on the sea, first discounts it as a small fishing boat, then realizes that no fishing dinghy would be out so far. They stop, and the sea delivers up to them, alone on its vast emptiness and barely alive, a beautiful blonde child.

Maurice Herzog, the first man to climb the forbidding Annapurna in the Himalayas alone, reaches the peak of that mountain after a grueling climb that has nearly killed him. Then, in his elation at succeeding, he lingers too long in the numbing cold and thin air of the summit taking pictures. Spent, he turns finally to descend and, as he does so, fumbles and drops his insulated gloves. He watches as they tumble down the mountain, knowing that all hope of avoiding frostbite has gone with them, and that, if he survives at all, he will never again be physically whole.

Mountaineer Joe Simpson survives a severe fall high in the Andes and breaks his leg. When his partner tries to lower him down the long, sheer side of the mountain, he loses control and both nearly fall to their death. His partner manages to anchor himself just above a cliff, leaving Joe dangling over a dark void for hours. Finally, his partner, who cannot move with Joe's dead weight on the end of the rope—and who probably assumes Joe is dead from this second fall—cuts the rope. Joe falls, bouncing off the side of the mountain and slamming to a stop on a ledge. As marooned as before, and realizing that his partner now surely believes he is dead, Joe cannot climb up by himself, and he cannot see what lies below him. After some hours he decides to lower himself on his rope, secured by a single ice screw, favoring the dark unknown over the certainty of death on the ledge. Before his rope runs out he reaches the bottom of a huge crevasse, which threatens to entomb him forever. Strangely, he is overpowered by the sense that the icy crevasse is a sacred place. He discerns what may be a way out, if he can only manage to crawl up the inside of the steep outer wall of the crevasse. Somehow he manages to do this and eventually tumbles through a hole in the wall to the outside world. And yet his ordeal has only begun. For the next three days he crawls, rolls, slides, drags himself, and hops (on one leg) back to his base camp. As he becomes more and more exhausted during his Long Crawl he begins to hear a disembodied voice that gives him orders and instructions. He obeys the voice.

Although it is not a solitary ordeal, surely one of the greatest survival dramas of all time is that of the crew of the fittingly named exploration ship *Endurance*, marooned for one and one-half years in the Antarctic after their ship is caught and then slowly crushed in pressure ice. Constantly wet and always cold, in danger of starving and drowning, they live at first in tents on ice floes until these begin to split apart under their feet. Then they take to their small boats and navigate the treacherous passages between the heaving floes. Finally they come to rest on a barren, isolated, windy island near the antarctic continent that might as well be the moon as far as chances of ever being rescued. Realizing this, their leader, Ernest Shackleton, takes one boat and a small crew and sets off to seek help, sailing and rowing across 800 miles of the world's most stormy, windy ocean toward the tiny island of South Georgia, which supports a small whaling station. His chances of finding that pinpoint of land in that frigid sea are remote, and both he and those he has left behind know it. But the marooned crew waits for months, constantly revising their estimates of how long before Shackleton could reach help, get a rescue ship, and return. Then one day, long after hope has dwindled, a ship appears offshore. On the deck, just discernible, is the silhouetted figure of their leader. Shackleton and his two companions have somehow reached the island (a monumental survival story in itself), trekked overland for three days across rugged mountains (professional climbers who have since tried it have marveled at this feat alone), and walked, gaunt and tattered specters, into the whaling station. And now he is returning to rescue his men, *all* of whom have survived nearly two years since their ordeal began. *Endurance* indeed. And leadership. Small wonder that it was said of Shackleton:

> For scientific leadership give me Scott; for swift and efficient travel, Amundsen; but when you are in a hopeless situation, when there seems no way out, get down on your knees and pray for Shackleton.

One of the most sadly tragic stories of solitary survival is that of Jan Little. Her life had been marginal and difficult for some time, as she and her husband, caught up in the Sixties search for alternative lives close to nature, had eventually isolated themselves with their young daughter on a lonely hillside homestead deep in the remote upper reaches of the Amazon, far from any other people. Jan was already nearly deaf and legally blind when fever struck all of them, causing her to lose still more sight and hearing. As if this were not enough, she had also to contend with the unreality caused by her delirium. Her daughter died first. This Jan discovered when she went to look for her outside of their hut and stumbled over the body. Her husband lingered for many days. After he died, Jan carried on by feeling her way around the hut and its food stores and by making her way by touch to their garden in the jungle. She managed like this in her dark and silent world for some months. One day as she was sitting and resting, a warm touch made her start. It was a human hand.

I could also add here a long list of hostages and prisoners and their ordeals. Stories of endurance and heroism abound. For example, there is Sir Geoffrey Jackson, an exceptionally articulate writer who was held prisoner for many months by South American guerrillas. There is also the case of Brigadier General James Dozier, a hostage of the Red Brigades in Italy, and the more recent cases of the American, French, British, and German hostages in Teheran and Beirut, such as Terry Waite and Terry Anderson.

The fact that so many works of survival fiction exist attests to how gripping a theme survival is. Indeed, it is one of the major themes in Canadian literature, befitting their long northern frontier and solitary pioneering history. (It is also, of course, a theme in American literature for similar reasons, though not to the same extent.)

The qualities portrayed and the emotions stirred in the scenes above are elemental: courage and fear, love and faith, despair and hope. The issue is primeval—survival. In that sense, the study of how people behave in extreme situations, and of how they cope with them, is nothing more than the study of what has been commonplace during much of human evolution: the constant, never-ending struggle to stay alive in trying circumstances. Surrounded by a cushion of culture, technology, and supportive institutions, most of us seldom face the issue of survival with the minute-to-minute, day-to-day immediacy of our ancestors—or of our less fortunate contemporaries. (Having spent two years of my life in Africa, I find it curious to observe that the American middle and upper-middle classes have by far the greater talent for complaining about life's supposed hardships.) We only see this aspect of the human heritage replayed in the heroic struggles of those who find themselves, whether by fate, personal choice, or the malicious design of others, torn loose from the protection of culture and social networks and abandoned in some remote, hostile, "uncivilized" environment.

Yet humans are all still equipped for such struggles. We are in many ways tough—evolution has made us that way—despite the popular psychology industry's attempts to play on our fragilities and dependencies. Many, indeed, seek out solitary ordeals, a fact that is one of the major themes of this book. In surviving ordeals, ancient mechanisms that are the product of the ancestral struggle against danger are activated: The "general adaptation syndrome" mobilizes the body to cope with threats to survival (heart rate goes up, eyes dilate, adrenaline flows). The body is prepared for "fight or flight." Over prolonged periods, however, this mobilization is wearing—it becomes *stress*. The tendency to flee from danger, or fight it, plus the tendencies to approach and consume food and to reproduce, are perhaps the most ancient of all animal survival behaviors—and they are still very much present, very much a part of the human character, as can be readily observed in people under duress. In fact, extreme stress can be helpfully understood as the prolonged mobilization of *both* "fight" (anger) and "flight" (fear) responses at the same time, without the ability to act them out overtly. Such a state of continuing conflicted arousal is extremely exhausting to the body and is one way of looking at post-traumatic stress disorder. Anger and fear are opposing emotions, and if both are continually aroused at the same time they both use up energy working against each other. Arousal that does not turn into activity merely exhausts.

Other bodily equipment also evolved out of the struggle to survive: humans' eyes face front and are stereoscopic, enabling them to gauge the distance between themselves and danger (or food); upright posture means hands are free for grasping clubs and rocks to use as weapons to protect the now-exposed midsection (or for using tools); the human mind weighs and balances options, formulates plans. Humans are, in part, *problem-solving creatures*, equipped by evolution to face and overcome concrete challenges that come from "out there." It is worth remembering that surviving is something that human beings have evolved to be "good at"—better at, perhaps, than at "understanding themselves," a much more recent focus in human history that has come about with "modern" self-consciousness (and which is the stuff of modern psychology). This may be one of the reasons for the popularity of wilderness survival programs such as Outward Bound, which enable us to get out of our modern self-involved mode and back into the mode of dealing with external challenges—obviously the mode that characterized humans during most of our history, until modern technology and modern self-consciousness.

What is an "ordeal"? I have chosen in this book to concentrate on survival stories—accounts of people placed in life-threatening situations as the result of plane crashes, mountaineering mishaps, imprisonment, solitary exploration, hostage taking, and the like. The episodes are mostly "outdoor" and many are associated with adventure of some sort.

There are many kinds of ordeals—both solitary and otherwise—that are not covered in this book. Many come from "domestic" life: surviving a long history of abuse, surviving rape, coping with severe long-term illness, being stalked, living with chronic intractable pain, surviving

mental illness, living alone in an urban apartment in terror of the crime
outside one's door. Indeed, many of these kinds of ordeals, even if occurring while surrounded by loved ones, are in some ways as solitary as
the ones I describe in this book. It was not a casual choice of title when
the great American sociologist David Riesman called his famous study
of the American character *The Lonely Crowd*.[1] Many people who have to
live with a painful secret kept hidden from those around them, or who
undergo the kind of psychic pain that others simply cannot understand,
go through their ordeals in a profoundly solitary way.

   Although most people will recognize an ordeal when they see one,
I will attempt a definition. By "ordeal," I am referring to the following
set of circumstances:

   1. A situation of prolonged physical suffering, pain, and debilitation
   2. A prolonged threat to life
   3. The prolonged stress of fear and arousal
   4. Being forced to live with one's freedom severely confined by
      circumstances
   5. Having to cope with prolonged and extreme uncertainty
   6. Facing demands that constantly threaten to overwhelm one's
      physical and psychological resources.

   It only remains to add that I am referring to situations where all of
the above are faced by someone utterly alone.

Surviving and Adapting

It is informative to view various psychological processes as mechanisms
for adapting to one's environment (and it is surprising to discover how
seldom such a perspective on psychology is taken).

Instinctive Behavior as Adaptive

Instinct and adaptation are two sides of the same coin, since instincts are
simply those behaviors that have evolved because they helped make
adaptation and survival possible. (Remember the logic of the theory of
evolution: Organisms that happen to have genetic traits that make their
survival more likely are the ones that will survive to mate and pass
those same traits on to following generations.) The simplest of the
evolved or instinctive behaviors are the protective (adaptive) reflexes—
eye blink, sneezing, grasping, sucking, and swallowing, for example—
which contribute to the survival of the organism by protecting against
or removing threatening stimuli or by acquiring essential food.

Another reflex critical to adaptation and survival is the so-called "orienting reflex"—the reaction of looking toward and focusing attention on the source of a sudden, new, or unusual stimulus (loud noise, sudden movement, looming shadow) in one's environment. The survival value of such a reflex is obvious, as is its essential role in the coping mechanisms of *vigilance*, *appraisal*, and *information gathering*.

There has also been speculation about a "maternal instinct" that helps to ensure that infants get proper care, the survival value of which is also obvious. Speculation has also centered on an "attachment instinct" in infants—a tendency to "bond" with, stay close to, seek out, and summon a mothering figure. Such an attachment or "bonding" instinct is said to be manifested in the visual fixation on the mother's face, in infant smiling, and in crying to attract attention—instinctive behaviors that elicit the maternal instinct and thus contribute to survival. Although the adaptiveness of such behaviors is clear, the case for their being inherited rather than learned has not been made convincingly.

Emotions and Adaptation

Emotions are important in the adaptive process as motives or "drives" that energize adaptive behavior—fear motivates avoidance ("flight"), anger motivates attack ("fight"), pleasure motivates approach.

The most primitive "emotions" may in fact be pleasure and pain. Pleasure motivates approach to food and to sexual partners. Out of the tendency to approach a sexual partner could well have evolved the additional emotion of "love," and out of efforts to recapture a lost love object could have evolved the emotion of "grief." The drive of pain led on the one hand to the emotion of fear, which motivated avoidance, and on the other hand to anger, which motivated attack. Similarly, the emotions of distaste and disgust could have evolved from the action of spitting out unpalatable food. The facial expression of disgust is in fact very similar to that for a bad taste in the mouth.

Fear and anxiety are of course major human emotions, and as Freud, Jung, and others have persuasively argued, humans fear themselves, or, more accurately, their own unconscious impulses or desires (by which Freud meant sex and aggression), as much as or more than they fear many external things. Thus there is a profound human tendency to avoid self-knowledge, especially of what lies on our own hidden darker side—the unconscious. Once patterns of avoidance are established they are difficult to get rid of, because such behaviors are always rewarded by the resulting reduction in anxiety or fear. Thus humans *continue* to avoid self-knowledge (as well as situations in their environments that provoke fear). Since ordeals are precisely the kind of situations where defenses can begin to get worn down, they are prime situations for the unconscious to begin to reveal itself and therefore for self-knowledge to develop—if one is open to what emerges from one's unconscious.

There is also the question of the effects of *levels* of emotional arousal on coping and adaptation. A great deal of research—and common sense—support the conclusions that moderate levels of emotional arousal are most successful in signaling and mobilizing effective coping behavior. Mild fear leads to complacency and little adaptive response; extreme terror leads to panic ("run in circles, scream and shout") or to paralysis, as well as to tunnel vision and disrupted thought processes. Moderate fear effectively mobilizes the body without disrupting vigilance, problem solving, and decisive action.

All of the same points could be made about levels of anger and passion as well. A "raging bull" is not very capable of thinking or acting in the most effective way, although in rare, no-choice-but-fight, back-to-the-wall situations, a desperate animalistic rage may be most effective. (Need I add that extreme "love" can also lead to highly maladaptive behavior!)

It is interesting in light of the above that military training seeks to evoke hate and anger and put them to use in the military arts, while at the same time trying to discipline and control these emotions. Military trainers know that anger ("hating one's enemy") is a powerful motivator but that uncontrolled anger leads to ineffective action. By the same token, the military provides a controlled outlet for the aggression of many (particularly young men, the most dangerous aggressors on the planet) who might otherwise go in other directions.

As has been said by others, adaptive behavior occurs at a cost. Prolonged arousal (stress) of the body is fatiguing to tissues and organ systems, and certain diseases of stress (hypertension, asthma, arthritis) may occur after long-term arousal of fear, anger, and/or grief. Some of the fatigue stems from the additional energy expended to control and suppress these feelings.

One major means of regulating emotions and avoiding emotional disruption in human beings, given our mental development, is *cognitive control*. We can use our mental abilities, for example, to label things in ways that are less emotionally disrupting than they might be otherwise.

Medical students, for example, don't use the familiar and upsetting term "dead person." They use instead the more clinical and dehumanized label "cadaver." When the Uruguayan rugby team stranded in the high Andes faced the prospect of eating their dead friends' bodies in order to survive, one device that helped them do so was to call their friends' flesh "protein"—a label even further removed than "cadaver" from "my dead friend Juan." (The various cultural taboos surrounding dead bodies, sexuality, and the like may similarly be means of insulating people from emotionally disruptive situations.)

Cognitive or intellectual abilities enter into the regulation of emotions in other ways. Our intellectual beliefs can have a profound impact on the state of our emotions. In close-knit, preindustrial societies, for example, the belief that one has been bewitched and therefore made totally outcast can create, in extreme cases, such a degree of terror that the normally steady autonomic nervous system ceases to function properly, the heart begins to beat irregularly and eventually starts to fibrillate (twitch irregularly), and the person dies—so-called "voodoo death."

The intellect thus can serve both to control emotions and to avoid them—or to release them in an overpowering flood if control fails. On the other side of the coin, however, the mind can function in just the opposite way: not as a series of mental devices for avoiding feelings, but as a means for *contacting* them and making them known so we can deal with them more effectively. Freud termed this "insight"—"where id is, let ego be also." The intellect can be applied to *understanding* the sources of our anxieties and can help in defusing them, because once we know what is bothering us, it emerges from the dark unknown and takes on less awesome dimensions, reducing our anxiety and also releasing some of the energy formerly used by the defense mechanisms to create new ways of dealing with the world.

Major questions for later consideration: What distinguishes people who use the mind to avoid the unconscious from those who use it to *seek* the unconscious? What role do ordeals play for those seeking to contact their unconscious?

Learned Behavior as Adaptive

What we learn—and the *ability* to learn has obviously also evolved—contributes directly to our ability to remain adapted to our environment, because learning involves either (1) responding to the demands of the environment and thereby becoming adjusted to it, (2) imitating the usually effective behavior of others (such as parents) in one's surroundings ("observation learning"), or (3) shaping behavior into more effective patterns based on its environmental consequences—in other words, behaving in ways that get rewarded ("operant conditioning"). To the extent that new environments resemble old familiar ones, old behavior will be adapted to them ("positive transfer of training"). In a new situation, one will adapt successfully if new responses can be acquired quickly enough; if not, old established habits may get in the way of the adaptation to a new situation ("negative transfer of training").

The fact that we respond in similar ways to similar circumstances ("stimulus generalization") has obvious survival value: It enables quick responses, and it saves a great deal of energy and memory storage capacity that would otherwise be used to completely catalog every tiny difference from situation to situation.

Thinking and Reasoning as Adaptive

Cognition, or thinking and reasoning about the world, also enables adaptation to the world. Cognition consists of internal images, or "maps," of the world. The more accurately these mental maps portray the environment, the more adapted one is—and the more likely that new ideas or solutions derived from the manipulation of these mental images ("problem solving") will lead to realistic, adaptive courses of action in the real world. Mental maps also contribute to adaptation because much of the time, if our maps are "close enough" to accurate, we make the world fit into our maps (as well as adjusting them to fit the world), and thus we can function as if the world and our maps match perfectly even when they don't. This makes us free to focus on other things that may be unusual and require special attention. This is highly adaptive because it enables us to deal with change, complexity, and new situations by seeing them as if they were old and familiar—an act of psychological economy that usually out-weighs the negative consequences of slight misreadings of the world.

Thinking relates to adaptation in more specific ways as well. The accurate understanding and labeling of things and events are important to adaptation, but sometimes we may need to protect ourselves from emotional trauma by not experiencing the full horrible truth about something; therefore we mislabel an event so as not to experience its devastating impact. In such cases the "horrible truth" may register only in the unconscious, and the powers of reasoning may be put to use to continue to disguise it (as in when we "intellectualize" about the trauma of war—talking about it in abstract terms of strategy, tactics, "casualties," "collateral damage," and the like rather than in terms of blowing living persons into bloody bits). Our powers of reasoning thus can allow us to detach ourselves from trauma. Later, intellectual powers may be used in the effort to gain insight into episodes and conflicts that cause us anxiety and that we blocked away in our unconscious. Once again, accurate labeling becomes important, as identifying our own emotional states helps us to realize what makes us anxious. The disguising (mislabeling, ignoring) of the contents of one's own unconscious is simply one of a store of protective devices known as *defense mechanisms*, which are discussed in the next section. Accurate labeling of both internal and external events, however, may be critically important in actively coping with the unusual during crisis situations, rather than trying to avoid dealing with such things.

Freudian Psychology and Adaptation

Viewed from the standpoint of the psychology of adaptation, Freudian psychology concerns itself with (1) regulation and control of feelings and circumstances (by the "ego" and "superego") and (2) how motivation (unconscious "id impulses" such as libido, or the "sex drive," and aggression) influences the way we adapt and cope. The theory also offers an intriguing interpretation as to how certain *adaptive styles* originate from early life experiences and, of course, has provided the all-important concept of defense mechanisms. Defense mechanisms are ways in which unconscious material is either repressed in the unconscious or disguised in some way so that we don't recognize what it really is when it does come out. (We may, for example, intellectualize our sexual desires by talking about sexuality and sexual morality, thus expressing some of our sexual feelings without realizing that they are what really motivates our "intellectual" interest.)

The ego (Freud's term for our perceiving, learning, and reasoning abilities) plays two key roles in adaptation: First, the ego is responsible for adapting to the world around us. It is also the executive decision maker within the personality, having the responsibility of finding outlets for id impulses (sex and aggression) that will not result in conflict with society or with the moralistic superego. The ego is therefore in the position of having to make perpetual *compromises* between the insistent needs of the id for expression and the demands of society and the superego for the regulation or even suppression of such impulses. In order to handle this state of conflict, the ego frequently relies on the protective devices of the defense mechanisms.

The above illustrates a major point concerning the psychology of adaptation: namely, that *adaptation is almost always a compromise*—one gains an adaptive benefit always at some psychological cost, in energy for example. If one relies heavily on defense mechanisms (to control anxiety-provoking impulses, for instance), one gains the benefit of reduced anxiety but at the cost of energy devoted to controlling one's impulses that is then not available to deal with problems of external reality. Highly "defended" (i.e., "neurotic") people are therefore less able to adapt to their worlds because they lack the energy to do so. The principle of compromise can be illustrated outside the framework of Freudian psychology as well: If one specializes in coping with certain problems well, one pays the cost of not being able to cope with different problems—what evolutionary theorists call "overspecialization." Many individuals' behavior is similarly overspecialized.

As far as the role *motivation* plays in adaptation, everything in life, according to Freud, is motivated ultimately either by sexual energy (libido) and the search for gratification or by aggression (or the "death wish"). In order for energy to be available for adaptation to the environment, sexual (and aggressive) energy must be "sublimated"—displaced into activities other than overt sex or hostility. Curiosity, for example, is adaptive, and it is motivated (believe it or not) according to Freud by rechanneled sexual desires. Striving to overcome obstacles and to become "successful" is also adaptive, and motivated perhaps by sublimated aggression. If, however, energy should become "fixated" on a certain primitive mode of gaining gratification (such as passively through the mouth, as is the dominant mode in infancy), then a great deal of energy will continue to be devoted throughout life toward seeking that same kind of "oral gratification" in the same primitive, passive way. Such an individual will tend always to cope with life by being passive and dependent and waiting for others to "feed" him what he needs. If energy has been thus fixated, the behavioral style has been made narrow and less flexible, and less energy is available to power other adaptive behaviors.

Fixations at any of the first three stages of life (oral, anal, and phallic) tend to produce lifelong personality traits or adaptive styles based upon the mode of behavior associated with that zone of the body (the mouth is associated with passively "taking in," the anus with stubbornly "holding on," the genitals [here Freud shows his male-centered bias] with actively "intruding"). In most people such fixations are usually mild, and the resulting rigidity in behavior and the cost of energy are usually slight. The individual whose approach to life is slightly cynical, pessimistic, distrustful, and one of never expecting to get much is likely to have a slight negative oral fixation stemming perhaps from severe weaning. The stubborn, stingy, miserly, obstinate, compulsively organized individual who tries to do everything "just so" is trying to cope by guardedly "holding on" to what he has. This coping style, according to the theory, stems from extreme assaults on one's sense of autonomy and control over one's own body, creating a profound sense of self-doubt for which one compensates by trying extremely hard to be in control of oneself (hence the obsessive-compulsive rituals). If a young child was rewarded positively for superficially sexual behavior, he or she is likely to have become fixated on the use of "intrusive" seductive charm as a way of getting along in life. (Such a style might work in some situations, but obviously would not be adaptive in all.)

All of the above styles are only narrowly adaptive.

Strong fixations, by siphoning off energy and rigidifying adaptive behavior into stereotyped modes of action (such as oral-dependent, anal-compulsive, phallic-seductive), take energy from the ego, making it harder for the ego to find reasonable ways to meet the needs of the id in the outside world. In order to keep the id under control, the ego begins to rely on the unconscious defense mechanisms, which use up still more adaptive energy.

The Freudian defense mechanisms have been exhaustively described in hundreds of places, so I will deal with them only in outline form. Essentially the defense mechanisms are means of *blocking* from awareness, *disguising*, or *rechanneling* impulses or memories within us that would provoke intolerable anxiety—at least we believe they would—if they were experienced for what they really are. Defense mechanisms, in short, enable us to avoid experiencing things that unsettle us. They are one of the major means of trying to cope with anxiety, but they exact the cost of consuming our energy, and they can lead into the lifelong patterns of anxiety-avoidance rituals that are commonly called neuroses. (When used in the short run to deal with a sudden trauma, however, defense mechanisms may be far more beneficial than harmful.)

The least sophisticated and most energy-consuming defense mechanism is simple *repression*. Repression is the damming up, by sheer expenditure of energy, of unsettling thoughts, memories, and impulses in the unconscious. Repression is the classic "blocking" defense mechanism. A related "blocking" mechanism is *denial*—refusing to perceive something that has happened ("Oh my God! I *didn't* cut my finger!").

The disguising types of defense mechanisms include *projection*, attributing one's own unacceptable sexual and/or aggressive impulses to someone else, and *reaction formation*, trying to replace what one really feels with the opposite emotion ("I just *adore* your brand new house!").

The rechanneling mechanisms include *displacement* (for instance, tearing up your garden instead of your boss) and *sublimation*, expending sexual and aggressive energy by using them to energize enterprises that are more acceptable to society.

The preceding defense mechanisms are usually used to ward off unpleasant feelings from within oneself, although denial is often applied to unsettling happenings from outside and frequently is used immediately after some personal trauma, such as the sudden unexpected death of a loved one.

In terms of coping with external crises, perhaps the most intriguing long-term defense mechanism besides denial is one observed in concentration camps. Certain prisoners seemed to try to adapt to their plight by becoming as much like their SS guards as possible, right down to putting makeshift SS insignia on their clothes. The unconscious reasoning seemed to be that, by becoming like their oppressors, they would remove all reason for being harmed ("If you can't beat 'em, join 'em."). This has been termed "identification with the aggressor."

Concerning coping, then, a major conclusion of Freudian psychology is that coping ability is hindered (1) by narrowly fixated adaptive patterns developed early in life and (2) by the fact that energy is used up keeping painful memories and anxiety-provoking feelings out of consciousness. In fact, energy is lost in *two* ways with respect to the latter, because energy is expended in defense mechanisms to bottle up the other energy of the unconscious impulses, creating a kind of loggerhead situation. (A repressed person may be tired and/or depressed a great deal because so much energy is locked up in the anger-repression loggerhead.) If the tendency to repress one's feelings can somehow be overcome—frequently through insight but sometimes through the sheer desperation of a crisis or ordeal—not only will the energy that has been used to keep the lid on one's impulses be available, but the energy of the impulses *themselves* can also be released to serve the process of adaptation. A prime example is anger. Many a "timid" or "mild" person is actually a very angry person who has repressed his or her anger. (Sometimes one gets a sense of this when someone seems *too* mild or controlled. Such apparently mild people are sometimes the ones who suddenly explode into a wild rage if something goes wrong in their lives.) If that anger were released, it could be mobilized to feed the determination to survive and become another source of the surprisingly tenacious "will to live" in some who are tragically beset, or it could account for some of the astonishing feats of strength that we occasionally read about. In an example of the latter, a tiny woman is able to lift a 3,000-pound car off her injured son because in her desperation she mobilizes both her anger *and* the energy that had been used to repress it.

Other resources that can be unlocked from the unconscious include stimulation for the ego, creative insight, and escapist fantasy. Almost paradoxically, an extreme stress situation is precisely the situation that breaks down the ego's ability to maintain the defense mechanisms and allows unconscious memories and impulses to become conscious—accomplishing the very release of energy that can enable people to do what is required in a crisis. On the other hand, the release of such emotions, energy, and painful memories can, if they occur abruptly, sometimes overwhelm the person and create panic, paralysis, or even psychosis, as fantastic hallucinatory images emerge along with terrifyingly powerful feelings to create an unhinging sense of unreality. Two things, therefore, might seem to separate those who will successfully mobilize their unconscious during ordeals from those who won't: (1) the ability to maintain some ego *control*, to understand what is happening to them, and (2) a predisposition to be *open* to and interested in one's inner life and feelings and to welcome them rather than to be in terror of them. This combination of maintaining control and being open to one's unconscious (Freud called it "regression in the service of the ego") seems, incidentally, to characterize the personalities of many survivors, as well as others such as solo mountaineers, test pilots, and the astronauts, who had extraordinary problem-solving and self-control aptitudes but who could also be open (and objective) about their feelings and anxieties when asked to do so. Control and openness, although seemingly almost opposites, are also major traits of such solitary adventurers as Charles Lindbergh, who is discussed in some detail later in this book. Lindbergh is an example of a person who could use his intellect to master and control his feelings but who was also intrigued by his inner "unconscious" life.

Jungian Psychology and Adaptation

The above is all largely according to Freudian theory, which is not of course the only theory. For instance, the Jungian view of the psychology of adaptation, although in general outline similar to the Freudian, sees the unconscious as containing not just memories from one's personal past and impulses from one's id but also ancient inherited wisdom and memories ("archetypes"), and as having a structure that is in many ways a mirror image of the conscious person. In other words, the unconscious contains a whole "other self" made up of opposites of our conscious self—an other self that is as complete as the conscious self, and (presumably) as capable of rational thought and action in a survival ordeal. (There is a great deal of literature that plays upon this notion of the unconscious having an "alter ego" that is opposite to the conscious self—Dr. Jekyll and Mr. Hyde, Dr. Frankenstein and his monster, for example. Students of literature call this the theme of the "double" or "doppelgänger.") Under stress, then, the breakdown of ego defenses could mean that not only energy but also an "other person," embodying perhaps evil but also ancient inherited wisdom, will emerge as a potential helpmate or even as a "new" self from the unconscious with the capability of functioning as fully (although in opposite ways) as the conscious ego. (The Jungian view of the unconscious as harboring an "other self" becomes interesting when we look later at the hallucinations experienced by people undergoing prolonged solitary ordeals.)

Humanistic Psychology and Adaptation

The twin themes of *control* and *openness* mentioned above also figure in what might be termed the humanistic approach to the psychology of adaptation. Control and openness are major features of what Csikszentmihalyi[2] has termed the "flow experience"—the subjective state that occurs when one is totally caught up or engrossed in some activity (a basketball player might call it "being unconscious"). One adapts most successfully when one is in a state of balance between being open and responsive to the demands of the situation and being in control of that situation. Neither person nor environment is dominating the other. There is a perfect balance between what the situation demands and one's skills in meeting those demands. This flow experience can come about only when there is such a match between the stimulating variety provided by one's surroundings and the ability of the individual to control and order that variety. People who are overwhelmed by environmental demands (an apparent feature of many survival ordeals) are paralyzed by extreme anxiety, while people whose abilities exceed environmental demands experience boredom. Chapter Eight examines the flow experience in more detail.

Humanistic psychology also stresses the fact that one *always* has some freedom to affect and control one's situation if one continues to remain open to possibilities that exist in even the most brutal and confining situations. The book *Man's Search for Meaning* by Viktor Frankl,[3] about the realization that even in the most oppressive and seemingly hopeless conditions (in his case a concentration camp) the person is fundamentally free, is a most powerful statement of this viewpoint. To the existentialists, the only difference between ordinary life and the solitary ordeal is one of degree: *In both situations the construction of a meaningful life is up to each one of us.* Frankl's book, incidentally, also teaches another powerful lesson about the psychology of surviving ordeals: We do not have to succumb to the status of being a victim, even when others put us in a situation that does victimize us in the most extreme sense.

Notes

[1] Riesman, David. *The Lonely Crowd.* New Haven: Yale, 1950.
[2] Csikszentmihalyi, Mihalyi. *Flow Experience.* New York: Harper & Row, 1990.
——— *Beyond Boredom and Anxiety.* San Francisco: Jossey-Bass, 1975.
[3] Frankl, Viktor. *Man's Search for Meaning.* New York: Washington Square Press, 1963.

CHAPTER TWO

The Theory of Coping

The way in which people adapt to and cope with ordeals depends on the nature of the situation, whether people are alone or in small groups, the extent of physical hardship and its duration, the prospect of reprieve and rescue, how prepared one is by training and "strength of character," the equipment at one's disposal, and a variety of other factors.

Nevertheless, if one were to construct in the abstract a list of psychological needs that must be met in order for an individual to cope successfully with adversity and maintain his or her sanity and humanity, one might turn to Robert White,[1] to Norris Hansell,[2] and to Erik Erikson.[3]

Robert White suggests the following:

1. There is a need for *information* concerning the new situation on which to base decisions for action. The individual must be vigilant and constantly appraise the situation. The vigilance and awareness of people facing extreme danger is sometimes quite remarkable, as will be shown.

2. People need to maintain themselves in a state of *equilibrium.* They cannot allow themselves or their bodies to be thrown too far out of balance by the stressful situation. Thus, body temperature must remain within certain limits, and the hunger and thirst and pain-avoidance drives cannot be allowed to become too strong lest the person's whole being be governed by the single-minded and

narrow obsession with getting water or food or reducing pain to the neglect of other essential survival needs. As was described earlier, emotions must not become extreme either.

3. Finally, people need to have a sense of *autonomy*—of freedom of action, of freedom from total domination by circumstances.

Hansell[4] provides a list of seven essential needs ("attachments") for coping. The list is not based on any single psychological theory.

1. *Supplies*. He lumps together under this heading food, water, and air on the one hand and information on the other. This category could obviously be broken down into a series of critical needs.

2. *Persons*. He is speaking here of a need for human relationship, contact, and intimacy. (Many solitary people do manage to meet even this need through "fantasy," as we shall see.)

3. *Identity*. By this he means a sense of who one is, of personal sameness and continuity, of positive self-concept, which brings with it a sense of perspective on one's life and a personal philosophy that can help to guide one through an ordeal. (I will talk at greater length about this need later.)

4. *Groups*. This is a need to *belong*, to experience solidarity with a collection of people, to feel that one is part of something that is larger than oneself (which gives one a feeling of security). In solitary ordeals this need is not easily met, except through memory and ritual.

5. *Roles*. This refers to a need to have something to *do*—to have a function in life, and to perform it well. One must somehow find a way to continue to practice one's life roles.

6. *Money*. While not as immediate a need as any of the preceding, and seemingly out of place in a psychology list, money (or purchasing or bartering power of some kind) is an important means of achieving many of the previous needs in the real world, especially "supplies." (Actually, the label "money" for this need is silly and trite, as money is usually not an issue. What is necessary is some means to gain what one needs in order to survive.)

7. *Meaning*. This may be the most powerful human need of all, especially in the modern era of "alienation" and absurdity. This is a need to sense and experience a deep purpose in life, a reason for existing and for continuing to exist. Frankl[5] addressed this need as the one most critical to survival in extreme ordeals. Frankl observes from his "existential" perspective that meaning can be created in three ways: through doing a deed (similar to Erikson's notions of

initiative, industry, and generativity below), through love (similar to Erikson's ideas of trust and intimacy below), and through suffering. This latter point has no parallel in most of the psychology literature, and is the outcome of Frankl's long and bitter, but in the end affirmative, experience in a concentration camp. Many other survivors would strongly attest to his notion that suffering leads not only to a sense of meaning, but indeed to profoundly deep meaning in many ways.

To Hansell's list could be added Erikson's "eight stages of man," a series of developmentally sequenced tasks, each of which poses a built-in crisis that must be resolved in order for a fundamental human need to be met. It will quickly be apparent that there is much overlap among Erikson, White, and Hansell.

Erikson's list of the eight fundamental needs of human beings refers to normal psychological growth and functioning, but these needs would also seem to be essential at any age. In a survival situation, meeting these needs becomes only more critical.

Basic Trust. The successful attainment of basic trust shows up throughout life in a sense of fundamental security, hope, faith, and optimism, a capacity to establish harmonious relationships with others (especially infant with mother), and a willingness to incorporate experiences from others. The opposite of basic trust is mistrust, manifested in cynicism, lack of hope, distrust of others, withdrawal from relationships, and even schizophrenia in extreme cases. Religion is an important institutional expression of the human need for trust, expressed as faith and hope. Being able to maintain a sense of basic trust in oneself, others, and reality is the foundation of all healthy psychological growth and functioning. Without this sense of trust, it is difficult to maintain hope, faith, and optimism. These may be strengthened during ordeals by religious faith, patriotism, or the memory of loved ones. (Trust, however, should be balanced by a healthy amount of mistrust appropriately applied.)

Autonomy. This is expressed in the exercise of will, will power, and willfulness, choice as to what to hold and what to reject, decision making, and self-control. Extreme attempts to assert autonomy can lead to negativism, a refusal to go along with (parental) authority; this refusal is the only thing a toddler can do to "assert" herself in the absence of acquired skills. The failure to establish autonomy will lead to the opposite pole of shame and doubt, both of which reflect a state of insecurity about one's separateness after leaving the mother-child whole. Doubt is a direct expression of this insecurity—of feeling alone and unsure of one's capacity to function successfully on one's own, and unsure of one's ability to exercise self-control in place of the caretaker's control. A certain amount of doubt is of course necessary and may show up in the form of "healthy skepticism." Likewise, shame in moderate doses is also healthy as it helps to keep people within bounds in their behavior. Shame reflects the insecure feeling that, now a separate being, one senses others observing him and feels exposed ("naked") to the critical eyes of the other(s) within whom one was previously immersed. One's bodily functions, feelings, and impulses may be troublesome not only because of one's struggle to regulate them, but also because one senses that they are now shamefully visible to others. One may attempt to avoid shame and doubt by practicing rigid, compulsive self-control.

The individual undergoing a life-threatening ordeal especially needs to maintain a certain amount of autonomy from his or her surroundings, a need also given great importance by Robert White. This means that he must have the ability to keep options open, a certain amount of freedom of action, and the ability to maintain some kind of control in order to prevent the situation from totally dominating, controlling, and crushing him. Survivors of imprisonment in degrading conditions such as concentration camps and penal colonies have written powerful accounts about how shame (the opposite of autonomy in Erikson's theory) is the most painful emotion in their ordeals, as they find themselves stripped of all dignity—and sometimes literally forced into nakedness and living in filth. In solitary confinement, autonomy may be found by a prisoner in his or her mind through fantasy life (see Papillon, later) or, if under strict surveillance to prevent autonomous action, in surreptitious and defiant finger exercises, the counting of flies, or any number of ways of subtly "refusing to go along" with authority (for example, by making a small change in the sequence of a series of acts one has been commanded to do that is inconsequential to one's jailer but is a moral victory for one's sense of control and autonomy). In concentration camps, autonomy might be manifested by a million tiny acts of symbolic defiance that prove one is not totally controlled by even these degrading circumstances.

To Erikson, maintaining autonomy means maintaining control of one's own life, mind, and body. Far from allowing the situation to control her, the survivor of a prolonged ordeal must control herself, and particularly her mental activities. The intellect needs to be kept functioning in good order in case quick decisions need to be made during a momentary flash of opportunity. Survivors faced with oppressive, debilitating ordeals have frequently hit upon ingenious mental exercises and games to provide intellectual stimulation, have made microscopically detailed studies of their surroundings, have arranged full-day schedules of intellectual activities with which to occupy themselves, and have even resorted to disciplining their minds by giving themselves highly authoritative verbal commands. (These actions obviously serve needs that go beyond autonomy and address some of Erikson's additional needs below.) By maintaining mental control of their routines and themselves, they preserve autonomy. And in preserving autonomy they also maintain a certain amount of detachment from the situation that threatens to overwhelm them. Thus they keep from being totally the *object*, or *victim*, and remain partly the observing agent, enabling the next need to be met.

Initiative. The desire to have effects or make a difference in one's world manifests itself in early childhood (and later as well) in ambition, aspiration, imagination, exploration, adventure, and many forms of intrusion into the world, into the unknown, and into the awareness of others. Extreme striving to establish a sense of initiative frequently results in overly intrusive ("out of bounds") behavior—the active breaking of, rather than simple refusal to go along with, conventions and constraints in order to assert one's ability to affect the world. Should initiative fail, the opposite is guilt, stemming from the feeling that "I may have gone too far" (or "not far enough") in striving to make things happen. This is the stage of conscience formation—the "voice" we hear when having "done wrong."

The individual during a prolonged solitary ordeal especially has to be able to exercise initiative—to feel that she can have effects on her situation despite the fact that it threatens to overwhelm her, that she can do something that will make a difference, however small this may be. A sense of initiative can be maintained by keeping active, by exercising one's creative imagination, by making small—even imperceptible—physical changes in one's surroundings, and the like.

Industry. The "school-years" stage is distinguished by the drive to be skillful, accomplished, and competent, the eagerness to learn systematically, the desire to know the reason for things, and the desire to make something work and work well. Extreme striving for industry creates an obsession with doing things "just so"—perfectionism—a frequent manifestation in the "child culture." Should industry fail to be established, a sense of inferiority and fear of failure are the result. Many people pursue industry in society through the pursuit of technology and other forms of skilled work. The individual under adversity must work extra hard to find a way to preserve this sense of industry, or competence, through finding some activities that still can be pursued with skill. This need is frequently satisfied through inventive ingenuity, the resourceful use of scarce materials to construct games (for example, chess pieces from bread dough), tools, clothing, and so on. Mental exercises and problem solving also help in the maintenance of industry. By exercising *some kind* of initiative and industry, individuals help to maintain a sense of themselves as vital, instrumental beings—and therefore as essentially non-victims—rather than as the passive objects of whatever besets them. Giving in to the situation is a major step away from surviving it.

Identity. This stage is characterized by a search for sameness, for continuity of self, and for a role for that self that has been created as the legacy of the previous stage. A major characteristic of this stage is fidelity, the need to belong to something and believe in something. The extreme striving for a sense of identity leads to a striving for *absolutes*, frequently in the form of a rigid ideology. (Ideology in general serves as the societal-level manifestation of the need for identity.) The opposite of identity is "identity diffusion," or meaninglessness and uncertainty about self, place, and future. Identity appears in social institutions in the network of social roles. Probably of major importance for survival is the need to maintain this sense of personal, conscious identity—of who one is, of where one is going in life, of a sense of perspective, and of what one stands for. The loss of identity means the victory of the ordeal over the self, the loss of sanity, and the loss of one's humanity. Reminiscing about one's past life, practicing significant cultural and religious rituals, and reminding oneself of past achievements are all ways to maintain identity, self-esteem, and a sense of worth. If one begins to lose confidence in oneself and the sense of who one is (a quite literal danger in situations of prolonged and intense stress and isolation), one may not make it. One witness to this is the death of otherwise healthy young POWs who seemed simply to "give up."

I will argue later that people who cope successfully may have a more "instrumental" identity than those who do not. They live more as an active "I" than a self-conscious "me."

Erikson also mentions the need to establish and maintain a sense of *intimacy* with another or others (or with a life-work of some kind); a sense of *generativity* (that one is still creating something that will endure after one has gone); and a sense of *integrity*, or dignity and self-respect—the belief that one has lived a full and good life, and is still living a life worth living. A sense of integrity translates to the idea that life has some meaning and purpose.

Another important trait of those who manage to survive extreme ordeals, and one of the most interesting, is the ability to make sense out of everything, even if things have gone beyond the sensible. Survivors are able to maintain a point of view, a way of looking at and understanding their situations. I want to stress how much a point of view really does matter, even to individual survival. In studying how people cope during solitary ordeals, I have come to appreciate how often survival can literally depend on the ability to maintain a constant way of looking at and making sense out of what is happening around oneself. I think, for example, of Bruno Bettelheim and Viktor Frankl in Nazi concentration camps who, because they were steady beholders who had firm, constant viewpoints, could make their own kind of sense and certainty out of even the utterly senseless and uncertain. It seems that the first thing they did was to accept their solitariness, their existence as solitary beholders, and go on from there. Their stable points of view enabled them to detach themselves from the horrors around them—almost as if the viewpoint were a *place* in which they could take refuge from a world gone mad. Bettelheim, for example, spent a great deal of time analyzing the behavior of his fellow prisoners from the perspective of psychoanalytic theory.

It seems that a way of making sense, if firmly held, is one of the last things to fall victim to an uncertain world. A stable "I" survives, monitoring what is happening, as indicated by the capacity of some people to recount and interpret in a rational way the meaningless, chaotic, and inhuman. If one has a constant way of looking at the world, one apparently does not so readily see oneself as a victim of the world. Indeed, self-consciousness and a concern with knowing the self as "me" makes an individual a kind of "victim in potentia," as it is not a great leap from the awareness of the self as an object *in* the world to the perception of the self as an object *of* the world.

In addition to the above points, I would suggest that one legacy of the millions of years of human survival struggle and evolution may also be a *need* to face and overcome external challenge in order to feel more completely alive, as well as to aid in meeting the needs for autonomy, initiative, industry/competence, identity, role-performance, and meaning. There may, in other words, be something of the hero-warrior-hunter-adventurer in all of us, what Carl Jung would call an unconscious archetype; and if we do not act out such tendencies in a straightforward way, they will find a perverse, distorted, bizarre form of expression on their own. (The recent "Iron John" movement of Robert Bly, in which men go through various tribal rituals of chanting and drumming in order to rediscover their ancient warriorhood, is perhaps one reflection of this. Whether it is a healthy or a distorted reflection could be endlessly debated.) The survival ordeal provides the opportunity to act on such tendencies—another way of saying that such ordeals can lead to new self-knowledge. (Concerning the controversy about Bly's movement and the concern that it could lead to more violent aggression among men, I have to add here that one of the most striking findings from my study of scores of solitary ordeals, and solitary adventures that became ordeals, is that men who have undergone real ordeals—not simulated ones such as Bly's—invariably emerge as much *gentler* men rather than as more violent.) Perhaps, as Carl Jung has argued, human beings are two-sided creatures, having gentle intellectual, contemplative, and introspective ("introverted") needs on the one hand and aggressive, heroic, adventurous, physical-action, problem-solving, and outward-looking ("extroverted") needs on the other, with the former probably being a more recently evolved feature of the human psyche. Surely the ancient ancestors of the human race were externally oriented problem solvers coping with physical challenge, not self-conscious introverts wondering about "who they are."

Another way of describing what Jung means is to speak of an "extroverted" and an "introverted" sense of identity. Some people relate to the world with a sense of self as "I"—producer, doer, observer of the world, and non-victim. Others relate to the world as "me"—consumer, receiver of experience, and therefore potential victim.

The current trend in this country toward "back to nature" activities (backpacking, camping, canoeing, exploring, outdoor living courses) and the popular fascination with adventures, disasters, and dangers may indicate that the balance had shifted too far inward (at least in some circles) toward the conscious expression and experiencing of the passive, introspective, "existential," and contemplative, and that this trend needed to be balanced by a counteremphasis on facing outward challenges—something we may be better equipped for than introspecting. Even some of today's most self-searching movements and institutions have begun to shift away from an exclusive emphasis on inward-looking exploration and meditation. Jogging, physical exercise, biking, wilderness excursions, and the martial arts—all of which involve training the body to handle external physical hardships as well as exploring and disciplining the mind—have become part of the scene at some of the best known of the centers for self-analysis and self-discovery. Perhaps this also indicates a search for balance between looking inward and looking outward.

It is sometimes suggested that people even *thrive* on danger, hardship, and ordeals. Such has been stated (or perhaps overstated) by the philosopher-mountaineer Woodrow Wilson Sayre:[6]

> Mere security is a barren ideal. We need to pay attention to what is done with that security. And we also need to ask whether security itself does not have its own dangers. Is a parent really better who tries to protect his child from every conceivable danger and difficulty? I think not. Neither, then, is a society better for trying to protect every one of its members from all dangers and difficulties. People grow through overcoming dangers and difficulties. They are not better off for being carefully wrapped in cotton batting. Deep within us I think we know that we need challenge and danger, and the risk and hurt that will sometimes follow. Dangerous sports would not be as popular as they are if this were not so. . . .[7]

David Lewis,[8] solitary explorer of the antarctic sea, adds his views:

> It is the enterprise itself that fires the imagination, driving you to go further than man has ever gone before. Naturally if you venture into the unknown you must be prepared to encounter unforeseeable dangers and, especially where these are not fully known, the sensible man is fearful and wary.
>
> None but the psychologically unbalanced are attracted to danger for its own sake. Risk is a disadvantage unfortunately often inherent in too many worthwhile ventures. Awareness of it may at best help promote that wild animal alertness upon which man's survival may depend when he steps off the pavements. The call comes to the adventurer and he must by his nature answer it. But he reduces any element of risk to an absolute minimum, acting out his destiny in spite of anxiety and fear.[9]

Interestingly, Csikszentmihalyi[10] describes the "flow experience" (the highly positive state of being "caught up" in what one is doing) as often occurring during dangerous activities, such as rock climbing. (The "flow experience" is discussed in Chapter Eight.)

Charles Lindbergh[11] takes a similar view:

> I didn't start on this flight to Paris because of its relative
> safety. I used that argument only to bolster my decision
> and to convince people that the hazard wasn't too great.
> I'm not bound to be in aviation at all. I'm here only
> because I love the sky and flying more than anything else
> on earth. Of course, there's danger; _but a certain amount of_
> _danger is essential to the quality of life._ [Emphasis mine—
> RDL] I don't believe in taking foolish chances; but nothing
> can be accomplished without taking any chances at all.[12]
>
> Why does one want to walk wings? Why force one's
> body from a plane just to make a parachute jump? Why
> should man want to fly at all? People often ask those
> questions. But what civilization was not founded on
> adventure, and how long could one exist without it? What
> justifies the risk of life? Some answer the attainment of
> knowledge. Some say wealth or power is sufficient cause.
> I believe the risks I take are justified by the sheer love of
> the life I lead. Yes, just being in the air on a flight across the
> ocean, to Paris, warrants the hazard of an ice field below.[13]

Is the overcoming of risks one of the major ways in which we can
come to sense ourselves as instrumental agents in a world dominated by
passive consumption?

A somewhat similar view is also incorporated into the philosophy
of the many wilderness programs, such as the Outward Bound School
(founded not incidentally by the same Ernest Shackleton who explored
and survived the Antarctic), which puts people through a weeks-long
series of physical trials with a view toward enhancing self-confidence
and building a fuller life. The effects on self-esteem are purportedly
great. It has also been noted that even in the harsh, involuntary ordeals
of concentration camps, where malnutrition, brutality, humiliation, and
filth are the rule, people can still in some sense "thrive." Frankl[14] noted,
for example, that in numerous inmates, many physical ailments simply
disappeared, as if they were just too insignificant to be bothered with.
(On another level, many of us are familiar with mothers who are so busy
coping with children that they simply "do not have time to get sick.")
Similar observations have been made on people living through natural
disasters, particularly the London blitz, where emotional breakdowns

and lowered morale were surprisingly rare. On the contrary, the ordeals seemed to have a galvanizing effect. High morale was also the rule rather than the exception among long-range bomber crews in World War II who sometimes experienced 50-percent casualty rates. And certainly many religious writers over the centuries have stressed the positive, spiritually enlightening consequences even of pain and suffering. (I do not cite this to subscribe to it.)

Ordeals and crises are not always *just* debilitating and destructive, although we definitely should not romanticize them. Consider the following quotation from Lauren Elder,[15] who survived a plane crash high in the Sierras, painful injuries, the gruesome deaths of her two companions, and then the long, torturous walk down out of the mountains. I submit her statement as "expert testimony," and she speaks for many others in the fraternity/sorority of lone survivors:

> "Horror does not manifest itself in the world of reality." Antoine de Saint-Exupéry, the French aviator and writer, wrote that, and I had discovered it to be so. In all the time it had taken me to descend the mountain I had not experienced horror. One [only] feels horror in anticipation or in retrospect; it needs a mental and a temporal distance.
>
> I had also discovered, that spring day [of her trek down the mountain], that there is little that cannot be endured. Much of the time I had felt as if I had been possessed of a special *grace*. That is all I could think to call it, *grace*. It was as if a transcendent power had been loosed in me as I made my way down the mountain. At times during the day I'd been filled with a peculiar sense of well-being, of elation. I had fallen out of the sky, had in the most primeval sense been lost in the wilderness, and it had not overwhelmed me. It had been even exhilarating.
>
> I had felt neither alone nor lonely; I was neither happy nor sad; I simply was.[16]

Speaking of Saint-Exupéry, after crashing in the Libyan desert and barely surviving several brutal days without water, he wrote:[17] "Never shall I forget that, lying buried to the chin in sand, strangled slowly to death by thirst, my heart was infinitely warm beneath the desert stars."[18]

Several points in Elder's comments are worth noting. To be sure, her "positive" view of her ordeal could be attributed to rationalization and/or the distortion caused in looking back at it by the euphoria of having been rescued. But her theme is too common among survivors, many of whom feel that the experience got them in touch with something significant— about themselves, about life, about spirituality, about meaning. Whatever it is, they find it hard to articulate (which is perhaps why they sometimes express themselves in unusual ways), and we find it even harder to grasp. For Elder, it seems to be something spiritual and existential—a whole new appreciation of life and existence that the routine of her previous life had covered over. This is one reason that, to a degree, there *is* a fraternity/ sorority of survivors; only they can understand what the others really mean, especially when they talk of their new cosmic consciousness and the like. That is one reason Elder quotes Saint-Exupéry, who wrote some of the most beautiful literature ever to come out of a solitary survival ordeal in the book *Wind, Sand, and Stars* (which recounts his ordeal) and the popular fairy tale *The Little Prince* (inspired by hallucinations he experienced during his ordeal).

Another encouraging point that can be derived from Elder's words is that most of us are capable of coping far better during a survival ordeal than we might expect, and that terror and helplessness do not have to be the rule.

Gary Mundell[19] reflects on how the experience of coping with an ordeal "puts things in perspective," for want of a better way to put it. He was sailing alone through the South Pacific when he ran aground on a small, remote atoll:

> "I'm from Alaska, and you have to learn to be tough in a cold place like that. When things get tough, I always consider it a sort of personal challenge. I've always thought of myself as a survivor and I knew I could make it. . . .
>
> Ninety percent of being a survivor is in the head. It's common sense and attitude. *After all, the difference between an adventure and an ordeal is attitude.* [RDL] Some people just give up. Why? I can't understand that. I mean I knew I was in trouble but in some ways I never felt so alive. I just took a good hard look at my needs versus my wants. I needed food and water and I had them. I wanted toothpaste and toilet paper and cold beer. But I could live without them. . . .[20]"

> [After a month of isolation, Gary had become] less
> emotional and was able to view the world without
> passing judgment on it. Having no human contact, he
> had become totally absorbed with the activities of the
> world around him. . . . Through—or perhaps because
> of—his ordeal, Gary had achieved the transcendental
> state. He had come to realize the most important lesson
> of all: that happiness is in the mind.[21]

Frankl,[22] writing from out of the depths of brutality and degradation
in the concentration camps, states:

> In a position of utter desolation, when man cannot
> express himself in positive action, when his only
> achievement may consist in enduring his sufferings in
> the right way—an honorable way—in such a position a
> man can, through loving contemplation of the image he
> carries of his beloved, achieve fulfillment. For the first
> time in my life I was able to understand the meaning of
> the words, "The angels are lost in the perpetual contem-
> plation of an infinite glory." [23]

I have found many survivors to be brilliant writers—far more
engaging than expert psychological discourse. I think one of the reasons
is that they *must* tell their story in order to put it into perspective and to
heal themselves—and to share what they have learned. I commend a
brilliant book by Janet Reno to readers who want insight into the survivor
from fiction: *Ishmael Alone Survived*,[24] her account of the lone survivor of the
Pequod in Melville's *Moby Dick*. It is Ishmael who narrates the story of the
ship's tragedy and his survival. Although her analysis is of a fictional
character, her interpretations are masterful:

> . . . when Ishmael succeeds in completing his story, he
> has triumphed over the given hardships of his life. A
> survivor needs to go through feelings of *sorrow, helpless-*
> *ness, rage, guilt, and loss* [RDL] to tell his story. . . . [This]
> permits Ishmael to triumph over senselessness . . . [and
> find] order and coherence in the world. . . . A disaster
> victim is often engulfed in a sense of chaos, but memoir
> writing permits one to make sense of things [and dis-
> cover] . . . a "metaphor of self" whereby one can [again]

perceive orderliness in the cosmos . . . [and have] the impression that one's self is orderly also.[25]

All in all, this adds up to a powerful set of incentives for the survivor to tell his or her story. It is well for us to keep Reno's points in mind as we read survival stories. Many survivors have obviously partially dealt with their sorrow, helplessness, rage, guilt, and loss *before* writing their accounts. The writing helps to further this healing.

On the important theme of the survivor needing to remake him or herself, as it were, Reno also says:

> . . . in order to move from perceiving himself as a victim and to grant that he is strong and ready for life, a survivor must . . . [quoting Terrence Des Pres] "make a radical shift in the sense of selfhood." Survivors are more aware of human limitations, such as time, than most people are. But, says Des Pres, they are also more aware of "the sustaining power which life itself provides when all else has been stripped away." [This is very much the point that Frankl makes.] From the experience of refusing to give up, the self gains "a special integrity, a clearness of vision indispensable to those for whom, outwardly, helplessness and victimization are major facts of existence."[26]

Much of what I would wish to say about ordeals and their survivors is contained in the above words from Reno and Des Pres. The theme of an altered self will come up again.

There are really two related questions involved in all of this: Why do at least some people do surprisingly well under the brutal conditions of ordeals? And why do certain other people actively *seek out* ordeals of great danger, suffering, and possible death in the pursuit of adventure? One reason some people may do well under adversity is that ordeals often recreate the kind of situation that humans have evolved to face, and the ordeal therefore satisfies an ancient need to overcome physical challenges, to take charge of one's own destiny, and to continue to be a challenge-mastering, problem-solving creature. Many psychological theories (including those of Erikson and White, mentioned earlier) do in fact suggest that "mastery" or "competence" motives are fundamental in human nature—that we are all motivated to solve problems, overcome challenges, and become competent. The kind of resourcefulness that evolved under ancient duress may still to some degree lead people today to seek danger and risk. Humans may to a degree have a need to face challenge and danger just as lions need to practice the hunt. The utter avoidance of physical challenge and of all forms of "stress" (a word that I think we toss around too easily today) may even be harmful—a body shaped by the evolutionary struggle to survive may deteriorate in a non-challenging environment. In fact, one might argue that video games, fast cars, amusement park thrills, sky diving, even the "rush" of drugs, create the illusion of just the kind of intensely challenging activity that humans find galvanizing.

A further reason may be that (as mentioned earlier) ordeals are precisely the kinds of situations that bring out and lead to the discovery of previously unconscious aspects of the self, which constitute a vast potential reserve that can be mobilized under stress and sent into the fray, later to be incorporated into a "larger" self.

Many other psychological theories could be offered to try to explain why adventurers and explorers seek solitary danger, hardship, and even pain in far-flung places. These are not all "positive" views.

1. Risk-taking solitary adventurers have strong self-hatred or have a powerful "death wish," the energy of which they have not been able to channel into more constructive pursuits and which is therefore taking its predestined course.

2. A similar view is that they are full of rage that they are unable to express outwardly toward the actual sources of their frustration (for example, a domineering parent), so they have turned their rage inward into a masochistic quest for self-destruction, a drive that motivates their risky adventures.

3. They have experienced rejection early in life and are acting out a childish "run-away" fantasy in the hope of punishing, through their own self-destruction ("you'll be sorry"), the parental (or other) figures who rejected them; or they are running away or risking harm in the fantasized hope of being "rescued" by those same figures.

4. They feel unworthy and consumed with guilt and are seeking self-punishment for their own real or imagined failures, trespasses, and shortcomings stemming from earlier in life.

5. They have been made to feel incompetent and inferior and they seek adventure to compensate for these inferior feelings and prove their worthiness.

6. They seek adventure as a way of proving themselves to some critical and demanding significant figure in their lives, such as a father, and also perhaps to prove themselves "man enough" to be worthy of a mother's or some other's affection.

7. They have a weak and uncertain sense of their identity and direction in life, so they confront dangerous situations as a way of feeling at least temporarily more intensely alive, whole, and worthy. They also seek to shore up a weak sense of identity through gaining the notoriety that often comes to adventurers (the "Evel Knievel" approach).

When one examines the belief that danger is "essential" (as Lindbergh and Sayre put it), or considers the fascination of some with risks and adventure, one has to be very careful to make some distinctions. Clearly there are very different reasons why people take risks. The seven reasons immediately above seem very self-centered—ways either of destroying or escaping a disliked self or of trying to build up a weak self. There may, however, be completely different reasons why some individuals seek danger and risks. Instead of doing so for defensive, escapist, or self-destructive reasons, they may be subjecting themselves to such ordeals in a quest (not necessarily conscious) *to discover more about themselves*, somewhat as in the "spirit quest" or "vision quest" of many traditional cultures, which invariably are major ordeals—and, interestingly, usually solitary. They may be on a quest for self-knowledge and their own unconscious, even if they do not realize it.

Even though ordeals involve coping with things outside of oneself as an instrumental and outward-looking figure in the world, they inevitably lead a person to become self-reflective. Therefore ordeals function as yet another of the ways in which modern man attempts to "search for his soul," for his unconscious—to find whatever it is that is missing that keeps him from feeling whole. The solitary ordeal may be uniquely suited to provide this kind of knowledge about what resides in the depths of one's own unconscious, as indicated by the hallucinatory visions that occur in the solitary "vision quest" of Native Americans, for example. (It is interesting in this connection that a feature of the two-week Outward Bound wilderness program is a three-day "solo.")

While it appears that those leading a contemplative, reflective, inward-looking life focused on "me" may benefit from the counterbalancing experience of coping less self-consciously with external challenges such as those provided by Outward Bound, it is interesting to note what seems to happen to many people of opposite temperament. During extreme ordeals, where one must constantly be oriented vigilantly outward toward threats to survival, a great many consciously pragmatic, problem-oriented people seem to demonstrate a tendency to move in the opposite direction and to become (sometimes profoundly) introspective, insightful, and contemplative. It is fascinating, for example, to read closely the writings of a seemingly tough, adventurous man like Admiral Richard Byrd during his isolation in Antarctica; of a meticulous problem solver like Charles Lindbergh on his solo flight; of a hardened underground military man like Christopher Burney during his solitary confinement; or of highly trained technicians like astronaut Michael Collins on his flight to the moon or astronaut Rusty Schweikart on a space walk in orbit around the earth. All of these men apparently were highly pragmatic people whose adult lives had been a series of calculated risks and training programs to cope with those risks. During their ordeals, however, the compensating introspective tendency emerges, and their writings become almost Zen-like as they dwell on the meaning of life, the expanded sense of self, and the feeling of oneness with the universe—as if they are seeking to balance the outward extreme with its inward opposite. Schweikart, for example, experienced an unexpected delay while on his space walk and found himself with time to think about large questions as he floated utterly alone, detached from Mother Earth. As he contemplated himself and where he was, all alone in the void of space, he found himself beginning to ask questions about consciousness, meaning, and existence: "Who am I? What is this thing called 'I'?" Few individuals have ever felt so profoundly solitary and so profoundly "cosmic" at the same time, I am sure, than Schweikart floating alone in the void of space.

Lindbergh, Byrd, Chichester, and other heroic survivors were not necessarily earlier-day Evel Knievels, daredevils seeking a great splash of notoriety in a series of dazzling stunts. Nor were they necessarily moti-vated by a mindless, thrill-seeking "machismo." They were for the most part more complex, quieter, and more self-effacing men than that.

Those who cope most successfully with solitary hardship seem, although very much focused on what is "outside," also to have been predisposed somehow by past experiences to be *open* to introspection, and thus are not distressed by specters that may emerge from the deep recesses of their minds under adversity. It is surprising, for instance, to see the apparent equanimity with which the young (age twenty-five)

Charles Lindbergh accepted the powerful hallucinations that occurred on his famous flight. (He accepted them much more readily than the rest of us did. When the movie was made of his book, no mention was made of his hallucinations and the change they made in his life. It would not have fit with our image of him as the consummate practical hero to see him communing with phantoms. The producers did, however, fit in a small fictitious scene of Lindbergh briefly conversing with a fly.) Though they instrumentally *control* their situations and their behavior, survivors remain open to discovering new things about their inner life. The nature of such a predisposition will be examined more fully later on.

A final necessity for survival is that one must also keep up his or her motivation and the will to survive. One of the fascinating things about real-life survival stories is the number of ways people in desperate straits help themselves to maintain their motivation: They threaten, insult, and goad themselves, flatter themselves, and frighten themselves; they reminisce about the good things they want to get back to, about scores they want to settle, about who they would let down (or who would gloat) if they succumbed; and they make themselves promises. The will to live has been fueled by love, by hate, by pride, by the desire to prove something, by fear, of course, and by sheer human obstinacy (in more than one instance in prisoner-of-war camps, for example, it was the tough, stubborn old birds who made it while the young greenhorns didn't). *One major additional motive may be the compelling drive toward self-discovery*, to uncover hidden, unconscious aspects of oneself that the ordeal begins to bring out. Some people may have greater determination to survive not only because they have been able to tap the hidden resources of their unconscious, but because they are then motivated to uncover still more.

In the coming chapters, examples of people who have undergone survival ordeals will be considered for what they can tell us about the limits of human adaptability. All of the stories are true, and some of them are famous. None is dull (at least not in the original recounting!). They are mostly first-person accounts—tales related by the survivors themselves, giving a highly personal and immediate sense of the nature of their ordeals. From these accounts emerges an understanding of how ordeals affect people and, more importantly, of how people cope psychologically with adversity.

Several kinds of prolonged solitary ordeals are examined, among them Charles Lindbergh—solitary twentieth-century man on a quest, striving to stay awake and alert for thirty-three hours in a fragile, unstable monoplane droning endlessly alone above the Atlantic; Admiral Richard Byrd struggling to stay alive for four and one-half months alone in a tiny hut buried in the ice during the frigid antarctic night; Christopher Burney, in solitary confinement for 526 days, trying to keep his mind well honed so that he will be prepared for intellectual duels with his Nazi interrogators; Edith Bone, in solitary confinement for seven years in communist Hungary; Sir Francis Chichester, sailing alone for weeks at a time, yet so embedded in the myriad tasks of sailing a ship that he doesn't seem to be as "alone" as the others; Christiane Ritter, a comfortable German housewife who suddenly finds herself living in a tiny shack in barren Spitsbergen, north of the Arctic Circle, where she must stay alone for weeks at a time in darkness and blizzard while her husband and his partner wander the wasteland tending their traps; David Lewis, New Zealand physician sailing alone around Antarctica; Joe Simpson, British mountaineer crawling back to his base camp after falling into a crevasse and being left for dead.

The similarities in the ways people react to ordeals and their efforts to cope with them are sometimes quite striking. One could interchange some of the writings of Byrd, Lindbergh, Burney, and Ritter without realizing that a switch had been made, so nearly identical are some of their descriptions.

Not all ordeals are identical, however, nor are the people who undergo them. In fact, four simple categories can be identified:

1. Some (such as Byrd, Lindbergh, and Chichester) choose to undergo ordeals *voluntarily* and are comparatively *prepared* (if one ever really can be) by training, temperament, and expectation for what is to confront them. These are the professional adventurers, the "seekers." The reasons they seek out ordeals may also be the reasons that they cope successfully. This highly select group is a primary focus of this book.

2. Others are forced to undergo ordeals *involuntarily* and, obviously, are mostly *unprepared* for what is to come. Plane crash and shipwreck survivors, imprisoned people, hostages, and victims of natural disasters usually fit into this category.

3. Nevertheless, not all involuntary sufferers are totally unprepared to cope with adversity; some *involuntary* sufferers are *prepared*. Christopher Burney, for example, was a highly trained military man with a background in espionage and underground resistance. This experience clearly was important preparation for solitary

confinement. Also, the survivors of the Andes plane crash were mostly members of a rugby team, and the crew of the *Endurance*, while having to undergo terrible trials not of their choosing, were "prepared" in some ways (by physical condition, training, familiarity with physical ordeals [rugby], group organization, and leadership) to face their situation. Similarly, some hostages have been military or foreign service personnel who had received at least some training in dealing with being held hostage.

4. Conversely, some people who *voluntarily* choose to subject themselves to extreme hardship are *unprepared* for what lies ahead. Here could be inserted a lengthy roster of history's foolhardy and naive explorers, adventurers, and soldiers of fortune who have blithely set off on some record-setting quest into ocean, jungle, or mountain range and have perished or disappeared. Many of these figures perhaps have the kinds of self-destructive, overstriving, risk-taking motives described earlier. Christiane Ritter is one example in this book of a voluntary yet seemingly unprepared survivor, yet she was able to find some previously untapped strengths of character within herself that helped to see her through. (The point is, of course, that all of us have such a reserve.) Ensio Tiira, a Finnish youth who joined the French Foreign Legion and then jumped ship in the Straits of Mollucca only to be drawn by the currents into the broad ocean where he languished for a month on a tiny raft (more like a life preserver), is another example of someone whose ordeal was voluntarily chosen but who was unprepared for what was to come. Yet somehow he too found an inner reserve of strength that pulled him through. It is the nature of such an inner reserve that this book, in part, attempts to investigate.

Notes

[1] White, Robert. "Motivation reconsidered: the concept of competence." *Psychological Review,* 66 (1959), pp. 297–333.

[2] Hansell, Norris. *The Person-In-Distress.* New York: Human Sciences Press, 1976.

[3] Erikson, Erik. *Childhood and Society.* New York: W. W. Norton, 1963.

[4] Hansell, Norris. 1976.

[5] Frankl, Viktor. 1963.

[6] Sayre, Woodrow W. *Four against Everest.* New Jersey: Prentice-Hall, 1964.

[7] Sayre, p. 219.

[8] Lewis, David. *Ice Bird.* New York: W. W. Norton, 1975.

[9] Lewis, p. 50.

[10] Csikszentmihalyi, 1975; 1990.

[11] Lindbergh, Charles. *The Spirit of St. Louis.* New York: Scribner, 1953.

[12] Lindbergh, p. 244.

[13] Lindbergh, p. 269.

[14] Frankl, 1963.

[15] Elder, Lauren. *And I Alone Survived.* New York: E. P. Dutton, 1978.

[16] Elder, pp. 163–164.

[17] Saint-Exupéry, Antoine de. *Wind, Sand, and Stars.* New York: Cornwall, 1939.

[18] Saint-Exupéry, p. 240.

[19] Quoted in Greenwald, Michael. *Survivor.* San Diego: Blue Horizons Press, 1989.

[20] Greenwald, p. 191.

[21] Greenwald, p. 195.

[22] Frankl, 1963.

[23] Frankl, 1963, p. 59.

[24] Reno, Janet. *Ishmael Alone Survived.* Lewisburg: Bucknell University Press, 1990.

[25] Reno, pp. 25–26.

[26] Reno, p. 24.

CHAPTER THREE

Solitary Ordeals

Many cases have been recorded of isolated individuals struggling interminably and heroically to survive. In the last century, the coal miner John Brown was found alive after being entombed in total blackness deep in a collapsed tunnel for twenty-three days with virtually no nourishment and only a tiny bit of moisture from the walls. When reached, he was lying bearded, emaciated, and barely conscious on the floor. His clothing was rotten and covered with cave mold, his skin a sickly yellow, like an exhibit in a house of horror. He greeted his rescuers with a wry, feeble comment about how he had been waiting for them for some time. He never told of the fantasies, reminiscences, and mental exercises that he may have indulged in. He died three days after his rescue—reputed to be possessed by the devil. In fact, he was probably just deranged. Many who have been trapped alone in tunnels and caves have gone mad in a much shorter time.

Jan Balsrud, a Norwegian patriot fighting the Nazis during World War II, once spent twenty-seven days buried in a sleeping bag under the snow before being rescued. Before his ordeal was over, he had to amputate his own toes. His only nourishment was melted snow.

Augustine Courtauld, a young upper-class Englishman with a taste—like so many others of his background—for adventure and solitude in faraway places, joined three separate Greenland expeditions. On the third one he volunteered (not unlike Admiral Byrd in Antarctica) to man an isolated meteorological station alone for two or three months. He ended up staying for five and barely survived to tell about it. By the time a relief party finally reached him, he had long since become imprisoned by the snow, which completely buried his hut. He was virtually out of food and had oil enough only to light his lamp for a few minutes a day to do the reading that helped him keep his sanity. He was lucky to be saved at all: Only the ventilator pipe of the hut was visible above the snow when the rescue party reached him. When his rescuers shouted down it into the still blackness, the shock must have made Courtauld feel his world was ending. And it was—he was returning to the other world of people, sounds, and light.[1]

Other equally dramatic solitary ordeals could be mentioned here: Howard Blackburn, young, barrel-chested Gloucester fisherman who rowed his dory and his dead companion through a North Atlantic winter ice storm for five days straight with no food or water, bending his ungloved hands into permanently frozen claws that could hold the oars; Martha Martin, abandoned alone on the Alaskan coast for months in her cabin, seriously mauled by a bear, and giving birth on her own to a child;[2] Douglas Mawson, his two companions dead, trekking alone and almost without food across the glaciers of Antarctica for weeks to get back to his base. So debilitated by the ordeal was he that when he did make it back, the first man to see him stared at the gaunt, aged face with tears in his eyes and said, "My God . . . which one *are* you?"[3]

Charles Lindbergh: The Struggle against Sleep

Charles Lindbergh was born in the small town of Little Falls, Minnesota, and grew up virtually as an only child (he had two half sisters) on a farm on the banks of the upper Mississippi River. Although he enjoyed a Tom Sawyer kind of childhood along that river, he was no simple country boy. His father was a progressive Republican Congressman who took Charles to Washington every winter. His mother was a high school science teacher and the "well-bred" daughter of Edwin Land, a prominent Detroit dentist and inventor, with whom Charles also spent significant time as a boy. Charles's childhood was very solitary, however, and he spent much time alone exploring, amusing himself, and tinkering with farm equipment. Indeed, he ran the farm all by himself from age fourteen to seventeen.

Charles Lindbergh's story—at least his momentous accomplishment—is almost too well known to tell again, but it remains a remarkable achievement. It was perhaps the last time that an adventurous, frontier spirit would be able to accomplish something quite so individually heroic in the machine age. (One of the biographies of Lindbergh was called *The Last Hero*.) Lindbergh bridged, perhaps uniquely, the rugged, individualistic, adventurous age of the frontier and the age of mass technology. He was at home in both. He lived early enough in the age of technology never to sense himself as a victim of it. For him, the machine was still an extension of himself in his endeavors. Airplanes were flown by seat-of-the-pants barnstormers (and Lindbergh did work as one), not by "by-the-numbers" technicians. Technology had not yet become master of the man.

Lindbergh's accomplishment of staying aloft and on course for thirty-three hours alone over the ocean had hardly even been contemplated. Yet he did it, and with a combination of self-assurance and modesty (Lindbergh was far more concerned with understanding the world as "I" than displaying himself as "me") that provided the world with a new hero figure.

Lindbergh's book, *The Spirit of St. Louis*,[4] is nearly as remarkable as his flight. It takes the reader on an excursion through the life and mind of the aviator, and the person who flew to Paris emerges in all of his fascinating complexity. An adventurous but surprisingly thoughtful man; an explorer and a latent philosopher; a technician and a dreamer. The picture that emerges is that of a man who already had been living a life that contained both inward- and outward-looking elements. Lindbergh's spare writing style—a direct reflection of the austerity of the man—won him the Pulitzer Prize for Literature (biography category) for the year 1954. His character was not without its flaws, however, as witnessed by his apparently favorable inclinations toward the Nazis, at least briefly, just before World War II.

Lindbergh flew a cloth and wood airplane over 3,000 miles of ocean for thirty-three hours without sleep (after not having slept for the previous twenty-four hours either). His enemies: dulled senses from the steady drone of engine and roar of wind, fatigue, sleep (instantly fatal), aircraft icing, getting off course, and his profound isolation, which, coupled with fatigue and tension, surely would have invited madness in many other people. The following excerpt provides one view of Lindbergh's precarious situation and of his intense awareness of it:

> I push my fingertips against quivering, drum-tight
> fabric of the cockpit wall. The plane's entire structure is

carried by this frail covering of cloth. Thousands of pounds are lifted by these criss-crossed threads, yet singly they couldn't restrain the tugging of a bird. I understand how giant Gulliver was tied so firmly to the ground. As he was bound to earth, I am held in air—by the strength of threads. Nine barrels of gasoline and oil, wrapped up in fabric; two hundred and twenty horse-power, harnessed by a layer of cloth—vulnerable to a pin prick, yet protecting an airplane and its pilot on a flight across the ocean, between the continents—suspended at this moment [fairly early in his flight] five hundred feet above a frigid, northern land [Labrador]. . . .[5]

A little later in the book, Lindbergh begins to speak of doing battle with fatigue and the overpowering urge to sleep:

Why does the desire to sleep come [when flying] over water so much more than over land? Is it because there's nothing to look at, no point different from all others to rivet one's attention to—nothing but waves, ever changing and yet changeless: no two alike, yet monotonous in their uniformity? Hold the compass needle on its mark, glance at the instruments occasionally; there's nothing else to do.

If I could throw myself down on a bed, I'd fall asleep in an instant. In fact, if I didn't know the result, I'd fall asleep just as I am, sitting up in the cockpit—I'm beyond the stage where I need a bed, or even to lie down. My eyes feel dry and hard as stones. The lids pull down with pounds of weight against their muscles. Keeping them open is like holding arms outstretched without support. After a minute or two of effort, I have to let them close. Then, I press them tightly together, forcing my mind to think about what I'm doing so I won't forget to open them again; trying not to move stick or rudder, so the plane will still be flying level and on course when I lift them heavily.

It works at first; but soon I notice that the minute hand of the clock moves several divisions forward while I think only seconds pass. My mind clicks on and off, as though attached to an electric switch with which some outside force is tampering. [Lindbergh may have been experiencing what researchers today have come to call "microsleep"—brief intermittent seconds of losing consciousness of which he is not fully aware.] I try letting one eyelid close at a time while I prop the other open with my will. But the effort's too much. Sleep is winning. My whole body argues dully that nothing, nothing life can attain, is quite so desirable as sleep. My mind is losing resolution and control.

But the sun is sinking; its brilliance is already fading—night lies ahead, not day. This is only afternoon, yet I'm experiencing symptoms I've never known in the past until dawn was closer than midnight. If sleep weighs so heavily on me now, how can I get through the night, to say nothing of the dawn, and another day, and its night, and possibly even the dawn after? Something must be done—immediately.

I pull the *Spirit of St. Louis* up two or three hundred feet above the water, shake my head and body roughly, flex muscles of my arms and legs, stamp my feet on the floor boards. The nose veers sharply left, and I have to put my toes back on the rudder to straighten it out. I breathe deeply, and squirm about as much as I can while still holding the controls.[6]

And there's the question of staying awake. Could I keep sufficiently alert during long, monotonous hours of flying with my eyes glued to the instruments, with nothing more to stimulate my mind than the leaning of a needle? It was difficult enough to stay awake over the ice fields southwest of Newfoundland, when my eyes could travel the whole horizon back and forth, and with the piercing light of day to stir my senses. How would it be with fog and darkness shutting off even the view of my wing tips? It would be like a dream, motionless yet rocketing through space, led on and on by those will-o'-the-wisp needles, those glowing dials in front of me, always two feet away. A dream that could turn into a nightmare fully as alarming as engine failure. [Even the most experienced veteran pilots can experience a detached feeling of unreality after a long period of being surrounded by visual nothingness except for their cockpit. Such is not uncommon when they have been flying straight and level for long periods at high altitudes where all they can see is the unchanging sky. Some pilots even have reactions akin to what we have now come to call "panic attacks."] After I'd been flying for an hour or two or three, might I find myself struggling to keep upright, to hold my altitude, to bring my plane back under control (flapping my sleep-bound arms with superhuman effort in a vain attempt to stop the sickening fall)? Might I awake from my stupor to hear air screaming past my cockpit and see the turn indicator moving sluggishly, its venturi clogged with ice?

Then there would be no waking in a soft and comfortable bed. That fall would end—how would it end? What do you feel in the rending, crashing instant that must exist between life and violent death? Do you experience excruciating pain? Have you time to realize that life itself has ended? Is all consciousness forever blotted out, or is there an awakening as from a dream, as from a nightmare; an awakening that for some reason you can't communicate freely back to living men—just as you can't communicate freely from a dream? What waits after life as life waits at the end of a dream? Do you really meet your God, or does blank nothingness replace your being?[7]

During the eighteenth hour of his flight (his forty-second hour without sleep), he describes how the ordeal is beginning to exact its toll just as his first dawn arrives:

With this faint trace of dawn, the uncontrollable desire to sleep falls over me in quilted layers. I've been staving it off with difficulty during the hours of moonlight. Now it looms all but insurmountable. . . .

I've lost command of my eyelids. When they start to close, I can't restrain them. They shut, and I shake myself, and lift them with my fingers. I stare at the instruments,

wrinkle forehead muscles tense. Lids close again regardless, stick tight as though with glue. My body has revolted
from the rule of its mind. Like salt in wounds, the light
of day brings back my pains. Every cell of my body is on
strike, sulking in protest, claiming that nothing, nothing
in the world, could be worth such effort; that man's tissue
was never made for such abuse. My back is stiff; my
shoulders ache; my face burns; my eyes smart. It seems
impossible to go on longer. All I want in life is to throw
myself down flat, stretch out—and sleep.[8]

Yet he is just over halfway there. He must fight off sleep in this debilitating and droning monotony for another fifteen hours. Fortunately,
with the brightness of a new day he becomes more alert. But it is essentially sheer will power (and his ingenuity for self-stimulation) that keeps
him awake.

Still later he relates:

I warn myself of relaxation's dangers. It's all very well,
I argue, to go half asleep in high clear air, but flying
blind at low altitude is a matter of life and death—life
and death! It's no use. There's a power beyond my will's
control which knows exactly where the danger limit lies,
and which realizes that as I become more skilled in using
instruments, the need for concentration accordingly
decreases. Simply telling myself that I must hold those
needles on their marks has no effect. That power, that
third being, has taken over the direction of my flight,
knowing better than I how far down the wing or nose
can drop before an emergency has to be declared and
the alarm given to my ordinary senses. [Lindbergh's
comment about the "third being" will be examined later.]
I looked forward with great apprehension to long
periods of flying blind under conditions of extreme
fatigue. I was afraid that needles would jump around
the cockpit more with each quarter-hour that passed,
and that the plane might get completely out of control.[9]

Lindbergh faces other enemies besides sleep:

It's a terrific strain on the mind also when it turns from long-proven bodily instincts to the cold, mechanical impartiality of needles moving over dials. For count- less centuries, it's been accustomed to relying on the senses. They can keep the body upright on the darkest night. They're trained to catch a stumble in an instant. Deprived of sight, they can still hold a blind man's balance. Why, then, should they be so impotent in an airplane? . . .

Wings quiver as I enter the cloud. Air roughens until it jerks the *Spirit of St. Louis* about as though real demons were pulling at fuselage and wings. No stars are over- head now to help, no clouds are below. Everything is uniform blackness, except for the exhaust's flash on passing mist and the glowing dials in my cockpit, so different from all other lights. What lies outside doesn't matter. My world and my life are compressed within these fabric walls.

Flying blind is difficult enough in smooth air. In this swirling cloud, it calls for all the concentration I can muster. The turn and bank indicators, the air speed, the altimeter, and the compass, all those phosphorescent lines and dots in front of me, must be kept in proper place. When a single one strays off, the rest go chasing after it like so many sheep, and have to be caught quickly and carefully herded back into position again.[10]

It's cold up here at—I glance at the altimeter—10,500 feet—-cold—good Lord, there are things to be consid- ered outside the cockpit! How could I forget! I jerk off a leather mitten and thrust my arm out the window. My palm is covered with stinging pinpricks. I pull the flash- light from my pocket and throw its beam onto a strut. The entering edge is irregular and shiny—ice! And as far out into darkness as the beam penetrates, the night is filled with countless, horizontal, threadlike streaks. The venturi tubes may clog at any moment!

I've got to turn around, get back into clear air—quickly! But in doing so those instrument needles mustn't move too far or too fast. Mind, not body, must control the turn.

My bodily senses want to whip the *Spirit of St. Louis* into a bank and dive it out of the thunderhead, back into open sky.[11]

The nose is down, the wing low, the plane diving and turning. I've been asleep with open eyes. I'm certain they've been open, yet I have all the sensations of waking up—lack of memory of intervening time, inability to comprehend the situation for a moment, the return of understanding like blood surging through the body. I kick left rudder and pull the stick back cornerwise. My eyes jump to the altimeter. No danger; I'm at 1,600 feet, a little above my chosen altitude. In a moment, I'll have the plane leveled out. But the turn-indicator leans over the left—the air speed drops—the ball rolls quickly to the side. A climbing turn in the opposite direction! My plane is getting out of control!

The realization is like an electric shock running through my body. It brings instant mental keenness. In a matter of seconds I have the *Spirit of St. Louis* back in hand. But even after the needles are in place, the plane seems to be flying on its side. I know what's happening. It's the illusion you sometimes get while flying blind, the illusion that your plane is no longer in level flight, that it's spiraling, stalling, turning, that the instruments are wrong.[12]

Lindbergh must rely on every ounce of his training and rationality not to follow that illusion, which is doubly difficult as his consciousness constantly hovers near the irrational realm of sleep, unreality, and hallucination brought on by both fatigue and sensory deprivation.

Admiral Richard Byrd: The Cold, Lonely Fight against Death

Admiral Byrd's story of surviving for several months in an isolated weather shack in the Antarctic is not quite so well known as Lindbergh's famous flight, although it was a considerably more grueling ordeal. Where Lindbergh faced sudden death for a day and a half and had to be highly vigilant from moment to moment, Byrd faced a slow, wasting death over many months from cold, starvation, exhaustion, and carbon monoxide poisoning. A more terribly lonely ordeal can scarcely be imagined.

Byrd was a Navy pilot and a veteran polar explorer when he undertook the solitary mission that he later described in his book *Alone*.[13] Unlike Lindbergh's account, which was reconstructed from memory years after his flight, Byrd's description of his ordeal was based on a daily diary—giving his account a particular immediacy for the reader. (Byrd was, like Lindbergh, also a decent writer. My view is that good *observers* often make good writers, as well as making good survivors.) Like Lindbergh, Byrd had been a pioneer aviator and, ironically enough, he and a crew were almost prepared to take off on a flight to Paris at the very time Lindbergh left—and from the same field. A month after Lindbergh's flight, Byrd and crew did fly the Atlantic nonstop to Europe, although they had to crash-land in fog just off shore.

Richard Byrd was a son of the Byrds of the Virginia aristocracy and a brother of Senator Harry Byrd. He attended a military school and then the U.S. Naval Academy and became a naval aviator, developing into a specialist in navigation. In 1924 he commanded a squadron of aircraft attached to an expedition to Western Greenland. This stimulated his interest in trying to fly to the North Pole, an accomplishment he claimed in 1926, though some have since disputed this. In the 1930s, after a tour of speech making and fund raising, he led an expedition to the Antarctic to do largely meteorological research. When it became apparent that enough supplies to support a whole party could not be moved to an advance weather station before the long, bitter polar night descended, Byrd decided to occupy the hut alone in order to operate the weather equipment that he deemed crucial to his whole mission. His five-month exile must rank as one of the most brutal solitary confinements of all time.

Byrd's enemies: the bitter cold (to -60°F) and the likely prospect of freezing to death when the stove failed (or carbon monoxide poisoning when the stove worked); starvation; physical exhaustion and debilitation; the mind-bending, endless polar night; and getting lost when venturing outside his hut. After being there for some time, Byrd describes his situation and the disorientation it engenders in the following excerpt as he awakens in the still, sub-zero utter blackness of his shack:

> At home I usually awaken instantly, in full possession
> of my faculties. But that's not the case here. It takes me
> some minutes to collect my wits; I seem to be groping in
> cold reaches of interstellar space, lost and bewildered.
> The room is a non-dimensional darkness, without

shadow or substance; even after all these days I sometimes ask myself: Where am I? What am I doing here? I
discover myself straining, as if trying to hear something
in a place where no sound could possibly exist. Ah, yes,
tick-tick, tick-tick-tick, tick. The busy, friendly voices of
the register and thermograph [weather recording instru-
ments] on the shelves . . . sounds I can understand and
follow, even as a mariner emerging from the darkness of
the boundless ocean can recognize and follow a coast by
the bell buoys offshore.[14]

Some weeks later he is suddenly overcome and nearly killed by carbon monoxide fumes from his faulty stove and gasoline generator. Even
under that kind of stress and loss of orientation, however, he seems to
have been capable of detaching part of himself and observing what was
happening to him, as if his personality had two parts. (Such detachment
from oneself is an important coping mechanism. It reflects the importance to survival of an enduring monitoring/observing part of the self.)

Two facts stood clear. One was that my chances of
recovering were slim. The other was that in my weakness
I was incapable of taking care of myself. These were
desperate conclusions, but my mood allowed no others.
All that I could reasonably hope for was to prolong my
existence for a few days by hoarding my remaining
resources; by doing the necessary things very slowly and
with great deliberation. . . . There was no alternative.
But you must have faith—you must have faith in the
outcome, I whispered to myself. . . .[15]

The outlet ventilator [of the stove] was two-thirds
filled with ice [one reason for his carbon monoxide
poisoning]: I could just reach it from the bunk with a
stick which had a big nail at the end. After every exer-
tion I rested; the pain in my arms and back and head
was almost crucifying. I filled a thermos jug with warm
water, added powdered milk and sugar, and carried
the jug into the sleeping bag. My stomach crawled with
nauseous sensations; but, by taking a teaspoonful at a
time, I finally managed to get a cupful down.

I won't even attempt to recall all the melancholy thoughts that drifted through my mind that long afternoon. But I can say truthfully that at no time did I have any feeling of resignation. My whole being rebelled against my low estate. As the afternoon wore on, I felt myself sinking. Now I became alarmed. This was not the first time I had ever faced death. It had confronted me many times in the air. But then it had seemed altogether different. In flying, things happen fast: the verdict crowds you instantly; and when the invisible and neglected passenger [death] comes lunging into the cockpit, he is but one of countless distractions. But now death was a stranger sitting in a darkened room, secure in the knowledge that he would be there when I was gone.[16]

(Note that Byrd has personified a possible outcome of his situation—death—as if it were another individual there with him. This personifying of features of one's circumstances is a common occurrence in solitary ordeals.)

He continues, later:

Afterwards, lying in the sleeping bag, I tried to analyze the possibilities. By then I had been through five days of [severe illness]—five everlasting, interminable days. I had been lost on a great plateau of pain where all the passes were barred. I had suffered and struggled; I had hoped and stopped hoping. Still, it is not in a man to stop, anyhow; something animal and automatic keeps him propped on his feet long after the light has gone from his heart. And as I lay there thinking, I finally asked myself: What are your assets? What might be done that has not already been done?

To begin with, there were two certainties. One was that no help was to be had from the outside—the Barrier [the antarctic ice plateau] was a wall between [him and base camp]. The other was that little could be done without improving the ventilation in the shack. Even if materials had been available to make a drastic change, I was palpably too weak to undertake anything of that order. Here the warmish weather had been an unexpected ally. I had been able to do without the stove for long intervals during the day; and the relief from the fumes had given my body respite. This was sheer luck, however. The greatest cold was yet to come, and might come any day.[17]

For the next three months, Byrd hung on to life like the last leaf that refuses to drop from a branch. He would simply not give up on his mission. Movement was agony, cooking a monumental chore, cranking his radio generator during transmissions a psychological Long March that left him weak and trembling.

How extreme was Byrd's ordeal? After he was rescued, an observer reported:

> Later they learned of the mess the [rescue] tractor men had found, the filth and litter in the shack, the appearance of this wild-eyed wraith whose eyes were sunk into his head, who looked twenty years older than his forty-six years, with lined, scabby face, dirty clothes and hands, scarecrow body and long disheveled hair. Byrd was put to bed and remained there. It was two months and four days before he was well enough [physically] to return to Little America [the base camp in Antarctica]. . . .[18]

Note that Byrd, despite the extremity of his situation and his perilous physical condition, writes that "at no time did I have any feeling of resignation." Somehow he found inner resources from which he gained the strength to endure. The inner strength surely must have been more than what Byrd himself called "something animal and automatic."

Sir Francis Chichester: The Lonely Struggle against Storm and Fatigue

Another kind of solitary ordeal is faced by that special and curious breed, the single-handed sailor. Perhaps the most famous and romantic recent example has been Sir Francis Chichester, most noted for sailing around the world alone in 1966–67 in a 53-foot sailboat at the age of sixty-five. (He followed the example of Joshua Slocum, the first person to sail alone around the world, in the 1890s.) Like both Lindbergh and Byrd, he also had been in his younger days a pioneering aviator (he flew from England to Australia and then to Japan in 1931). Also like the former figures, he was a crack navigator who made major breakthroughs in aerial navigation that were the equal of Lindbergh's finding Paris and

Byrd's locating the North Pole. (The navigation theme bears examination later.) He was fifty when he took up ocean sailing.

Chichester's ordeal: trying single-handedly to sail a 53-foot boat for fifteen months. His enemies: injury, equipment failure, storms and capsizing, getting lost, starvation, and isolation.

A glimpse of Chichester's hardship is provided in the following excerpts:

> It was a tiresome and trying period of the voyage. If I kept *Gipsy Moth* going fast on the wind, she slammed damnably into the seas, which worried me for the safety of her hull. Yet I had to keep going as fast as I could if I was not to fall hopelessly behind the [speed record of the fast nineteenth-century sailing vessels called] Clippers. I could make no good radio contacts, and I had trouble trying to charge the batteries. . . . At night I was troubled with cramp in my legs which would hit me after I had been asleep about two hours, and would let go only if I stood up. This meant that I never got more than about two hours sleep at a time. . . .[19]
>
> Suddenly there was a major crisis. I suppose I should not have let myself get caught, but due to fatigue I was not at my best for dealing with emergencies. As I was trying to eat some breakfast, a particularly fierce squall struck. . . .
>
> The boom came over with an almighty "wham," the [self-steering] vang tearing a stanchion out of the deck. . . .
>
> One's thoughts at these moments of crisis are sometimes curiously detached. My chief personal worry during the gybe and the troubles that followed it [which put his very life at risk] was that, without a cap to protect them, my spectacles would blow away. . . .[20]
>
> I think I was awake when the boat began to roll over. If not, I woke immediately she started to do so. Perhaps when the waves hit her I woke. It was pitch dark. As she started rolling I said to myself, "Over she goes!" I was not frightened, but intensely alert and curious. [Again, not an uncommon reaction.] Then a lot of crashing and banging started, and my head and shoulders were being bombarded with crockery and cutlery and bottles. I

had an oppressive feeling of the boat being on top of me. I wondered if she would roll over completely, and what the damage would be; but she came up quietly the same side that she had gone down. I reached up and put my bunk light on. It worked, giving me a curious feeling of something normal in a world of utter chaos. . . .[21]

I was fagged out, and I grew worried by fits of intense depression. Often I could not stand up without hanging on to some support, and I wondered if I had something wrong with my balancing nerves. I felt weak, thin and somehow wasted, and I had a sense of immense space empty of any spiritual—what? I didn't know. I knew only that it made for intense loneliness, and a feeling of hopelessness, as if faced with imminent doom. On November 5 I held a serious conference with myself about my weakness. When I got up that morning I found that I could not stand on my legs without support, just as if I had emerged from the hospital after three months in bed. I was exhausted after a long struggle with the radio on the previous evening, and a long-drawn battle with the mainsail during the night finished me off. Then I thought, "Husky young men on fully crewed yachts during an ocean race of a few days have been known to collapse from sheer exhaustion. I have been doing this singlehanded for more than two months. Is it any wonder that I feel exhausted?" That cheered me up a bit.[22]

What was Chichester seeking on his solo circumnavigation for which he was willing to subject himself to such hardship? Was he simply a masochist, or did he have some more fundamental goal?

Note how both Byrd and Chichester show a certain degree of detachment, as if one part of the self observes another. And note for future reference how Chichester is comforted by the ordinary-world act of turning on a light, and how he motivates himself by comparing his lot with that of others.

David Lewis: Alone on the Antarctic Sea

David Lewis[23] was a New Zealand physician and avid sailor with a penchant for adventure. He had taken several long ocean voyages and written books about them before deciding, in 1973, that he wanted to do something no one had ever done—sail solo around Antarctica. He confronted many potentially deadly situations from storm, the freezing cold, and injury. The following gives a flavor of what he faced:

But this storm was something altogether new. By evening the estimated wind speed was over 60 knots; the seas were conservatively forty feet high and growing taller—great hollow rollers, whose wind-torn crests thundered over and broke with awful violence. The air was thick with driving spray.

Ice Bird was running down wind on the starboard gybe (the wind on the starboard quarter), with storm jib sheeted flat as before. Once again I adjusted the windvane to hold the yacht steering at a small angle to a dead run, and laid out the tiller lines where they could be grasped instantaneously to assist the vane. This strategy had served me well in the gale just past. . . . But would it be effective against this fearful storm? Had any other precautions been neglected? The Beaufort inflatable life raft's retaining straps had been reinforced by a crisscross of extra lashings across the cockpit. Everything movable, I thought, was securely battened down; the washboards were snugly in place in the companionway; the hatches were all secured. No, I could not think of anything else that could usefully be done.

Came a roar, as of an approaching express train. Higher yet tilted the stern; Ice Bird picked up speed and hurtled forward surfing on her nose, then slewed violently to starboard, totally unresponsive to my hauling at the tiller lines with all my strength. A moment later the tottering breaker exploded right over us, smashing the yacht down on to her port side. The galley shelves tore loose from their fastenings and crashed down in a cascade of jars, mugs, frying pan and splintered wood. I have no recollection of where I myself was flung— presumably backwards on to the port bunk. I only recall clawing my way up the companionway and staring aft through the dome.

The invaluable self-steering vang had disappeared and I found, when I scrambled out on deck, that its vital gear-ing was shattered beyond repair—stainless steel shafts twisted and cog wheels and worm gear gone altogether. The stout canvas dodger round the cockpit was hanging in tatters. The jib was torn, though I am not sure whether it had split right across from luff to clew then or later. My recollections are too confused and most of that day's log entries were subsequently destroyed.

I do know that I lowered the sail, slackening the halyard, hauling down the jib and securing it, repeatedly unseated from the jerking foredeck, half blinded by stinging spray and sleet, having to turn away my head to gulp for the air being sucked past me by the screaming wind. Then lying on my stomach and grasping handholds like a rock climber, I inched my way back to the companionway and thankfully pulled the hatch to after me.

I crouched forward on the edge of the starboard bunk doing my best to persuade Ice Bird to run off before the wind under bare poles. She answered the helm, at best erratically, possibly because she was virtually becalmed in the deep canyons between the waves; so that more often than not the little yacht wallowed broadside on, port beam to the sea, while I struggled with the tiller lines, trying vainly to achieve steerage way and control.

And still the wind kept on increasing. It rose until, for the first time in all my years of seagoing, I heard the awful high scream of force thirteen hurricane winds rising beyond 70 knots.

The remains of the already-shredded canvas dodger streamed out horizontally, flogging with so intense a vibration that the outlines blurred. Then the two stainless steel wires supporting the dodger parted and in a flash it was gone. The whole sea was white now. Sheets of foam, acres in extent, were continually being churned anew by fresh cataracts. These are not seas, I thought: they are the Snowy Mountains of Australia—and they are rolling right over me. I was very much afraid.

Sometime later—I had no idea how long—my terror receded into some remote corner of my mind. I must have shrunk from a reality I could no longer face into a world of happier memories, for I began living in the past again, just as I had in my exhaustion in the gale two days earlier. It is hard to explain the sensation. I did not move over from a present world into an illusory one but temporarily inhabited both at once and was fully aware of doing so, without feeling this to be in any way strange or alarming. My handling of the tiller was quite automatic.

I was not wearing my safety harness, for I often omitted it these days; after all, the precaution seemed rather pointless when the ship itself was doomed. The breaking sea caught me unawares, the shock catapulting me through the air towards the vanished starboard guard wires. Here I brought up agonizingly, if providentially, against the tip of a stanchion. I felt ribs go in a blaze of breath-stopping agony and my right arm went numb as the elbow shared the impact. I can't stand any more pain, I thought, as I writhed in the scuppers, gasping for breath. But there was also relief that I had not gone over the side, where five minutes in the -1°C water would have brought oblivion. Such is the mark of our humanity. There is no foreseeable way out of your predicament; you have come to the end of your tether; yet some unsuspected strength within you drives you to keep on fighting.

I dragged myself, moaning and groaning and making a great to-do, along the side deck and down below. As the wind was from the south-south-west there was no need to steer. Bilge water was overflowing the floorboards, though. Cursing mentally—drawing each breath meant stabbing pain enough without aggravating it by speech—I prized up the floor and scooped up twenty-two buckets from the well to tip them into the cockpit. The rest of that pain-fringed day and a restless, chilly night I spent on my bunk, increasingly aware of the vast difference between a merely damp sleeping bag and one still soaked from the recent capsize. . . .[24]

The knife-stabs in my right side that had greeted any sudden body movement during this work on deck became less frequent once I had returned below where

I could move with greater caution. But my hands! I rocked back and forth, tears squeezing out from under my eyelids. Would they never mend? Extravasated blood ballooned out each finger end grotesquely so that the finger nails were acutely angled. The bases of the fingers were, in contrast, pale but so swollen that my hands looked like flippers. On the credit side, there was as yet no sign of gangrene. The antibiotics must be taking effect, then, and the healing process beginning, though how complete it would be only time would tell—if time were allowed me. But the pain! The agony resulting from only the briefest moment of chill was worse, much worse than it had been and was lasting longer.

This was the day that my sheepskin trousers, which had shown signs of falling apart, finally disintegrated. Damp and smelly though they were, I was sorry to see the last of them; sorrier still to have to go through the awkwardness and discomfort of getting them off, then pulling over my shivering limbs the mildewed and half-frozen Dacron flying suit I had earlier discarded. How much more of this recurrent misery could I stand? Would it not be easier just to give up the hopeless struggle? And fresh trouble was in store: as I lit the hurricane lamp that evening, I saw with a sinking heart that the glass was dropping again.

I spent a sleepless night as the weather worsened. The number two storm jib, despite the knots that reduced its length to fit the short mast, was setting so badly that periodically it threshed violently. This was my best and strongest sail, a brand-new one, but because I could not immediately think up any way of saving it from the damage it was sustaining, I did not even venture outside to look. Had I done so, ways of dealing with the trouble surely would have become apparent. I would rather not record this, but the sorry fact of the matter is that I had become so demoralized and my dread of pain from fingers and ribs was so great that I did not once go on deck to experiment with the sail's sheeting for three whole days. . . .[25]

By now the cabin was well awash and fresh spurts of water were continually being forced under pressure through the split coach roof. It must be got rid of even at the risk of swamping when unbattening the hatchway. Twenty-seven bucketfuls were lifted out, every one paid for in pain: pain in my right ribs with each gasping breath; in my hands as always; from a new bruise whenever a wave smashed me against the side of the cabin. At length it was done, though a worse task awaited me. For a record three days I had held off using the toilet bucket. Now it could not be delayed a moment longer. This was a dreaded chore and a difficult feat of balance at the best of times. In a gale it was a hundred times harder. I dreaded removing my flying suit and, even more, stumbling into my filthy tattered clothes again with one wary eye on the bucket without spilling its contents all over the cabin, myself, the cockpit or the deck was the most delicate operation but, more by luck than otherwise, it was always successfully accomplished.[26]

Christiane Ritter: The Struggle against Loss of Self

Christiane Ritter was a German housewife whose husband made a living trapping in the icy wastes north of the Arctic Circle in Spitsbergen, a group of islands north of Norway. They had lived much of their married life apart from each other until her husband suggested that she come north to live with him and his partner in a tiny hut along one of the frozen inlets of the Arctic Ocean. She traveled north by one of the infrequent steamers. Of all of the survivors examined in this chapter, Christiane Ritter was probably the least prepared by training and experience (though not by character, as one who reads her book will see) for the struggle she was to face. She was shocked by the Spartan conditions she discovered. She spent several periods of days and even weeks alone in the closet-sized hut while her husband and his partner walked their far-flung traplines. During such periods she had to cope with isolation, with the numbing stillness and sameness of the Arctic, with the task of gathering wood for the all-essential fire, and with the gathering of snow to melt for water. In addition, she faced blizzards that buried the hut and forced her to tunnel her way out the door; and she faced the haunting twenty-four-hour polar night, which, together with her isolation, combined to produce extreme emotional stress. Further, there was always the possibility of running out of food, or of confronting a marauding polar bear that might be blown her way on the moving ice floes.

Christiane Ritter tells her story this way:

> To live in a hut in the Arctic had always been my husband's wish-dream. Whenever anything went wrong in our European home, a short circuit, a burst pipe, or even if the rent was raised, he would always say that nothing like that could happen in a hut in the Arctic.
>
> But for me at that time, as for all central Europeans, the Arctic was just another word for freezing and forsaken solitude. I did not follow at once.
>
> Then gradually the diaries that arrived in summer from the Far North began to fascinate me. They told of journeys by water and over ice, of the animals and the fascination of the wilderness, of the strange light over the landscape, of the strange illumination of one's own self [remember this phrase] in the remoteness of the polar night. In his descriptions there was practically never any mention of cold or darkness, of storms or hardships.
>
> The little winter hut appeared to me in a more and more friendly light. As housewife I would not have to accompany him on the dangerous winter excursions. I could stay by the warm stove in the hut, knit socks, paint from the window, read thick books in the remote quiet, and, not least, sleep to my heart's content.[27]

The phrase "strange illumination of one's own self" is interesting, as it reflects the radical changes in understanding oneself that can occur in prolonged solitary ordeals. The term "strange illumination" hints at the unworldly kinds of changes in consciousness that can occur.

Upon arriving in the Far North, the appalling dimensions of the ordeal she is about to face begin slowly to define themselves to her:

> How quiet it is here on the island; the beat of the ship's engines is still in my ears. The waves break monotonously on the rocky strand, cold and indifferent. Involuntarily the thought comes into my mind: Here we can live, we can also die, just as it pleases us; nobody will stop us.

The scene is comfortless. Far and wide not a tree or shrub; everything gray and bare and stony. The boundlessly broad foreland, a sea of stone, stones stretching up to the crumbling mountains and down to the crumbling shore, an arid picture of death and decay.

The hut stands in the middle of a small promontory, whose banks drop steeply down to the sea. It is a small, bleak, square box, completely covered in black tarpaulin. A few boards, nailed higgledy-piggledy over the tarpaulin, provide the only light touch in all this blackness. A solitary stovepipe rears up from the roof into the misty air. Chests and tubs, sleighs, oars, old skis lie against the walls, and around lie the bones of mysterious animals. . . .[28]

It takes all my self-control not to betray the horror and dread I feel at all the new impressions crowding in on me. I am amazed at my husband, who seems to have quite forgotten how a European woman is accustomed to live. He seems to take completely for granted that I will feel quite at home in this wretched hut, with beasts of prey for company. Anyhow, this way of introducing me to the wilderness does not seem very considerate.[29]

Before long, she faces her first crisis:

I am alone in the furious drumfire of a hurricane. I think these are called blizzards in books about the Arctic. In any case I have never been through anything like this in Europe. From within the hut it sounds as though an express train were being driven endlessly over iron bridges and through screaming tunnels.

For nine days and nine nights the storm rages without respite, and the worst of it is that the men are away. The storm broke a few hours after they left. . . .[30]

The wind rose rapidly. . . . I thought with a shock of fear of all the things out of doors that had to be secured against the storm. I dressed quickly, and without giving it much thought, dashed out of the hut.

Never had I seen Spitsbergen looking like that. The entire country was in an uproar. The snow was driving like a broad stream of water over the land and over the hut and in clouds over the black sea. The swell was going out seaward. High above, the storm was booming like a deep, long-drawn organ note.

The window shutters were already buried under snow. I had to shovel them out, and put them in the passage.

There was not too much fuel in the hut. I set about chopping the sawn logs which were lying against the wall of the hut. From the stories the men had told me, it seemed that a storm like this could last three weeks. I chopped away for dear life.

The storm was still increasing in violence. The hollow roaring undertone had swelled into intermittent thunder. Now and again I could hear the first dull rumbling blows of the approaching storm at sea beating on the cliffs. It was cheerless in the hut. The stove smoked and although stoked high, the room remained cold. The wind whistled through the wooden walls and the hideous foxes swung gently. In spite of my fur jacket and fur hood I froze.

The fire burnt down quickly, and what could I do in order not to burn still more precious fuel, but go to sleep? I felt my way into my little room. It was ice-cold, and I crept fully clothed into my little bunk. But it was easier to think of sleeping than to fall asleep, for here the noise if anything was still greater. To the crashing thunder of the storm was added the knocking and rapping of all the boards and posts leaning against the east wall. The wind was howling in the stovepipe, and on the roof the frozen corpses of the skinned foxes, left up there for heaven knows what reason, were tapping and knocking.[31]

Christopher Burney: The Struggle for Sanity

Christopher Burney, a British underground fighter and intelligence agent, was captured by the Nazis in France in World War II. He describes his ordeal, but little of his background, in the book *Solitary Confinement*.[32]

Burney's ordeal consisted of 526 long days in oppressive solitary confinement, brutal interrogations, starvation rations, the prospect of execution, unheated cells, and lack of stimulation. He was placed in a five-by-ten cell with one small window and a board bed with one blanket.

He also had a mug and a spoon. Coffee was given to him each morning, and bread and soup for lunch.

He describes his situation after being imprisoned:

> I lay awake for a long time that night, pricked into consciousness and fury by the banderillas of might-have-beens and hunger. And when I woke again in the morning, they returned in a sudden solid on-rush as I looked round me at the walls of concrete and remembered what had happened yesterday. It was then, too, that the more remote parts of my life started to parade before me, each marked with its little label, on which was written, "I am past and cannot return." Whereas yesterday I had cursed an interruption to the current chapter of my life, now I found myself obliged to say goodbye to everything that had gone before. Fate, as it were, had tired of the plot which it had woven around me, of the people and places past which it had led me, and had torn up the script, undone the world it had created, and was now wondering whether or not to do the same with me. From this farther side, the world that was gone presented a new and unfamiliar face. What my eyes had once looked upon as things or scenes in themselves complete and independent of me, my memory saw as unfinished sketches on a single canvas, drawn higgledy-piggledy in the mood of each minute, then abandoned, and needing more generous and skillful artistry than I had given them and an eye of a wider view than mine to bring them together in harmony and endow each and all with beauty and meaning. . . .[33]

Of the following days I remember little in particular, because nothing happened, and days in prison are distinguishable only by such rare incidents as from time to time make one of them memorable among its fellows. . . .[34]

Throughout the summer, while it was fine and warm, I slept bare between my two blankets, and when in the early morning I heard the trolley rattling round the floor with the "coffee" (a euphemism, but it will serve), I put on my trousers and washed under the cold tap. This was an operation which required some skill, for the tap was of the push-button kind and had to be pressed with one hand while the water was scooped up with the other. And when I had done that, my active day was ended. As Economic Man my small doings were quite passive, and as *homo artifax*, I was incapacitated by lack of the wherewithal to draw, write or make anything; nor could I even be a student, however poor, since I had nothing to read. The fourteen or more hours of daylight could be filled only by the aimless movement of my body in the cell or by the meandering of thoughts within my head.[35]

Edith Bone: Seven Years' Solitary

Edith Bone[36] was a sixty-year-old Englishwoman who was arrested by the Hungarian Communist government in 1949 and sentenced to fifteen years in solitary confinement. (She served seven years, being freed during the Hungarian uprising of 1956.) Although she had been a believing Communist, she was accused of being a spy for the British. Her uplifting book is an especially insightful documentation of means of coping in the most limited, dehumanizing, and confining kinds of circumstances. Interestingly, and in keeping with her proactive character during her ordeal, you will note in the excerpts below that she chooses not to dwell on "atrocities" she experienced. She describes her first cell:

It was quite dark in there. There was no means of ventilation and no natural light at all, only electric light. In the cell itself the mortar was crumbling from the ceiling, spiders' webs hung in festoons, and on one side the wall had a sort of fur coat of fungus. On the other side, for some reason, there was no fungus, but to make up for this, there was water seeping down the wall. This water later froze into a thin coat of ice. My bed was attached to this wall and I could not pull it away; so I was in cold storage, so to speak, on ice. There was not only no heating but no means of heating at all. There was, on the other hand, a lot of very nasty dirt, human and rat droppings, and a perfectly infernal stink. There were two iron-framed plank beds, a very small table screwed down to the floor and a small stool about a foot square, also screwed down, and of course in the corner the inevitable bucket. I was given an aluminium wash basin, a three-pint jug, an aluminium mug, a small cake of soap, a towel and a packet of toilet-paper.

I was very tired. . . . My arthritis had not been improved by my sojourn in various cellars, and I was all in. So I just put down one blanket and covered myself with the other, thinking that I would have a good sleep in the pitch darkness. In this I was mistaken, because somebody clumped down the iron stairs and switched on a light in my cell. The dazzling light after the utter darkness hurt my eyes very much. The man also banged on the door with some sort of knobkerrie with the idea, I suppose, of preventing me from sleeping. This very unpleasant procedure was repeated every half-hour or so, and, at first, when they put on the light I shielded my eyes with my hand to protect them. But when I realized that one of the purposes of this sort of thing was to make me move, I decided to turn around and lie face downwards, so that my eyes at least would be protected, after which I did not react at all to their antics.[37]

After my rescue and return to England, knowledgeable and experienced friends were disgusted with me when they heard that I did not propose to describe any lurid atrocities in this book, and I was warned that this would greatly jeopardize its success. But I do not believe so; and even if I did, it would make no difference. I made up my mind to record only facts. Other people have harped sufficiently on the atrocity string.

In any case, I considered it a sufficient atrocity to railroad me to prison practically for life—since at the age of sixty, fifteen years means life—when I had not committed even the vestige of any act that could have justified so much as a ten-shilling fine; and to keep me in solitary confinement in a total isolation far exceeding even the solitary confinement imposed on those who had in fact committed crime. Even the worst criminals were allowed to write and to receive letters, and, at certain intervals, visitors. But I, who had committed no crime, was for seven years completely deprived of all contact with the outer world, not because of any action of mine, not because of any particularly abominable conduct or attitude on my part, but because, having once denied all knowledge of me, they had to, or thought they had to, stick to this lie.[38]

As we will see later, Edith Bone made absolutely the most out of her prolonged solitary ordeal.

There is much for the "alienated," uncertain, self-conscious, directionless twentieth-century person to identify and empathize with in the vulnerability and isolation of the preceding cases—almost as if they are a metaphor for the modern human condition, and for the modern individual's search for meaning and belonging. That is perhaps part of their appeal as literature. (Burney and Bone, too, are good writers.) However, these particular individuals also stand apart and distinct, for they all seem to possess, in (because of? prior to?) their ordeals, their own internal compasses that will lead them from alienation and uncertainty toward internal harmony and self-knowledge. While we may see them as victims, they still manage to sense themselves as instrumental agents, and they work at doing so.

Joe Simpson: Alone on a Mountain

Joe Simpson, an English mountaineer who suffered a severe fall while climbing in the Andes, went through one of the most extreme ordeals ever suffered by a mountaineer. His account of the ordeal is equally remarkable:

> As the hammer came out there was a sharp cracking sound and my right hand, gripping the axe, pulled down. The sudden jerk turned me outwards and instantly I was falling. . . .[39]
> I was facing into the slope and both knees locked as I struck it. I felt a shattering blow in my knee, felt bones splitting, and screamed. . . .[40]
> I hung, head down, on my back, left leg tangled in the rope above me and my right leg hanging slackly to one side. I lifted my head from the snow and stared, up across my chest, at a grotesque distortion in the right knee, twisting the leg into a strange zigzag. . . .[41]

Something terrible, something dark with dread occurred to me, and as I thought about it I felt the dark thought break into panic: "I've broken my leg, that's it. I'm dead. . . ."[42]

I kicked my right leg against the slope, feeling sure it wasn't broken. My knee exploded. Bone grated, and the fireball rushed from groin to knee. I screamed. I looked down at the knee and could see it was broken, yet I tried not to believe what I was seeing. It wasn't just broken, it was ruptured, twisted, crushed, and I could see the kink in the joint and knew what had happened. The impact had driven my lower leg up through the knee joint.

Oddly enough, looking at it seemed to help. I felt detached from it, as if I were making a clinical observation of someone else. . . .[43]

I looked south at the small rise I had hoped to scale quickly and it seemed to grow with every second that I stared. I would never get over it. Simon would not be able to get me up it. He would leave me. He had no choice. I held my breath, thinking about it. Left here? Alone? I felt cold at the thought. . . .[44]

The rope which had been tight on my harness went slack. Simon was coming [down toward him]! He must know something had happened. . . .[45]

"What happened? Are you okay?"

I looked up in surprise. I hadn't heard his approach. He stood at the top of the cliff looking down at me, puzzled. . . .[46]

"I fell. The edge gave way." I paused, then I said as unemotionally as I could: "I've broken my leg."[47]

"Are you sure it's broken?"

"Yes.". . .[48]

Already he had begun to dig out his belay seat. I grabbed the two ropes, knotted them together and tied myself into the free end. The other end was already attached to Simon's harness. In effect we were now roped together with one 300-foot line, which would halve the time spent digging belay seats and double the distance lowered. Simon could control the speed of my descent by using a belay plate, and so reduce any sudden jerks of weight and avoid having the rope run away from him if he couldn't get a grip on it with his frozen mitts. The one problem was the knot joining the two ropes. The only way to get it past the belay plate would be by disconnecting the rope from the plate and then reconnecting it with the knot on the other side. This would be possible only if I stood up and took my weight off the rope. I thanked my stars that I hadn't broken both legs. . . .[49]

Simon nodded at me and grinned. Encouraged by his confidence I lifted my feet and began to slide down. It worked!

He let the rope out smoothly in a steady descent. . . .[50]

The sense of weight on my harness increased, as did the speed. I tried braking with my arms but to no effect. I twisted round and looked up into the darkness. Rushes of snow flickered in my torch beam. I yelled for Simon to slow down. The speed increased, and my heart jumped wildly. Had he lost control? I tried braking again. Nothing. I stifled the rising panic and tried to think clearly—no, he hadn't lost control. I'm going down fast but it's steady. He's trying to be quick. . . .[51]

A sense of great danger washed over me. I *had* to stop. I realised that Simon would hear nothing, so I must stop myself. If he felt my weight come off the rope he would know there must be a good reason. I grabbed my ice axe and tried to brake my descent. I leant heavily over the axe head, burying it in the slope, but it wouldn't bite. The snow was too loose. I dug my left boot into the slope but it, too, just scraped through the snow.

Then abruptly my feet were in space. . . .[52]

Looking between my legs, I could see the wall dropping below, angled away from me. It was overhanging all the way to the bottom. . . .[53]

There was no chance of Simon hauling me up.

I waited silently, hugging the rope with my arms to stay upright, and feeling shocked as I stared between my legs at the drop.

It was impossible to reach the wall. . . .[54]

The rope slipped. I bounced down a few inches. Then again. Had he freed the knot? I slipped again. Stopped.

Then I knew what was about to happen. He was coming down [i.e., he was sliding, in danger of falling]. I was pulling him off. I hung still, and waited for it to happen [both of them to fall]. Any minute, any minute. . . .[55]

[The night stars] seemed far away; further than I'd ever seen them before. And bright: you'd think them gemstones hanging there, floating in the air above. Some moved, little winking moves, on and off, on and off, floating the brightest sparks of light down to me.

Then, what I had waited for pounced on me. The stars went out, and I fell. Like something come alive, the rope lashed violently against my face and I fell silently, endlessly into nothingness, as if dreaming of falling. I fell fast, faster than thought, and my stomach protested at the swooping speed of it. I swept down, and from far above I saw myself falling and felt nothing. No thoughts, and all fears gone away. So this is it!

A whoomphing impact on my back broke the dream, and the snow engulfed me. I felt cold wetness on my cheeks. I wasn't stopping, and for an instant blinding moment I was frightened. Now, the crevasse! Ahhh . . . NO!!

The acceleration took me again, mercifully fast, too fast for the scream which died above me. . . .

The whitest flashes burst in my eyes as a terrible impact whipped me into stillness.

I lay still, with open mouth, open eyes staring into blackness, thinking they were closed. . . .

I was alive.[56]

I was on a ledge, or a bridge. I wasn't slipping, but I didn't know which way to move to make myself safe. Face down in the snow I tried to gather my confused ideas into a plan. What should I do now?

I had to hammer an ice screw into the wall without pushing myself off the ledge I was perched on.

As I began to hammer the screw into the ice I tried to ignore the black space beyond my shoulder. . . .[57]

> I tugged on the loose rope. It moved easily.
>
> I saw the rope flick down, and my hopes sank. I drew the slack rope to me, and stared at the frayed end. Cut! I couldn't take my eyes from it. . . .[58]
>
> I fastened a Prussik knot to the rope above the screw. I would climb while still attached to the screw.
>
> An hour later I gave up trying. I had made four attempts to climb the vertical ice wall. Only once had I managed to get myself clear of the ledge.[59]

Later, he decides that if he remains on the ledge he will surely die, and his only remote chance is to lower himself into the dark void beneath him and take his chances with the unknown:

> I let myself slide off the ledge and watched the Prussik get smaller as I abseiled down the slope to the drop. If there was nothing there I didn't want to come back. . . .[60]
>
> The desire to stop abseiling was almost unbearable. I had no idea what lay below me, and I was certain only of two things: Simon had gone and would not return. This meant that to stay on the ice bridge would finish me. There was no escape upwards. . . .[61]
>
> I abseiled slowly over the drop until I was hanging vertically on the rope. The wall of the drop was hard, clear, water ice. . . .
>
> I wanted to cry but couldn't. I felt paralysed, incapable of thinking, as waves of panic swept through me. The torment of anticipating something unknown and terribly frightening broke free, and for a helpless immeasurable time I hung shaking on the rope with my helmet pressed to the ice wall and my eyes tightly closed. I had to see what was beneath me because, for all my convictions, I didn't have the courage to do it blind. . . .
>
> The decision to look down came as I was in the process of turning. I swung round quickly, catching my smashed knee on the ice wall and howling in a frenzy of pain and fright. Instead of seeing the rope twisting loosely in a void beneath me, I stared blankly at the snow below my feet not fully believing what I was seeing. A floor! . . .[62]

I yelled again and again, listening to the echoes, and laughed between the yells. I was at the bottom of the crevasse. . . .

[He sees a possible way out of the crevasse if he can only climb up the slope of the inside of its outer wall.] In seconds my whole outlook had changed. The weary frightened hours of night were forgotten, and the abseil which had filled me with such claustrophobic dread had been swept away. The twelve despairing hours I had spent in the unnatural hush of this awesome place seemed suddenly to have been nothing like the nightmare I had imagined. I could do something positive. I could crawl and climb, and keep on doing so until I had escaped from this grave. Before, there had been nothing for me to do except lie on the bridge trying not to feel scared and lonely, and that helplessness had been my worst enemy. Now I had a plan.

The change in me was astonishing. I felt invigorated, full of energy and optimism. I could see possible dangers, very real risks that could destroy my hopes, but somehow I knew I could overcome them. . . .

A powerful feeling of confidence and pride swept over me as I realised how right I had been to leave the [ledge]. I had made the right decision against the worst of my fears. I had done it, and I was sure that nothing now could be worse than those hours of torture on the [ledge]. . . .[63]

I stood up gingerly on my left leg letting my damaged limb hang uselessly above the snow. It had stiffened during the night and now hung shorter than my good leg. At first I wasn't sure how to set about climbing the slope, which I had guessed to be 130 feet high—ten minutes work with two legs. . . .

Pain flared up as I leant down and dug a step in the snow. . . .

Then I bent down to dig another two steps and repeat the pattern. Bend, hop, rest; bend, hop, rest. . . .

After two and a half hours the slope had steepened considerably, and I had to be especially careful when I hopped. There was a critical moment when all my weight was on the axes driven into the loose snow, and the angle forced me to balance my movements precisely. I had nearly fallen on two occasions. . . .

It took another two and a half hours to reach a point ten feet below the hole in the roof. . . .[64]

If anyone had seen me emerge from the crevasse they would have laughed. My head popped up through the snow roof and I stared gopher-like at the scene outside. . . .

Slowly it dawned on me that my new world, for all its warmth and beauty, was little better than the crevasse. I was 200 feet above the glacier and six miles from base camp. The tranquility evaporated, and a familiar tension returned. The crevasse had been only a starter! How foolish to have thought that I had done it, that I was safe! . . .

I sat up and looked bitterly at the frayed rope-end which I had carried up from the crevasse. . . .

The horror of dying no longer affected me as it had in the crevasse. I now had the chance to confront it and struggle against it. . . .

In a peculiar way it was refreshing to be faced with simple choices. It made me feel sharp and alert, and I looked ahead at the land stretching into the distant haze and saw my part in it with a greater clarity and honesty than I had ever experienced before.

I had never been so entirely alone, and although this alarmed me it also gave me strength. An excited tingle ran down my spine.[65]

Simpson went on to crawl back to his base camp.

Don O'Daniel: The Drowning Man

A solitary survival ordeal of greater immediate intensity and trauma than any of the preceding comes from the annals of psychology. The recollections of a young man, Don O'Daniel, who survived several hours in a raging ocean were, by great good fortune, recorded verbatim during his post-trauma delirium when he repeatedly relived and "worked through" the ordeal.[66] Like Lindbergh, he needed to be alert moment by moment, and as in Byrd's case, the ordeal took a terrible physical toll.

Unfortunately, not a great deal is recorded about this young man's background.

> The ordeal began at Wakonda Beach, Oregon, on the Pacific Ocean. It was 4:30 P.M. on an unusually stormy Saturday afternoon in late fall [1942]. Don O'Daniel, a 19-year-old student at Oregon State College, was jumping the breakers, when suddenly he was swept out to sea by the powerful undertow of the outgoing tide. His anguished companions gave him up for lost, never dreaming that anyone could possibly survive for many hours far out from shore in those huge, battering ocean waves.
>
> At 8:30 P.M. Don was found unconscious on the beach. He was put to bed in a friend's cottage, where he lay inert except for sporadic groaning accompanied by convulsive contractions of his bruised body. After 3 hours, Don began writhing as though he were in great mental agony. With his eyes still closed, he began verbalizing in his delirium a detailed account of the disaster, as though he were reliving it in a dream and talking aloud in his sleep.[67]
>
> Time and again during his delirium Don suddenly became frantic; his body became tense and rigid, as if he were preparing for superhuman exertion. After regaining consciousness, Don explained that he had suddenly found himself knocked off his feet by a wave and had fought hard to regain his upright position, but was knocked down over and over again: "Like when you roll down a hill—you regain your feet, but you keep on rolling. . . ."
>
> Dive under it—dive under the breaker to get back— don't drink any salt water—don't swallow any salt water—take off your pants and shirts—they will help you float—don't take them off it will help you float— keep them on—take it easy—you will be all right—try to hold your own until the tide turns—you will be O.K., but you're getting tired—you were crazy to come out in the first place—you have gone out too far—you know better than that—don't swallow any water—it'll choke you. . . .

> You must have stepped in a hole—the tide took you
> out—it's a good thing you know how to swim—but
> don't swim too hard—get out past the breakers before
> you get caught—you thought you had it figured out—
> how you'd make it—now's your chance.[68]

Note in the preceding that one is hearing entirely from the self as
command giver and not command receiver—from the "instrumental I,"
not the "me."

Notes

[1] Noyce, Wilfrid. *They Survived.* New York: E. P. Dutton, 1963.
[2] Martin, Martha. *O Rugged Land of Gold.* Leicester: Ulverscroft, 1953.
[3] Bickel, Lennard. *Mawson's Will.* New York: Stein & Day, 1977.
[4] Lindbergh, 1953.
[5] Lindbergh, p. 227.
[6] Lindbergh, pp. 233–234.
[7] Lindbergh, pp. 305–306.
[8] Lindbergh, p. 354.
[9] Lindbergh, p. 378.
[10] Lindbergh, p. 324.
[11] Lindbergh, pp. 326–327.
[12] Lindbergh, p. 374.
[13] Byrd, Richard. *Alone.* New York: Putnam, 1938.
[14] Byrd, p. 94.
[15] Byrd, p. 173.
[16] Byrd, p. 177.
[17] Byrd, pp. 188–189.
[18] Hoyt, Edwin P. *The Last Explorer: The Adventures of Admiral Byrd.* New York: The
    John Day Company, 1968, pp. 327–328.
[19] Chichester, Sir Francis. *Gipsy Moth Circles the Globe.* New York: Coward-Mc-
    Cann, 1967, p. 49.
[20] Chichester, 1967, p. 76.
[21] Chichester, 1967, pp. 125–126.
[22] Chichester, 1967, pp. 80–81.
[23] Lewis, David. *Ice Bird.* New York: W. W. Norton, 1975.
[24] Lewis, pp. 77–78.
[25] Lewis, pp. 78–79.
[26] Lewis, pp. 80–81.
[27] Ritter, Christiane. *A Woman in the Polar Night.* New York: Dutton, 1954,
    pp. 9–10.
[28] Ritter, pp. 28–29.
[29] Ritter, p. 34.
[30] Ritter, p. 88.
[31] Ritter, pp. 89–92.

[32] Burney, Christopher. *Solitary Confinement*. London: Macmillan, 1952.
[33] Burney, pp. 11–12.
[34] Burney, p. 13.
[35] Burney, p. 14.
[36] Bone, Edith. *7 Years' Solitary*. New York: Harcourt, Brace, Jovanovich, 1957.
[37] Bone, pp. 106–107.
[38] Bone, p. 119.
[39] Simpson, Joe. *Touching the Void*. New York: Harper & Row, 1988, p. 63.
[40] Simpson, p. 63.
[41] Simpson, p. 63.
[42] Simpson, p. 64.
[43] Simpson, p. 64.
[44] Simpson, p. 64.
[45] Simpson, p. 65.
[46] Simpson, p. 65.
[47] Simpson, p. 65.
[48] Simpson, p. 65.
[49] Simpson, p. 70.
[50] Simpson, p. 71.
[51] Simpson, p. 82.
[52] Simpson, p. 82.
[53] Simpson, p. 83.
[54] Simpson, p. 83.
[55] Simpson, p. 86.
[56] Simpson, p. 94.
[57] Simpson, p. 95.
[58] Simpson, p. 98.
[59] Simpson, p. 99.
[60] Simpson, p. 100.
[61] Simpson, p. 111.
[62] Simpson, p. 112.
[63] Simpson, p. 114.
[64] Simpson, pp. 116–117.
[65] Simpson, pp. 118–120.
[66] Janis, Irving. *Stress and Frustration*. New York: Harcourt Brace Jovanovich, 1971.
[67] Janis, p. 6.
[68] Janis, p. 8.

CHAPTER FOUR

The Psychological Effects of Prolonged Solitary Ordeals

Ordinarily when we read of ordeals, we think—quite rightly—of hardship and suffering. This chapter should properly begin with a description of these negative effects of ordeals. People who have undergone the kinds of ordeals described so far undoubtedly suffer great physical and psychological pain. And it is worth remembering that those who don't survive obviously don't write books about *their* experiences. It is likely, in fact, that those who survive to write about their experiences have, at least in some ways, suffered less than most—they did, after all, survive to tell about it. And it should also be remembered that survivors generally write their stories well after the fact. By the time of writing they have had a chance to work through and come to terms with at least some of their most destructive emotions, such as their rage at what had been done to them, their "survival guilt," and their feelings of helplessness, sorrow, and loss. Thus the serenity conveyed by some may not have been present in the moment of the ordeal. Yet the extremes that some people do manage to live through remain remarkable, and in some cases even uplifting. They are also enlightening.

Some psychological effects of extreme ordeals include anxieties, phobias and nightmares that may remain twenty to thirty years later, constituting what may be termed a "traumatic neurosis" (or nowadays "post-traumatic stress disorder"). Survivors of train crashes, for example, have been known to experience panic at the mere sight or sound of a train decades after the event. Concentration camp survivors have shown fears, anxieties, and "survival guilt" a generation later, as well as paranoid reactions and "persecution manias." Some veterans of Vietnam's jungle fighting still suffer flashbacks and panic attacks twenty-five years later. Amnesia, ordinarily interpreted as an unconscious attempt to block from conscious memory events that are too horribly painful to bear, is also a common reaction in the survivors of trauma. Some may even have long-term psychoses, more extreme forms than amnesia of what psychiatry terms "dissociation."

A commonly observed immediate reaction to sudden, unexpected, traumatic disasters (crashes, tornadoes, explosions, earthquakes, etc.) is the *staring reaction*—survivors who stand still and impassively, sometimes for hours, with blank stares on their faces, looking at nothing in particular. I can recall precisely this reaction in friends numbed by the sudden news of President Kennedy's assassination; they stood in small groups around radios staring blankly as they listened to the reports. One interpretation of this reaction is that the trauma has so disrupted the normal routines and the surroundings of these people that they are "stuck" in the initial process of simply trying to take in the flood of new information. The phase of mobilizing the brain to pay attention to and make sense of something that has just happened is ordinarily momentary in everyday life. In the startle reaction, for example, the individual startles in the first instant, then integrates ("collects himself"), then attends to (looks toward) possible danger, and finally responds adaptively if necessary. If instead of a startling event, however, there is sudden overwhelming, devastating trauma (such as one's house and neighborhood flattened by a tornado), the individual may have great difficulty in even integrating and attending to what has just happened, let alone beginning to respond effectively. The person's functioning is arrested, therefore, in the phase of trying to attend or "take it all in," which is manifested in the staring reaction, a distorted and prolonged version of what is ordinarily vigilant visual attentiveness, a critically important coping and survival mechanism. This phenomenon probably accounts for some of the ineffective behavior shown in the aftermath of a major disaster—people wandering and accomplishing nothing. Specialized training for combat, police work, disaster control, fire fighting, and the like prepares individuals to respond effectively in the initial moments to those very circumstances that disorient the untrained.

(SWAT teams and commandos not only train so as to deal effectively with sudden disorienting events, they also study how to create the kinds of events that will momentarily disorient an enemy.)

In terms of emotional reactions to sudden crises and disasters, it is intriguing to discover how frequently (judging from many accounts) a sudden life-threatening crisis provokes anger rather than terror—anger at oneself for stupidity, anger at life, the world, fate; and how often a crisis (such as flying one's fighter plane into a hillside) provokes, as one's last utterance on this earth, words of *embarrassment:* "God, what a jerk!" "Is this going to look stupid." In many such situations where one realizes that he has bought it, the last words are simply "Oh shit." Because people wish not to appear foolish, they may even hesitate to scream for help in a crisis until it is too late. Similarly, bystanders may not yell to get help when seeing a drowning person, either because they don't want to believe what they're seeing or because they are hesitant to stand out, even if it could cost a life. (I once observed at a crowded beach a young boy beginning to thrash in the water and go under within only feet of other bathers, and I saw several people look anxiously at him and then look away, as if sensing impending danger but not wanting to believe that someone could actually begin to die right there in front of them. Being only too aware of this "bystander phenomenon," I hollered, "Grab that kid!" and several people immediately did.)

Another common reaction to a sudden, life-threatening crisis (such as going through an auto accident) is one of *detachment,* as if one is watching a movie of the event rather than actually experiencing it. (Chichester described having this reaction when his boat overturned. A friend of mine who survived the high-speed rollover of his car and being thrown clear described the experience as like watching a slow-motion silent movie of his car tumbling over and over down the highway—as he was tumbling down the roadside himself. He felt neither pain nor fear.) The psychological protection afforded by such a reaction seems obvious, introducing the concept of coping, which will be taken up in the next chapter.

The more drawn-out kinds of solitary ordeals that are the primary focus of this book do not create all the same kinds of effects as the immediate traumas above.

Sensory Deprivation

Experimental investigations of sensory deprivation—a condition in which subjects are isolated for long periods in an unchanging situation (solitary confinement, marooned alone) with very little external stimulation—have documented a number of psychological effects of prolonged isolation: a craving for stimulation, the occurrence of hallucinations, the appearance of psychotic behavior, and so on. (It should be noted that experiments on the effects of depriving people of stimulation have also involved prolonged social isolation, physical immobility, and frequently great physical discomfort as well, not just simple sensory deprivation. So it is unclear which of these factors accounts for the effects, if indeed they all do not contribute.) Naturally occurring cases of solitary ordeals can share these same features of the sensory deprivation experiments, only they are more acute—for example, if a person is held in solitary confinement or trapped in a cave for a long time. As the following excerpts show, our survivors were not immune to these effects, but neither were they slouches about describing them. Consider Christopher Burney writing on the need for stimulation of the isolated man held in solitary confinement:

> I soon learned that variety is not the spice, but the very stuff of life. We need the constant ebb and flow of wavelets of sensation, thought, perception, action and emotion, lapping on the shore of our consciousness, now here, now there, keeping even our isolation [i.e., keeping our isolation even, balanced] in the ocean of reality, so that we neither encroach nor are encroached upon. If our minds are thus like islands, they are of many shapes, some long and straight, others narrow and bent, a few nicely rounded, and yet others round and hard, impervious to the sea and belching from deep unapproachable cones, the universal warmth which lies beneath us all. We are narrow men, twisted men, smooth and nicely rounded men, and poets; but whatever we are, we have our shape, and we preserve it best in the experience of many things.[1]

Could a psychologist describe man's need for stimulation any better? (Note that Burney, like so many other survivors, uses words in unusual ways to create unusual images, as if wrestling to use ordinary language to capture an extraordinary realization that has come to him through the altering of consciousness created by his ordeal. What is he trying to get across when he describes some people as "belching from deep unapproachable cones, *the universal warmth that lies beneath us all*"? Like many survivors of solitary ordeals [compare Lindbergh and Byrd later], he has experienced a sense of universal or cosmic connectedness akin to what others have claimed to get from drugs or Buddhist enlightenment, and he is trying to convey this profound realization in mere words.)

Byrd, isolated in the Antarctic, describes an incident that also aptly illustrates the need for stimulation and the deadliness of monotony:

> A moment ago there came a tremendous noise, as if tons of dynamite had exploded in [the ice of] the Barrier. The sound was muffled by distance; yet, it was inherently ominous breaking through the silence. But I confess that any sound which interrupts the evenness of this place is welcome.[2]

Byrd describes not just the effects of the absence of stimulation per se, but how it feels to be utterly isolated in Antarctica:

> One may be a long time realizing it, but cold and darkness deplete the body gradually, the mind turns sluggish and the nervous system slows up in its responses. This morning I had to admit to myself that I was lonely. *Try as I may, I find I can't take my loneliness casually; it is too big.* [RDL] But I must not dwell on it. Otherwise I am undone.[3]

What could be a more telling description of being overwhelmed by extreme loneliness than to call it "too big," as if it were some kind of tangible looming dark monster?

There is also the unprepared Christiane Ritter's description of how loneliness and the absence of stimulation affect her alone in the Arctic, a description that also provides a further glimpse into the nature of her ordeal and its effects:

> I have now been alone for nine days. . . . Out-of-doors the country lies white, rigid and absolutely quiet. . . . But for human beings this stillness is horrible. It is days since I have been outside the hut. Gradually I have become fearful of seeing the deadness of the land. I sit in the hut and tire myself out with sewing. It makes no difference whether the work is finished today or tomorrow, but I know what I'm doing. I do not want to

have my mind free for a moment to think, a moment in which to become aware of the nothingness outside. I have become conscious of the power of thought, a power which up here can bestow life or death. I have an inkling, or rather I know with certainty, that it was this, this terror of nothingness, which over the past centuries has been responsible for the death of some hundreds of men up here in Spitsbergen.[4]

Ritter is describing something akin to what many would recognize as "cabin fever" and the sensory deprivation that comes with it, only more extreme. Note how Ritter, like Byrd, mentions how important it is not to dwell on the fact of her isolation, otherwise the "terror of nothingness"—of the loss of her sense of self in the vast emptiness—might lead her to be, in Byrd's description, "undone." Do all isolated people face this terror of nothingness? Keep Chichester and especially Lindbergh in mind.

Hallucinations

Another common effect of prolonged sensory deprivation in solitary ordeals is hallucinations, as if the mind's need to be stimulated by interesting things is so great that it conjures them up (although this is not the only interpretation of hallucinations). Lindbergh has the following hallucination about halfway through his flight as he continues the fight to stay awake after more than a day without sleep:

Last night [in the hotel before flight] I couldn't go to sleep—Tonight I can barely stay awake—if only I could balance the one against the other—awake—asleep— which is it that I want to be?—But look—there's a great black mass ahead—its ears stick up—its jaws gape wide—It's a cloud—or—maybe it's not a cloud—It could be a dragon, or a tiger—I could imagine it into anything at all—What's that whitish object, moving just beyond the window of my room—no, my cockpit—no, my room—I push goggles up to see more clearly—No, they're bedsheets I'm peeking out between—I'm in the nursery of my Minnesota home, and I'm afraid of the dark![5]

At other points Lindbergh was accompanied by "phantoms" with whom he had long conversations. Single-handed sailors on long voyages and mountaineers have also had their share of hallucinations, some of them quite extraordinary. There will be much more to say about hallucinations later.

Loss of Self and Cosmic Unity

Individuals isolated for long periods have another common reaction: a sense of oneness and harmony with the basic rhythms of the universe. An excerpt from Richard Byrd introduces and illustrates this theme:

> The day was dying, the night being born—but with great peace. Here were the imponderable processes and forces of the cosmos, harmonious and soundless. Harmony, that was it! That was what came out of the silence—a gentle rhythm, the strain of a perfect chord, the music of the spheres perhaps.
>
> It was enough to catch that rhythm, momentarily to be myself a part of it. In that instant I could feel no doubt of man's oneness with the universe. The conviction came that the rhythm was too orderly, too harmonious, too perfect to be a product of blind chance—that, therefore, there must be a purpose in the whole and that man was part of that whole and not an accidental offshoot.[6]

In a like vein, Eric Shipton, the British explorer and expedition leader, describing the reactions of men to adversity, speaks of "rare moments of intellectual ecstasy which appear to be the result of a happy coincidence in the rhythm of mind and scene."[7] Burney, in his quote about the "universal warmth that lies beneath us all" (above), may have been alluding to a similar feeling.

Christiane Ritter also describes a feeling of harmony and oneness with the universe but at the same time introduces the corollary, as it were, of this experience—the loss of a sense of the boundaries of the conscious self. For to feel one with the universe, the self must cease to be an island within experience, and the boundaries of the self must break down and a larger wholeness become the anchoring center of experience. Here is the way Ritter describes it:

I myself stand forlornly by the water's edge. The power of this world-wide peace takes hold of me although my senses are unable to grasp it. And *as though I had no real existence, was no longer there* [RDL], the infinite space penetrates through me and swells out, the surging of the sea passes through my being, and what was once a personal will dissolves like a small cloud against the cliffs.

I am conscious of the immense solitude around me. There is nothing that is like me, *no creature in whose appearance I might retain a consciousness of my own self* [RDL—note, again, the unusual mode of expression; her precise meaning is difficult to grasp]; I feel that the limits of my being are being lost in this all-too-powerful nature. . . .

With an effort I return to the hut, fasten my skis and go to the distant headland. I move because I have ordered myself to move, but I do not feel that I am moving. I am as weightless as the air.[8]

She seems to experience the breakdown of the boundaries of the conscious self as more a matter of loss—a "terror of nothingness"—than a reaching out into a new realm of consciousness.

Later, Ritter develops this theme further as she describes the effects on her of the bright full moon during the seemingly endless twenty-four-hour arctic night:

We cannot escape the brightness. I take it particularly badly, and the hunters [her husband and his partner, who have returned briefly] maintain that I am moonstruck. What I would like best of all is to stand all day on the shore, where in the water the rocking ice floes catch and break the light and throw it back to the moon. But the men are very strict with me. They do not let me out of their sight and often keep me in the house. And then I lie down in my little room, where the moonlight filters green through the small snowed-up window. Neither the walls of the hut nor the roof of snow can dispel my fancy that *I am moonlight myself, gliding along the glittering spines and ridges of the mountains, through the white valleys. . . .*[9] [RDL]

Here her feeling of oneness with the universe—a feeling engendered by her isolation and lack of stimulation and the psychological stress they have produced—has been stated more as an *expansion of consciousness* outward into the far reaches of her surroundings, as she fancies she has lost her identity and has become moonlight. (Note how she alludes to the loss of the boundaries of herself by referring to the failure of the walls and roof of her house to contain her consciousness.) Feeling like she has become a part of her surroundings to this degree could easily become, if it has not for her already, the kind of madness that occasionally destroys solitary individuals. For others, it could be experienced as a kind of cosmic spiritual insight akin to that sought by Zen masters and those on a "vision quest."

Sometimes a sudden and particularly traumatic solitary ordeal can be so overwhelming that it produces an even more profound loss of self. Consider the effects of Don O'Daniel's[10] four-hour battle against the ocean after being swept out to sea and exhausting himself in the struggle against the stormy waves. Later, he was found unconscious on the shore. Before he came to, he apparently relived the entire experience, and the words he spoke while unconscious were recorded. As he relives his experience in his delirium, he seems to have lost his sense of personal orientation in a desperate way and is unable to get reoriented psychologically in the throes of his struggle:

> Where are you?—I don't remember this—this is all new to me—where is this?—where were you before you came here?—where was I before I came here?—where are your folks?—where do they live?—wait till you come to—you don't know anyone—they are all strangers—can't I remember where I am?—better go back and see where you lost your senses. . . .
>
> I can't remember where I've been or where I'm going—where is this? Wakonda Beach? where is that?—where am I going?—home?—where is home?—I go to school?—No. I finished school!—*who are you?* [RDL]—Chuck?—how did I get here?—Is this the Navy?—this is like the time in football when I was knocked out for 5 hours—Corvallis?—I remember when I used to go to Corvallis [the town in which his college was located] when my brother was down there—but have I ever gone to school there?—ocean?—swimming?—have I been to the ocean?

—how could I get here and not know a thing?—all I
can remember is my folks trying to talk me out of going
into the Navy—we're going to Corvallis tomorrow?—I
am going to school there?[11]

Lindbergh also deals with the expansion of consciousness as he
speaks of the vivid sensations he could have if he "left" his plane:

At moments I forget I'm in a plane. It's as though the
wings and thinly covered framework no longer suspend
me in air or separate me from the ice I skim across. I feel
I could reach down and plunge my hand into freezing
water, or close my fingers on a chunk of ground-up ice.
I'm conscious only of the desolate solitude, as though I
were standing alone and isolated on one of those cakes.[12]

Another excerpt from *The Spirit of St. Louis* provides a further description of the isolated individual's feelings of expansion of consciousness,
of oneness with the universe and of leaving the self—although to Lindbergh and others, it is not a "loss" experience. It seems remarkably similar
to the descriptions of Ritter, even though their circumstances are very
different:

On a long flight, after periods of crisis and many hours
of fatigue, mind and body may become disunited until at
times they seem completely different elements, as though
the body were only a home with which the mind has been
associated but by no means bound. Consciousness grows
independent of the ordinary senses. You see without
assistance from the eyes, over distances beyond the visual
horizon. There are moments when existence appears
independent even of the mind. The importance of physical desire and immediate surroundings is submerged in
the apprehension of universal values.
For unmeasurable periods, I seem divorced from my
body, as though I were an awareness spreading out
through space, over the earth and into the heavens,
unhampered by time or substance, free from the gravitation that binds men to heavy human problems of the

world. My body requires no attention. It's not hungry.
It's neither warm nor cold. It's resigned to being left
undisturbed. Why have I troubled to bring it here? I
might better have left it back at Long Island or St. Louis,
while this weightless element that has lived within it
flashes through the skies and views the planet. This
essential consciousness needs no body for its travels. It
needs no plane, no engine, no instruments, only the
release from flesh which the circumstances I've gone
through make possible. . . .

While my hand is on the stick, my feet on the rudder,
and my eyes on the compass, this consciousness, like a
winged messenger, goes out to visit the waves below,
testing the warmth of the water, the speed of the wind,
the thickness of intervening clouds. It goes north to the
glacial coasts of Greenland, over the horizon to the edge
of dawn, ahead to Ireland, England, and the continent
of Europe, away through space to the moon and stars,
always returning, unwillingly, to the mortal duty of seeing that the limbs and muscles have attended their
routine while it was gone.[13]

Lindbergh, in yet another instance of an unusual use of language to
convey a new consciousness, captures the sense of oneness with the
universe in the interesting phrases "existence appears independent
even of the mind" and—even more striking—"submerged in the apprehension of universal values." The first phrase seems to suggest that he
is experiencing a kind of consciousness very different from the usual.
Concerning the second, how could he have learned something new about
"universal values" simply from being alone? Yet he seems persuaded
that he has. And many other survivors of solitary ordeals have similar
things to say. Bear in mind that this is a young and only technically
trained Lindbergh talking, not one schooled in philosophy or spirituality
nor interested in the least in mysticism. (Needless to say, he later on became
mightily interested in questions of this kind.) Lindbergh was nothing at
that point if not a total pragmatist and realist whose world was practical
technology. He is also an example of the fact, as mentioned in the preface,
that the *self* comes to experience—and to be experienced—in a different
way during and after an ordeal.

Admiral Byrd also describes his ordeal in language that implies a diffusion of the sense of self outward into his surroundings. One such excerpt sounds strongly negative, much like the experience of Don O'Daniel and something like that of Ritter:

> At home I usually awaken instantly, in full posses-
> sion of my faculties. But that's not the case here [in his
> blacked-out hut]. It takes me some minutes to collect
> my wits; I seem to be groping in cold reaches of inter-
> stellar space, lost and bewildered. The room is a non-
> dimensional darkness, without shadow or substance;
> even after all those days I ask myself: Where am I?
> What am I doing here?[14]

I sense that Byrd might be on the verge of asking, like Don O'Daniel above, "*Who* am I?"

It is intriguing to note how often isolated individuals begin to rely on "oceanic metaphors" (recall the Burney example earlier) in describing their new state of consciousness and their views. Do they use oceanic metaphors because they convey both some sense of their isolation and also their closeness to the rhythms of nature and their oneness with the universe? Are they a way of expressing a state of solitariness that is embedded within a larger whole—the feeling of being in a state of cosmic union ("ocean") but at the same time of being alone ("island")? This is a reminder that to be profoundly isolated and solitary is not necessarily to feel overwhelmingly alone.

Byrd writes the following description of a highly significant event—the coming of night:

> . . . the coming of the polar night is not the spectacular
> rush some imagine it to be. . . . Rather, the effect is a
> gradual accumulation like that of an infinitely prolonged
> tide. Each day the darkness, which is the tide, washes
> in a little farther and stays a little longer; each time the
> day, which is a beach, contracts a little more, until at
> last it is covered.[15]

Byrd at other points writes:

Ah, yes . . . The busy, friendly voices of the register and thermograph on the shelves . . . sounds I can understand and follow, even as a mariner emerging from the darkness of the boundless ocean can recognize and follow a coast by the bell buoys offshore. . . .[16]

The last half of the walk is the best part of the day, the time when I am most nearly at peace with myself and circumstances. Thoughts of life and the nature of things flow smoothly, so smoothly and so naturally as to create an illusion that one is swimming harmoniously in the broad current of the cosmos. During this hour I undergo a sort of intellectual levitation, although my thinking is usually on earthy, practical matters. . . .[17]

At the end only two things really matter to a man, regardless of who he is; and they are the affection and understanding of his family. Anything and everything else he creates are insubstantial; they are ships given over to the mercy of the winds and tides of prejudice. But the family is an everlasting anchorage, a quiet harbor where a man's ships can be left to swing to the moorings of pride and loyalty. . . .[18]

Time was no longer like a river running, but a deep still pool. It was enough to immerse myself in it, quietly and unresentfully, and not struggle any more. The past was done, and the future would adduce its own appropriate liquidation. . . .[19]

There are other interpretations, of course, as to the meaning of feelings of "cosmic unity" and the reliance of survivors on oceanic metaphors. To Freudians, "oceanic feeling" indicates a wish to return to a womblike state of gentle harmony and security. To Jungians, water may be a symbol for the unconscious and therefore for contact with the wisdom of the ages that resides there in the form of archetypes, or ancient inherited memories. (Jungians interpret the hallucinations that occur during prolonged ordeals as the emergence of ancient memories of godlike guiding figures, warriors, demons, tricksters, the Earth Mother, and the like.)

The "loss of self" experience can be either of two extremes: an unhinging experience or a spiritually enlightening one, depending on many other circumstances. I think it tends to be a spiritually enlightening one if the individual has defined him or herself as an instrumental agent in the world rather than an object or victim of it.

Heightened Awareness

Another effect of prolonged isolation related by solitary survivors is an extreme heightening of sensory awareness—as if vigilance (a coping mechanism to be explored later) reaches unheard-of levels in highly unusual situations. Robert Manry,[20] alone in a tiny 12-foot boat crossing the Atlantic, experienced one such instance, which must either be genuine heightened sensory awareness or an experience much more mystical in nature. He also again raises the theme of oneness with one's surroundings:

> It was Saturday, June 12th, and one of those "God's-in-His-heaven-all's-right-with-the-world" mornings that come along every once in a while to give you a taste of how wonderful life can be. And then, just as I was beginning to slip into utter harmony with the delights of the environment, I became conscious of a subtle something. I heard nothing whatever that could be termed alien or out of place and yet, gradually, imperceptibly, I was infused with an eerie feeling that *Tinkerbelle* and I were not alone, that we had company. It was an uncanny sensation, as if I were on the receiving end of a telepathic message.
>
> I opened the hatch and went topside. Good Lord! There was another vessel![21]

(It is of course possible that he had actually heard something, perhaps as subtle as the muted echo of the sound of moving water reflected off the side of the other vessel.)

Chichester,[22] another single-handed sailor, relates some very similar incidents:

> The night of 23rd–24th of June I was fast asleep, with *Gipsy Moth* sailing [in the Grand Banks] at 4 knots through fog on a dark night. [For no apparent reason] I woke up and stepped into the cockpit, rubbing my

eyes, to see a huge fishing steamer across the bows. It was vague in the fog. I grabbed the tiller . . . and pushed the tiller hard down to bring *Gipsy Moth* up into the wind to avoid the steamer. . . .[23]

At 5:25 in the morning I woke and rolled my eye to the telltale compass beside my berth. What I saw was the letter N, for North. It meant that I was headed right for Long Island. I was out of my bunk and into the cockpit in record time. Day was breaking and there was land dead ahead, but still two miles ahead, thank God. . . . After I calmed down, I pondered on why I had woken up then instead of thirty minutes later. I believe that the instinct for danger is latent in man, and becomes active as the senses sharpen during a long period alone. It was this same instinct which woke me when I was near the fishing steamer on the Grand Banks.[24]

Chichester's analysis of the reasons for heightened awareness is as good as any, and many instances of sharpened senses during long periods alone could be cited. Or (is it possible?) can the consciousness of isolated individuals—as many of them seem to feel—*literally* expand outward into one's surroundings to function as a sort of distant early warning system? (Many traditional and Eastern societies take it for granted that consciousness/the spirit can leave the body and often does so during vision quest types of experiences.) Is there some kind of heightening of the intuitive sense in such circumstances that counterbalances the preoccupation with conscious problem solving, just as introspection begins to counterbalance excessive outer preoccupations? Or, in being more vigilant generally, do people simply learn how to be much more finely attuned through their senses to their environments?

Chichester[25] expands on his heightened sensory awareness or vigilance elsewhere in his writings and also speaks of some benefits of prolonged solitude:

I was bursting with fitness and *joie de vivre* that seemed to build up after a few weeks alone. Perhaps it had taken three weeks to shed the materialism of everyday living. I had become twice as efficient as when with people; my sensations were all greater;

excitement, fear, pleasure, achievement all seemed
sharper. My senses were much more acute and everything seemed much more vivid—the shape and colour
of sky and sea; feeling spray and wind, heat and cold;
tasting food and drink; hearing the slightest change in
the weather, the sea or the ship's gear. I have never
enjoyed anything more than that marvelous last 1,000
miles sailing along the eastern seaboard of North
America.[26]

Many others who have been alone for long periods also talk about
shedding their materialism. Note for later reference that the good feeling
Chichester is experiencing is partly associated with the experiencing of
contrasts and opposites in a balanced way. This is suggested by the
writing style that lists a series of opposites and near-opposites ("fear,
pleasure . . . shape and colour . . . sky and sea . . . spray and wind, heat and
cold . . . food and drink"). He is mastering and enjoying the contrasts
and opposite poles of experience, and he consequently feels in balance
and whole as a person.

Byrd also discusses his heightened sensory awareness, and sounds
very much like Chichester:

It was queer business. I felt as though I had been
plumped upon another planet or into another geologic
horizon of which man had no knowledge or memory.
And yet, I thought at the time it was very good for me; I
was learning what the philosophers have long been
harping on—that a man can live profoundly without
masses of things. For all my realism and skepticism
there came over me, too powerfully to be denied, that
exalted sense of identification—of oneness—with the
outer world which is partly mystical but also certainty.
I came to understand what Thoreau meant when he
said, "My body is all sentient." There were moments
when I felt more alive than at any other time in my life.
Freed from materialistic distractions, my senses sharpened in new directions, and the random or commonplace affairs of the sky and the earth and the spirit,
which ordinarily I would have ignored if I had noticed
them at all, became exciting and portentous.[27]

After the sun has dropped below the horizon for good and the long polar night has begun, Byrd observes: "These are the best times, the times when neglected senses expand to an exquisite sensitivity."[28]

Christiane Ritter details an experience similar to Chichester's as she awakens on the morning of a day when the men are scheduled to start their return to the hut from a place many miles distant:

> . . . I am aroused suddenly from sleep. I can hear the scraping of rapid, long-drawn ski strokes out in the snow. Have the hunters already come home? I listen, but everything is quiet again. Nothing is stirring. Nor, when I step out of the hut later, can I find any trace of them in the snow.
>
> What could it have been? An hallucination? I had looked at my watch, and it said nine o'clock. If the men had really been able to keep to their schedule, they might have started on their journey home at nine that morning from their last station [many miles distant]. . . .
>
> I cannot get it out of my head that the men are coming. They must have been speaking about me, and I, the only receiving station up here, must have picked up their thoughts. In eight hours, I am certain, they will be back.[29]

She turned out to be right; they had indeed started on their return at 9:00 A.M.

Alexander Solzhenitsyn,[30] who suffered hardships over a number of years, many of which were also solitary, talks about another form of heightened sensitivity—the emergence of extraordinary abilities to evaluate people even on the briefest of meetings:

> I had not yet even heard the word "nasedka"—"stool pigeon"—nor learned that there had to be one such "stool pigeon" in each cell. And I had not yet had time to think things over and conclude that I did not like this fellow Georgi Kramarenko. But a spiritual relay, a sensor relay, had clicked inside me, and it had closed him off from me for good and all. I would not bother to recall this event if it had been the only one of its kind. But soon, with astonishment and alarm, I became aware of the work of this internal sensor relay as a constant, inborn

trait. The years passed and I lay on the same bunks, marched in the same formations, and worked in the same work brigades with hundreds of others. And always that secret sensor relay, for whose creation I deserved not the least bit of credit [meaning that it was simply a heightened natural intuition?], worked even before I remembered it was there, worked at the first sight of a human face and eyes, at the first sound of a voice—so that I opened my heart to that person either fully or just the width of a crack, or else shut myself off from him completely. This was so consistently unfailing that all the efforts of the State Security officers to employ stool pigeons began to seem to me as insignificant as being pestered by gnats: after all, a person who has undertaken to be a traitor always betrays the fact in his face and in his voice, and even though some were more skilled in pretense, there was always something fishy about them. On the other hand, the sensor relay helped me distinguish those to whom I could from the very beginning of our acquaintance completely disclose my most precious depths and secrets—secrets for which heads roll. Thus it was that I got through eight years of imprisonment, three years of exile, and another six years of underground authorship, which were in no wise less dangerous. During all those seventeen years I recklessly revealed myself to dozens of people—and didn't make a misstep even once. (I have never read about this trait anywhere, and I mention it here for those interested in psychology. It seems to me that such spiritual sensors exist in many of us, but because we live in too technological and rational an age, we neglect this miracle and don't allow it to develop.)[31]

While imprisoned by the North Koreans for three years in the early Fifties, General William Dean[32] on two different occasions found himself possessed by the conviction that friends had been killed. He was not able to verify his intuitions until his release, whereupon he discovered that he had been correct. He had no explanation.

Solzhenitsyn's intimation that spirituality and intuition are opposite to technology and rationality, and that the latter can drive out the former, is in fact a prominent feature of Jungian thought. If our conscious relies on our senses, then our unconscious relies on intuition—and vice versa. As the boundaries of the conscious self are pushed ever outward during prolonged solitude, is it possible that there is an expansion of the intuitive sense along with them? Is intuition the data-gathering sense of an expanded consciousness upon which solitary persons "attuned to the cosmos" come to rely? If this is so (or even if it isn't), are there *other* hidden aspects of the psyche that might come to the surface under prolonged and/or intense duress?

Confrontations with "Others"

Many isolated individuals eventually become possessed by the conviction that they are not really alone. This is one of the most striking findings of all from the study of prolonged solitary ordeals. Not all solitary individuals actually hallucinate that they have a human companion—some of them have a vaguer but still compelling sensation as if some sort of "presence" is at hand. Consider, for example, Christiane Ritter, who describes returning from her self-imposed daily walk in the days when the twenty-four-hour arctic night is closing in:

> In the distance the dark outlines of the little hut emerge. Here, always on the same spot, I have for some time been startled by a remarkable fantasy. I imagine that something has risen out of the unquiet water in the last inlet before the hut, a dark form which is making its way toward me, bent, noiseless, and ineluctable. Again and again I try to banish this phantom, clear and sharp though its outlines may be in my imagination.[33]

Just as Ritter seems to have personified and given form to the darkness, Byrd in his five-month solitude during the antarctic night personifies the silence as if it were an "other." Just after waking up in the darkness of his hut, Byrd comments:

> The silence during these first few minutes of the day is always depressing. It seems real, as if a gloomy critic were brooding in the shadows. I merely grunt a good morning. My exercises help to snap me out of this.[34]

Lindbergh during his 1927 solo flight also begins to sense the presence of "others," but they seem to be more humanlike than the vague presences sensed by Ritter and Byrd:

> While I'm staring at the instruments, during an unearthly age of time, both conscious and asleep, the fuselage behind me becomes filled with ghostly presences—vaguely outlined forms, transparent, moving, riding, weightless with me in the plane. I feel no surprise at their coming. There's no suddenness to their appearance. Without turning my head, I see them as clearly as though in my normal field of vision. There's no limit to my sight—my skull is one great eye, seeing everywhere at once.
>
> These phantoms speak with human voices—friendly, vapor-like shapes, without substance, able to vanish or appear at will, to pass in and out through the walls of the fuselage as though no walls were there. Now, many are crowded behind me. Now, only a few remain. First one and then another presses forward to my shoulder to speak above the engine's noise and then draws back among the group behind. At times, voices come out of the air itself, clear yet far away, traveling through distances that can't be measured by the scale of human miles; familiar voices, converging and advising on my flight, discussing problems of my navigation, reassuring me, giving me messages of importance unattainable in ordinary life.[35]

Other survivors begin to sense companionship that seems real, though unseen. Ensio Tiira,[36] a Finnish would-be soldier of fortune who lived for thirty-two days on a raft, describes the "strange feeling that someone else was with me."

The mountaineer Hermann Buhl,[37] after spending nearly forty hours alone above 20,000 feet climbing the Himalayan peak of Nanga Parbat, described the "extraordinary feeling that I was not alone . . . [an] 'other man' would hold me on the rope."

Another mountaineer, this one in far more desperate straits, heard a voice that stayed with him throughout his ordeal. The voice Joe Simpson heard, however, never materialized into a personlike companion. In his account, interestingly, Simpson does not introduce or describe the voice. It is suddenly simply there in his narrative, much as it was suddenly simply there in his consciousness. It becomes quite clear from his account that the voice he is hearing is not experienced as his own. His experience is clearly different from that of talking to oneself or giving oneself orders. The *voice* (he puts it in italics) is introduced this way after his devastating accident and desperate struggle to crawl to safety:

> There was silence, and snow, and a clear sky empty of life, and me, sitting there, taking it all in, accepting what I must try to achieve. There were no dark forces acting against me. A voice in my head told me this was true, cutting through the jumble in my head with its coldly rational sound.
>
> It was as if there were two minds within me arguing the toss. The *voice* was clean and sharp and commanding. It was always right, and I listened to it when it spoke and acted on its decisions. The other mind rambled out a disconnected series of images, and memories and hopes, which I attended to in a daydream state as I set about obeying the orders of the *voice*. I had to get to the glacier. I would crawl on the glacier. . . .
>
> Reaching the glacier was my aim. The *voice* told me exactly how to go about it, and I obeyed while my other mind [note how he senses the voice as separate from his mind] jumped abstractedly from one idea to another.[38]
>
> It took some experimentation before I found the best method of crawling. The soft wet snow made it hard to slide. . . .
>
> From time to time I stopped to eat snow and rest. Then I would stare vacantly at the huge West Face of Siula Grande above me and listen to the strange thoughts echoing in my head. Then the *voice* would interrupt the reverie and I would glance guiltily at my watch before starting off again.
>
> The *voice*, and the watch, urged me into motion whenever the heat from the glacier halted me in a drowsy exhausted daze. . . .
>
> It didn't seem to concern me that I was moving like a snail. So long as I obeyed the *voice*, then I would be all right. I would look ahead and note some features in the

waves of snow, then look at my watch, and the *voice* told me to reach that point in half an hour. I obeyed. . . .

As I inched over the sea of snow I listened to other voices that wondered what people were doing in Sheffield and remembered the thatched-cottage pub in Harome where I used to drink. . . .

I sang lyrics of a pop song incessantly to the tune of my crawling. . . .

Then the *voice* would tell me I was late, and I would wake with a start and crawl again. *I was split in two.* [RDL] A cold clinical side of me assessed everything, decided what to do and made me do it. The rest was madness— a hazy blur of images so vivid and real that I lost myself in their spell. . . .[39]

A film of weariness enveloped everything. . . .

When I stopped I would make an excuse for it, so as not to feel guilty. My frostbitten fingers became the most common excuse. I had to take my mitts and inner gloves off to check that they were not getting worse. Ten minutes later the *voice* would jolt me back to reality, and I would pull on the glove I had only half managed to remove and tug my mitt over it, and crawl. My hands were always deep in the snow as I crawled, and when they had gone numb I would stop again and stare at them. . . . I just stared at them blankly until the *voice* called me.

After two hours the circular crevasse was behind me and I had escaped the shadow of Siula Grande. I followed the footprints in a crescent under Yerupaja's South Face, passing the broken side of a crevasse. . . .

I drifted [he is actually crawling—the word "drifted" captures the dreamy unreality of what he is doing] slowly by, staring at the bared ice. I seemed to be drifting with it on a current. It didn't strike me as odd that I wasn't overtaking the ice cliff. I gazed at figures in the broken ice of the cliff. I was unsure whether I could really see them. Voices argued with the commanding *voice*, and decided I *was* seeing [the figures]. . . .[40]

I was less dazed now, and the voice had banished the mad thoughts from my mind. An urgency was creeping over me, and the *voice* said: "*Go on, keep going . . . faster.*

You've wasted too much time. Go on, before you lose the tracks," and I tried hard to hurry. . . .

There was snow in the air above. Fresh falling snow! My stomach tightened as panic threatened. The snow and wind would hide the footprints. The *voice* said I would lose my way, said I would never get through the crevasse without the prints, and told me to hurry on. . . . I clawed feverishly through the gusting snow. . . . The light faded quickly. . . . I lay down in the snow defeated. . . . I wanted to sleep. . . . I nearly slept, dozing fitfully, edging close to the dark comfort of sleep, but the wind kept waking me. I tried to ignore the *voice*, which urged me to move, but couldn't because the other voices had gone. I couldn't lose the *voice* in daydreams.

". . . don't sleep, don't sleep, not here. Keep going. Find a slope and dig a snow hole . . . don't sleep."

I dug the snow hole in a confusion of pain and exhaustion. . . .

The other voices returned once I was sheltered from the wind, and I dozed off with their images idly flitting through my mind. . . .[41]

I awoke with a start—*"get moving . . . don't lie there . . . stop dozing . . . move!"* The *voice* came through the wandering idle thoughts of pop song lyrics, faces from the past, and fantasies of empty value. I set off crawling. . . .

With frequent stops to stand and check the route, I slowly entered the crevasse zone. . . .

A mounting horror of falling into a crevasse forced me into frantic guessing at the best path through the maze. . . .

In a state of nervous exhaustion I collapsed on a narrow bridge of snow between two crevasses. . . .[42]

I lolled against the rock, feeling luxuriously warm and relaxed in the sun. I promised myself a good rest before attempting the moraines and immediately nodded into sleep. After half an hour the *voice* rudely disturbed my peace, coming into my dreams like the distant murmur of flowing water, with the same insistent message I had so far been unable to ignore:

"Come on, wake up! Things to be done . . . long way to go . . . don't sleep . . . come on."

I sat up and stared confusedly at the dark river of rock flowing away from me. For a moment I felt disoriented. . . .

I lay back against the boulder and closed my eyes, but the *voice* kept calling. Instructions tumbled in, repeated commands of what I must do, and I lay back listening and fighting the instinct to obey. I just wanted to sleep a little longer. I lost the fight and obeyed [the *voice*]. . . .[43]

When I stood up and leant heavily on the boulder, my head spun with giddiness and I gripped the rock harder to stop myself falling. . . .

There was no question of crawling. Walking was also out, so it would have to be hopping [on one leg].

At the first attempt I fell flat on my face. . . .

After covering ten yards I had managed to perfect my hobbling technique. . . .[44]

The *voice* kept urging me on, *"Place-left-brace hop . . . keep going. Look how far you've gone. Just do it, don't think about it. . . ."*

I did as I was told [by the *voice*]. Stumbling past and sometimes over boulders, falling, crying, swearing in a litany that matched the pattern of my hopping. I forgot why I was doing it; forgot even the idea that I probably wouldn't make it. . . .

Now I staggered blind in the dark . . . ignoring the *voice* which [now] told me to sleep, and rest. . . . At ten o'clock I tripped and fell heavily on to the rocks. . . . Now, I couldn't stand up. . . . There was an over-ride stopping me. The *voice* prevailed. I shuffled into my sleeping bag and immediately fell asleep. . . .[45]

I opened my eyes and flinched at the sharp glare of sunlight. . . .

I shook my head from side to side, trying to wake myself and drive the lethargy away. . . . I wanted to move but couldn't. . . .[46]

I hoisted my sack on to my back and crouched to make the first tentative hop of the day. The moment I jumped I knew I would fall. My arm buckled and I pitched forward. . . . Fifteen minutes later I was still within sight of where I had slept. . . . At every hop I fell. . . .[47]

Part of me cried out to give up and sleep, and accept that I would never reach camp. The *voice* countered this. I lay still and listened to the argument [between his "mind" and the *voice*]. I didn't care about the camp or getting down. It was too far. Yet the irony of collapsing on the moraines after having overcome all those obstacles angered me. The *voice* won. My mind was set. It had been from the moment I got out of the crevasse.

I would keep moving. . . .[48]

The *voice* still urged me on but without the insistent commanding tone of yesterday. Now it seemed to suggest that I might as well get on with it for want of anything else to do. I found it easier to ignore it and slump on the ground in a sleepy daydream. Yeah, sure, I'll move, but I'll rest a little longer first . . . and the *voice* would fade into a background of hazy dreams. . . .[49]

I resorted to a forward belly-crawl. . . .[50]

A part of me hesitated, paralysing any thought of moving. I didn't want to get [back to base camp] before dark. It would destroy me if I saw that the tents had gone. [It was by now two or three days after his partner would have returned to camp, thinking him dead, and therefore having little reason to stay around.]

The *voice* said, *"Don't be a fool, hurry on; two hours' light left."*[51]

Some hours later, Joe Simpson did manage to crawl and hop all the way back to base camp where his partner—who had miraculously not yet left—heard his cries for help in the dark.

Michelle Hamilton,[52] lost at sea when her small outrigger canoe drifted too far from land and then was overturned in a powerful storm, was debating with herself whether or not to abandon the canoe and swim for land when a "commanding voice" loudly ordered her, "Don't leave the boat!" Douglas Mawson, struggling back alone to his base camp in the Antarctic, experienced a "presence" that he believed guided him safely through his ordeal. There is clearly a sharp distinction here between the experience of "talking to oneself" during a hardship situation (to be taken up later), the experience of hearing random voices as one begins to become hallucinatory, and the experience of hearing a singular, constant, authoritative voice such as these survivors are relating. The explanation for this singular kind of experience during a prolonged ordeal is not easy to come by, but one can see why some people claim to have spiritual experiences during ordeals.

People in small groups have experienced the phenomenon of sensing "others" also. Commander H. G. Stoker, fleeing with two companions across Turkey after escaping from a World War I POW camp, relates that all three of them independently felt a "fourth man" was accompanying them. Stoker also relates that his experience was virtually identical to that of the antarctic explorer Sir Ernest Shackleton and two companions crossing South Georgia island after nearly two years' isolation in Antarctica. They also sensed a "fourth man."[53]

Lauren Elder,[54] lone survivor of a plane crash high in the Sierras, describes the following meetings with "others" during her long trek down from the mountains. After climbing down for many hours:

> I sat on a rock to take a short rest and raised my eyes to scan the mountain. That was when I saw them.
> They were curved along a ridge of rocks, directly across from me—a row of houses built of beautifully mellowed redwood, skillfully integrated into the landscape. . . .
> I took off, trying to lope in the snow, tremendously excited. . . .
> I saw him and stopped short. A man with long, light hair was standing on the deck of the highest house, stretching. He was wearing a robe. His arms were out and the white robe billowed around him.
> "Hello!" I called, out of breath. "I've been in a plane crash. I need help."
> He did not turn at my call. I noticed a large black cross hanging around his neck. I was confused. And then I realized that it was not a man at all, but a statue. . . .
> I stood there for a long time, rubbing my hand over the rock. There was no house, only the massive rocks curving into the land. I blinked. There were no houses, no statue.[55]
> Before long I began [again] to feel that people really were close by. I was sure that when I made my way around the next bend I would discover some tangible evidence. . . .

The feeling swelled, filling me with such certainty that I wasn't at all surprised to come upon a small hut with broad, flat leaves thatched over a framework of branches, the kind of shelter a camper might put up. I didn't stop to examine it, since I was sure the ranch would be around the next bend.

I hurried on. Just as I had hoped, I saw a farmhand working on a hillside above me, a Mexican wearing loose white clothes and a straw hat.

"Hello," I called out to him.

He didn't turn around but kept working in the garden. Maybe he didn't understand English.

"Hola!" I tried again in Spanish. "Hablas espanol? Socorro! Me duelen las piernas!"

Still he did not turn around.

I knew then that he was another fiction. Like the man in the white robe. . . . It was as if I didn't exist. I thought to myself: *You don't, not for him.*[56]

A little later:

She was sitting on a rock ledge just above my head, in the shade of an overhanging boulder; a middle-aged woman with a sketchbook and a tool kit fitted out with paints. . . . She was sketching wildflowers and she looked the part perfectly. . . .

She did not look up. She continued sketching and I understood that she was not going to acknowledge me. . . . Somehow I knew that phantoms were peripheral to my purpose, which was to get myself off the mountain and home again.[57]

Lindbergh, in the eighteenth hour of his flight, sensed another kind of presence or "other," but this time it was not ghostly humanlike forms. Instead he was explicitly *aware of a newly surfaced part of himself:*

My mind strays from the cockpit and returns. My eyes close, and open, and close again. But I'm beginning to understand vaguely a new factor which has come to my assistance. It seems I'm made up of three personalities, three elements, each partly dependent and independent of the others. [First] there's my body, which knows definitely that what it wants most in the world is sleep. [Second] there's my mind, constantly making decisions that my body refuses to comply with, but which itself is weakening in resolution. And [third], there's something else, which seems to become stronger instead of weaker with fatigue, an element of spirit, a directive force that has stepped out from the background and taken control over both mind and body. It seems to guard them as a wise father guards his children; letting them venture to the point of danger, then calling them back, guiding with a firm but tolerant hand.[58]

The "directive force" described by Lindbergh that "takes control" also describes very aptly the disembodied guiding voice experienced by Simpson. That phenomenon plus the vague sense of the presence of an "other" and the more explicit images of human companions may be simply indirect, symbolic expressions and personifications of what Lindbergh experienced more directly—a newly surfaced part of his own personality coming into consciousness. If these images do not come from some other more "spiritual" realm, then they clearly must come from the unconscious. The fact that Lindbergh and others felt no surprise at their hallucinations may be evidence of preexisting openness to communication from the "other side" of themselves, a point that deserves further attention later.

It is perhaps no accident that spirit quests among Native Americans (and others) usually involved prolonged solitary ordeals of wandering, fasting, cold, and so forth—ordeals not unlike those examined here. Such conditions would seem to be ideal for producing a confrontation with an "other," either as a concrete hallucination or as a disembodied voice. The same would presumably hold true for the harsh, solitary, unchanging lives of the monks and holy men and women of many cultures who have sought spiritual enlightenment over the centuries. The literature on near death experiences is full of examples of people who have apparently "died" and, after being resuscitated, reported that they had met a variety of guiding figures.

Notes

[1] Burney, p. 16.
[2] Byrd, p. 101.
[3] Byrd, p. 94.
[4] Ritter, p. 171.
[5] Lindbergh, p. 338.
[6] Byrd, p. 86.
[7] Quoted in Noyce, Wilfrid. *The Springs of Adventure.* New York: World Publishing Co., 1958, p. 226.
[8] Ritter, pp. 99–100.
[9] Ritter, p. 133.
[10] Janis, 1971.
[11] Janis, p. 18.
[12] Lindbergh, pp. 241–242.
[13] Lindbergh, pp. 352–353.
[14] Byrd, pp. 94–95.
[15] Byrd, p. 83.
[16] Byrd, p. 95.
[17] Byrd, p. 103.
[18] Byrd, p. 179.
[19] Byrd, p. 268.
[20] Manry, Robert. *Tinkerbelle.* New York: Harper & Row, 1966.
[21] Manry, p. 115.
[22] Chichester, Sir Francis. *The Lonely Sea and the Sky.* London: Pan Books Ltd., 1964.
[23] Chichester, 1964, p. 367.
[24] Chichester, 1964, p. 372.
[25] Chichester, 1964.
[26] Chichester, 1964, p. 368.
[27] Byrd, p. 120.
[28] Byrd, p. 83.
[29] Ritter, p. 103.
[30] Solzhenitsyn, Alexander. *The Gulag Archipelago.* New York: Harper & Row, 1973.
[31] Solzhenitsyn, pp. 185–186.
[32] Dean, William F. *General Dean's Story.* New York: Viking, 1954.
[33] Ritter, pp. 114–115.
[34] Byrd, pp. 96–97.
[35] Lindbergh, p. 389.
[36] Tiira, Ensio. *Raft of Despair.* London: Hutchinson, 1954. New York: Dutton, 1954.
[37] Buhl, Hermann. *Lonely Challenge.* New York: E. P. Dutton, 1956.
[38] Simpson, p. 120.
[39] Simpson, pp. 123–124.
[40] Simpson, p. 124.
[41] Simpson, pp. 125–126.
[42] Simpson, pp. 133–134.
[43] Simpson, pp. 135–136.

[44] Simpson, p. 137.

[45] Simpson, p. 141.

[46] Simpson, p. 147.

[47] Simpson, p. 148.

[48] Simpson, p. 149.

[49] Simpson, p. 151.

[50] Simpson, p. 153.

[51] Simpson, p. 154.

[52] Hamilton, Michelle. *A Mighty Tempest*. Texas: Word, Inc., 1992.

[53] Stoker, H. G. "The Fourth Man." In *On the Run: Escaping Tales*, edited by H. C. Armstrong. London: Rich and Cowan, 1934.

[54] Elder, 1973.

[55] Elder, pp. 120–121.

[56] Elder, pp. 132–133.

[57] Elder, p. 134.

[58] Lindbergh, p. 361

CHAPTER FIVE

Coping with Solitary Ordeals

Having examined some (and only some) of the effects of prolonged solitary ordeals, what psychological coping mechanisms can be found in the writings of solitary survivors? To what devices did they turn to keep from being done in by their hardships? Is there knowledge to be gained from their experiences that can be used by others when they face hardship?

The coping devices or techniques described below are categorized somewhat arbitrarily, because these are conceptual categories and not real-world categories. Some of the examples cited would actually illustrate more than one way of coping, and the categories obviously overlap as well. My intent is to try to capture both some of the range and some of the flavor of the kinds of things that people do in order to keep their heads and to survive.

Adaptation

Most of the coping mechanisms in this chapter represent some form of control of one's behavior and situation. But another important aspect of coping with prolonged hardship is that, within limits, one simply gets used to it, no matter how extreme it is. With the passage of time, one's frame of reference changes, the extreme situation becomes the new norm, and the formerly bizarre, unbearable, and incredible become almost matter-of-fact. (One of the most striking examples of the abominable becoming matter-of-fact is the famous case of the Andes plane crash survivors' gradual acceptance of the eating of human flesh, raw.) Admiral Byrd[1] captures this process of adaptation in relating an incident prior to his isolation in Antarctica:

> The tolerable quality of a dangerous existence [i.e., what makes a dangerous existence tolerable] is the fact that the human mind cannot remain continuously sensitive to anything. Repetition's dulling impact sees to that. [Psychologists would term this "habituation," but they would describe it no better.] The threat of sudden death can scare a man for only so long; then he dismisses it as he might a mealy-mouthed beggar. [Note the contempt!] When Floyd Bennett and I were on our [flight] to the North Pole, and not quite halfway there, something let go in one of the [aircraft] engines, and ropy streaks of oil, whipped by the wind, coated the cowling. Bennett went white, and into my throat came a choking feeling like suffocation. Then the feeling vanished . . . the outcome was out of our hands. Presently an angling wind fetched Bennett's attention back to the problem of holding his course, and mine to the drift indicator. And throughout the rest of the flight we paid little more attention to the leak.[2]

In many ordeals and crises there seems to be much greater acceptance of things about which nothing can be done than of less onerous things that might possibly be changed. Survivors quickly learn not to expend energy on things that can't be changed. It has been noted, for example, that there is less panic among people who are trapped with no way out, as in a sunken submarine, than there is when people are trapped with even a slim hope of finding an exit, as in a crowded theater that is on fire.

Solzhenitsyn[3] also shows how all things become relative in extreme situations, and how one begins to focus on those things that seem good if only by virtue of being compared to the abominable:

> And how much it had cost you to last out until that first cell! You had been kept in a pit, or in a box, or in a

cellar. No one had addressed a human word to you. No one had looked at you with a human gaze. All they did was to peck at your brain and heart with iron beaks, and when you cried or groaned, they laughed.

For a week or a month you had been an abandoned waif, alone among enemies, and you had already said good-bye to reason and to life; and you had already tried to kill yourself by "falling" from the radiator in such a way as to smash your brains against the iron cone of the valve. Then all of a sudden you were alive again, and were brought in to your friends. And reason returned to you.

That's what your first cell is!

You waited for that cell. You dreamed of it almost as eagerly as of freedom.[4]

Christopher Burney,[5] in a Nazi prison, provides a similar, though more subdued, example:

A strange sergeant came to my cell and told me to collect my things, of which I had none, and ordered me out of the door. For once I was not paralyzed, though I felt cold when I discarded the blanket I had been wearing as a cloak, and I asked him where I was going more out of curiosity than of fear. . . .

Cell No. 239 was no different from the others, but I had the same feeling of being uprooted as if I had been living for a long time in a warm Georgian house and had to move to a draughty villa. Yet, when I had examined the appointments of my new home, I found much to recompense me for the change. The floor was shiny, the cement round the lavatory was clean and not yet crumbling and, best of all, the blankets were new, full-size and with all their hair. The plug pulled, the tap flowed, and there was even a pane of transparent glass in the skylight, which gave me many square inches [!] of extra light and extra sky to look at. It was wonderful to look at the sky, whatever the weather. Little clouds lit like southern islands in the sunset, or fast grey scurries, or the blue fullness of invisible things were all beauty to me. I knew why we put Heaven up there, and could not tire of looking at it.[6]

Note how attentive Burney is to tiny details in finding things to be positive about. To him a tiny pane of glass has the impact of a giant picture window. To him, one can truly "see a universe in a grain of sand."

Edith Bone[7] describes her experience of moving from one isolation cell to another, where the second cell was merely a little less atrocious than the first, this way:

> But scarcely had I lain down and packed myself in my blankets when the duty officer came again and said, "Take all the things. You are leaving this cell." And so I gathered up the things and was taken to another cell, on the ground floor. This cell was another Ritz Hotel compared with the one downstairs. First of all there was a straw palliasse on the bed. There was a stove; and there was no filth, only dust such as collects in a place which had not been inhabited for a long time. One of the guards was kneeling in front of the stove, making a fire. And there was the governor, saying to him, "Mind you keep that fire up. This cell hasn't been used for a long time. It's damp and chilly." Here was a surprise! But in prison one has to take things as they come, so I turned in and slept quite well. The guard kept up the fire all night; he had made a fire fit to roast an ox to start with.[8]

She even manages to find other positive features in her intensely deprived situation, such as time to think and freedom from other cares:

> For many, many years this was the first opportunity I had had to think over and digest all the things I had absorbed in more than sixty years of life, and which I had never yet had time to digest properly under the stress of circumstances, the necessity of making a living, and the pressure of new things cropping up all the time.
>
> But in my specially isolated cell I was, to a very considerable extent, undisturbed, especially in the first five months after the sentence, when I was in the dark and therefore necessarily inactive physically. In the dark

there is little one can do except think, and the absence
of anything to divert one's thoughts gives them an intensity seldom experienced in normal conditions. . . .[9]

The first thing I tried, while still in complete darkness,
was to recite poetry and afterwards to translate poems
from one language into another. While doing this I discovered that rhymes came easily to me, and from there
to composing doggerel of my own was but a step. . . .[10]

While I [had been] in the black hole underground,
there was little else I could do. There was not even the
prisoner's eternal resource—the walking to and fro—
because I had a horror of treading in the stinking muck
on the floor.

For certain reasons I did not eat at all during the nine
days I spent down there, and found that I was not hungry.
I experienced instead a strange lightness of the body and
clarity of thought—which possibly I only imagined—
rather like one feels in the first stages of getting tight.
(Were the medieval churchmen right in recommending
fasting as an aid to prayer?) There was also a feeling of
relief—the black hole was a respite from constant alertness, expectation of unknown troubles and preparedness
for them.

In fact, strange as it may seem, those nine days were
something in the nature of a holiday, a relaxation of tension. The only trouble was the cold, which was getting
worse every day.

When after nine days downstairs I was transferred to a
cell on the ground floor, still dark but much less disgust-
ing in other respects, I was just beginning to get tired of
a mental diet consisting entirely of poetry.[11]

A more concise instance of a change in the frame of reference in
extremity is provided by Byrd at Advance Base. After having repaired
the pipes for his stove during 60-below weather, Byrd writes: "Next
morning, when I got up, the inside temperature was [only!] 30° below
zero. The new arrangement was working quite nicely indeed."[12]

A factor related to adaptation that helps some solitary individuals
survive is simply the knowledge, gained from arduous past experience,
that certain trials of the flesh will pass with time. Lindbergh speaks of

this during the fourth hour of his flight, and at the same time displays a remarkable talent for being a detached observer of himself:

> My legs are stiff and cramped. But that won't last more than three or four hours. The dull ache will get worse for a time, and then go away altogether. I've experienced the feeling before. It begins after about three hours of flying, and ends at about seven. After the seventh hour, my muscles will cease complaining of their restrictions and accept the mission they've been given to fulfill. I wish the desire for sleep could adapt itself to a long-distance flight as easily.[13]

Vigilance

Another coping device is vigilance. This mechanism has been briefly discussed previously. In order to survive an ordeal, one must remain alert to possible dangers. Lindbergh suggests the heights that vigilance can attain when called for:

> The engine's even vibration, shaking back through the fuselage's steel skeleton, gives life to cockpit and controls. Flowing up along the stick to my hand, it's the pulse beat of the plane. Let a cylinder miss once, and I'll feel it as clearly as though a human heart had skipped against my thumb.[14]

The French aviator Antoine de Saint-Exupéry (the "French Charles Lindbergh")[15] makes a similar statement as he wings alone above the Sahara: "We [he and his plane] were truly alone in the Universe—a thought that caused me not the least worry. If my motor were to cough, that sound would startle me more than if my heart should skip a beat."[16]

Many of the previously cited examples of sensory sensitivity and "intuition" could also be cited here as examples of the heightening of vigilance and information seeking under stress.

It is not enough simply to be vigilant during adversity, however, particularly during isolated, monotonous adversity. One must find ways to stimulate the mind into constant alertness, flexibility, and vigilance so that one can be in control. Survivors of prolonged and tedious hardship have used many techniques to stimulate themselves, making use of whatever happens to be at hand for the purpose. Lindbergh describes one means of providing varying and stimulating experiences during his flight—subjecting himself to blasts of cold air to stay awake:

> I shake myself violently, ashamed at my weakness, alarmed at my inability to overcome it. I never before understood the meaning of temptation, or how powerful one's desires can become. I've got to alert my mind, wake my body. I can't let anything as trifling as sleep ruin the flight I spent so many months in planning. . . .
>
> I cup my hand into the slipstream, diverting a strong current of air against my face, breathing deeply of its gusty freshness. I let my eyelids fall shut for five seconds; then raise them against tons of weight. Protesting, they won't open wide until I force them with my thumb, and lift the muscles of my forehead to help keep them in place. Sleep overcomes my resistance like a drug.
>
> I draw the flying suit's wool collar across my throat. Should I put the windows in now? Why not shut off the world outside, relax in the warmth of a closed cockpit, and gain that last mile or two of speed from streamlining? . . . If I shut myself off even partially from outside air and clouds and sky, the lure of sleep may prove beyond resistance. The coolness of the night is a guard against it; the clarity of moonlit clouds helps to overcome it; the exhaust of the engine, barking in through open windows, serves to ward it off.[17]

He recognizes that discomfort is a stimulus to alertness and is willing to suffer it for that reason, in a kind of trade-off within this new frame of reference that makes added discomfort a positive, desirable thing because of its stimulating quality. In ordeals, many such trade-offs become possible and rational because of the new frame of reference. (For example, it makes perfect sense during an ordeal to make yourself suffer even more if that is the only way to keep yourself alert and increase your survival chances. Byrd, for example, when faced with the choice between using his stove to stay warm—but breathing its carbon monoxide—and freezing in fresh air, opts for enduring the brutally painful cold as the positive choice.)

A little later on, Lindbergh speaks more explicitly of the overriding importance of finding mental stimulation and in the process writes some good practical advice on the psychology of coping with stimulus deprivation:

> The brilliant light and the strangeness of the sea awaken me—make my mind the master of my body once again. Any change, I realize, stimulates the senses. Changing altitude, changing thought, even the changing contours of the ice cakes [on the ocean below] help [me] to stay awake. *I must look for differences, and find ways of emphasizing them.* [RDL] I can fly first with my right hand and then with my left. I can shift my position a little in the seat, sitting stiff and straight, slouching down, twisting sidewise. *I can create imaginary emergencies in my mind* [RDL]—a forced landing—the best wave or trough to hit—the stinging wetness of the ocean. I can check and recheck my navigation. A swallow of water now and then will help. And there's the hourly routine of fuel tanks, heading, and instrument readings. All of these tricks I must use, and think of others. Similarity is my enemy; change, my friend.[18]

Still later, Lindbergh puts one of these methods of stimulating himself—anticipating emergencies—to work as he mentally rehearses with his characteristic attention to detail:

> What would I do now if my engine failed? How could a pilot land on such a surface [a broken ice field on the ocean]? Well, God and gravity would take care of that. If an essential part of my engine broke, I'd be down in thirty seconds. I'd have only time to bank left into wind, cut the switch, pull my stick back, and pancake onto ice. The landing gear would be wiped off the moment it hit a cake's edge. But possibly the fuselage would skid along without smashing up too badly and, with real good luck, end up on ice instead of water.
>
> What then? There'd certainly be no rescue ships steaming through an ice field. I might use fabric and framework from the plane to erect a shelter, if the wind didn't blow too hard. Ribs, engine oil, and spar splinters would make a good fire. But staying with the wreckage

would mean only a few more days of life. I'd have to start traveling as soon as my clothes were dry.

I'd cut a strip of covering from the wing to wrap up in at night. I'd cut a second strip to catch rain or snow for extra drinking water. I'd lash my equipment on my back, and hold the raft in front of me so I could fall on top of it if footing gave way. My eyes pick out the best routes to follow as I imagine walking over the ice field. There's a quarter-mile stretch where cakes are jammed together without a crack of water in between. By traveling straight north I should strike the coast of Newfoundland within a hundred miles. For sustenance, I have with me five quarts of water, lacking a few swallows, five sandwiches, and five eight-ounce cans of Army rations. Possibly I could make ten miles a day on foot, using the rubber raft to cross patches of water.[19]

Note the attention to small detail in Lindbergh's thinking as he reasons through an entire scenario of how to handle the possibility of crash landing on the ice and anticipates and plans for remotely possible emergencies: "I would hold the raft in front of me so I could fall on top of it if footing gave way." The more particularly he thinks about things, the more intellectual stimulation he can extract from them—an example of "seeing a universe in a grain of sand." This "compulsive" attention to detail in preparing to face danger is a trademark of Lindbergh's character and of his coping that crops up again and again. His character seems also to be built upon the challenge of overcoming danger by anticipating all possible scenarios.

Lindbergh's rehearsing the minute details of various scenarios as a means of gaining mental stimulation is paralleled in the experience of Vietnam POWs who passed their time for hours on end observing the tiniest details of the mating, hunting, eating, fighting, and territorial behavior of geckos, rats, and spiders—even training some of these tiny creatures by rewarding them with crumbs of food. The individual who copes primarily by becoming an "observer" of the surrounding scene is relying on both detachment and vigilance at once, while at the same time gaining intellectual stimulation through the act of observation.

Byrd has his own version of setting up stimulating little mental challenges to keep himself sharp: "I wound up the battered green victrola

. . . and jumped simultaneously for the dishes. The idea is to finish the dishes before the victrola runs down."[20]

I would warrant that many of us would acknowledge doing similar sorts of small challenging things. (Other examples of mental stimulation will be found in the later chapter on the flow experience.)

Maintaining Autonomy and Self-Control

Autonomy may at first seem like a paradoxical need in a situation where someone is already profoundly alone. Yet the ordeal threatens to take away one's sense of psychological autonomy at every turn. During adversity, psychological autonomy is maintained through techniques of self-control and by imposing one's own control over the situation, sometimes if only in tiny ways. Thus one keeps oneself from succumbing psychologically (and perhaps physically) to the situation with which one is trying to cope.

Sometimes autonomy can be achieved by doing *nothing*—nothing, that is, in the sense of what Erikson termed "refusing to go along," or passive resistance. Edith Bone[21] practiced this a great deal during her seven-year solitary confinement. She describes how she decided to react to having a dazzling light in her cell twenty-four hours a day and to her guards banging on her cell door at regular intervals:

> This very unpleasant procedure was repeated every half-hour or so, and, at first, when they put on the light I shielded my eyes with my hand to protect them. But when I realized that one of the purposes of this sort of thing was to make me move, I decided to turn around and lie face downwards, so that my eyes at least would be protected, after which I did not react at all to their antics. Fortunately for myself I am not at all noise-sensitive. I used to live in a place where a tube-train roared past every few minutes; and if one can stand that, one is immune to noise.
>
> Apparently this attitude of mine, this immobility, made them uneasy. The sergeants and sergeant-majors who were on duty there were not ordinary prison service officers but secret police men; nevertheless they were not allowed to come into my cell, except with an officer of commissioned rank. They must have reported, "The

prisoner doesn't move," because presently a sub-lieutenant came in and spoke to me. I did not answer. He came and shook me by the shoulder, but I did not respond and went quite limp. He stood by my bed for a while and then went away, but after this they stopped banging on the door. They came and switched on the light, looked in, and went away again about every hour.[22]

Having no appetite gave me an idea. I decided to go on a complete general strike, as a sign, as a sign of protest against such impermissible treatment—impermissible in any case, but especially impermissible in a Communist State, where a humane attitude, not only to those who are prisoners at large (i.e. all citizens) but also to prisoners actually in custody, has always been the boast of the government. The strike was to include a speech strike, a hunger strike, a cleaning strike. In short, I decided to refrain from absolutely everything except lying on my bed and sleeping. This I carried out quite thoroughly. I did not eat, I did not answer when I was spoken to, I did not move when the sergeant brought in a broom in the morning and I did not do any of the other chores either. I found that for some mysterious reason my behavior alarmed my guards, and on the third or fourth day of this stunt I had a visit.[23]

The visit was from a high-ranking officer who informed her she would be moved to the cell that she described as the "Ritz Hotel" in the excerpt I quoted earlier under Adaptation. By doing "nothing" she had actually exerted rather strong control.

Maintaining Mental Control

Lindbergh describes the need to maintain mental control over his reactions, his sleepiness, and even his thought processes. Sometimes he keeps such control by sheer force of determination. He begins by describing the ways in which he is virtually imprisoned:

My body is shaped by the seat's design. My hand is tied to the stick and my feet to the rudder by cords of instability. Even the angles of my joints are fixed. But shaking clarifies my mind a little—enough to make new resolutions. I will *force* my body to remain alert. I will *force* my mind to concentrate—never let it get dull again. I simply can't think of sleep. I have an ocean yet to cross, and Paris to find. Sleep is a trivial thing, insignificant compared to the importance of this flight. It has no business bothering me now. It will interfere with my judgment, my navigation, my accuracy of flying. . . .[24]

The clouds are thickening. I'm down to nine thousand feet. Should I climb back up where valleys [between clouds] are wider? No, I've got to get under these clouds where I can see waves and windstreaks. I *must* find out how much the wind has changed. I must take hold—begin to grapple with problems of navigation. The rising sun will bring strength—it *must*. Half the time, now, I'm flying blind. . . . All my remaining energy, all the attention I can bring to bear, must be concentrated on the task of simply passing through.[25]

Byrd also talks about maintaining mental control, but he links it to the necessity of finding stimulation:

I practiced my preachments of a disciplined mind. Or perhaps discipline isn't exactly the right word; for what I did, or tried to do, was to focus my thinking on healthy, constructive images and concepts and thus crowd out the unhealthy ones. I built a wall between myself and the past in an effort to extract every ounce of diversion and creativeness inherent in my immediate surroundings.[26]

Lindbergh's best statement of the need to maintain mental control may be the following. It displays the utter faith in reason and in technology ("trust your instruments") that characterizes all great pilots who know that bodily sensations while flying can play deadly tricks, even though they convey with apparent certainty what the aircraft seems to be doing. Many small aircraft accidents occur when people follow their bodily sensations, as when an inexperienced pilot blundering into clouds senses that he is losing altitude and so pulls back on the stick; in fact what has happened is that he has drifted into a slow descending spiral, and by pulling back on the stick he goes into a tighter and fatal spiral dive. A disciplined mind can overrule bodily sensations, much like a trained mind can overcome the disorientation that comes with a sudden crisis. Many who are trained in this way view the body and its sensations as a kind of irresponsible emotional and impulsive child, to be brought into line by the responsible, rational adult mind:

> The body must be informed sternly that the mind will take complete control. The senses must be drafted and lined up in strictest discipline, while logic replaces instinct as commander. If the body feels a wing dropping, and the mind says it is not (because the turn indicator's ball and needle are still centered), the muscles must obey the mind's decision no matter how wrong it seems to them. If the eyes imagine the flicker of a star below where they think the horizon ought to be, if the ears report the engine's tempo too slow for level flight, if the nerves say the seat back's pressure is increasing (as it does in a climb), the hands and feet must still be loyal to the orders of the mind.[27]

Giving Oneself Commands

At other points, Lindbergh "regresses" to what may be one of the most primitive means of remaining an agent and maintaining control over one's own behavior: simply talking to oneself, arguing with oneself, and giving oneself commands, as if one part of the self (the adult) is trying to control another (the child). Talking to oneself is not uncommon in people who are trying to solve problems under conditions of stress. Many of us do it when we are merely trying to solve difficult math problems, for example. Indeed, it occurs all the time in students trying to solve test problems under the stress of an examination. Lindbergh actually carries on an inner argument between two parts of himself:

> I pull the flashlight from my pocket and throw its beam onto a strut. The entering edge is irregular and shiny—*ice!* . . .

Kick rudder hard—no time to lose—the turn indicator's icing up right now.

But the mind retorts, "Steady, steady. It's easy enough to get into a steep bank, but more difficult to get out of one and on your course again. If you turn too fast, you'll lose more time than you save; the plane may get entirely out of control."

"If the turn indicator ices up, it'll get out of control anyway. There's no time—only a few seconds—quick—quick—harder rudder—kick it. . . ."

"Don't do anything of the sort. I've thought all this out carefully and know just what's best to do. You remember, you are to obey my orders!"

"Yes, yes—but just a little faster, then—just a little. . . ."

"No, no faster; turn just the right amount. You're to do exactly what I say; no more, no less!"

"Just a little!"

"No, none! . . ."

"Turn faster! You see the air speed's dropping. It's ice doing that! Quick, or it'll be too late!"

"No, it's not ice—at least not very likely. It's probably just the normal slowing down in a bank."[28]

And, when Lindbergh finally approaches Le Bourget airport, he once again falls back on giving himself orders in order to maintain control over his behavior under stress:

It's only a hundred yards to the hangars now—solid forms emerging from the night. I'm too high—too fast. Drop wing—left rudder—sideslip—careful—mustn't get anywhere near the stall. I've never landed the *Spirit of St. Louis* at night before. It would be better to come in straight. But if I don't sideslip, I'll be too high over the boundary to touch my wheels in the area of light. That would mean circling again—still too high. I push the stick over to a steeper slip, leaving the nose well down—below the hangar roofs now—straighten out—a short burst of the engine—over the lighted area—sod coming up to meet me—deceptive highlights and shadows—careful—easy to bounce when you're tired—still too fast—tail too high—hold off—hold off—but the lights are far behind—the surface dims—texture of sod is gone—ahead, there's nothing but night—give her the gun and climb for another try?—the wheels touch gently—off again—No, I'll keep contact—ease the stick forward—back on the ground—off—back—the tail skid too—not a bad landing, but I'm beyond the light—can't see anything ahead—like flying in fog—ground loop?—No, still rolling too fast—might blow a tire—the field *must* be clear—uncomfortable though, jolting into blackness—wish I had a wing light—but too heavy on the take-off—slower, now—slow enough to ground loop safely—left rudder—reverse—stick over the other way—the *Spirit of St. Louis* swings around and stops rolling, resting on the solidness of earth, in the center of Le Bourget.

I start to taxi back toward the floodlights and hangars—but the entire field ahead is covered with running figures! [The rest is, of course, history.][29]

Compare Lindbergh's telegraphic instructions to himself with those from the verbatim recording of the drowning man, Don O'Daniel, reliving his ordeal in delirium:

Dive under it—dive under the breaker to get back—don't drink any salt water—don't swallow any salt water—take off your pants and shirts—they will help you float—don't take them off, it will help you float—keep them on—take it easy—you will be O.K., but you're getting tired—you were crazy to come out in the first place—you have gone out too far—you know better than that—don't swallow any water—it'll choke you. . . .[30]

It's getting dark—the tide's turning—see the light—it's getting plainer—take it easier—you are going to make it to the breakers—swim with the breakers—you are going to make it. . . .

That sand stings my face—it's cold—drag yourself—why doesn't somebody come?—take it easy—you're out of the water—I can't yell—why doesn't my flashlight

work?—I can't yell—my voice doesn't work—my
throat is all stopped up—crawl out of the water before
it takes you back out.[31]

Steven Callahan,[32] adrift alone in a life raft for seventy-six days,
also describes talking to himself and giving himself commands:

I talk to the lazy vagrant in control of my body. I coax
him to kneel by the entrance to await another dorado.
At first my body is slow. I clumsily splash down [with
his makeshift spear]. Miss. Another. Miss. But the
pumping of blood helps to revive my other self, the
physical part. On the third shot I ram my weapon
through the fish's back.[33]

Later, after fifty-two days at sea, Callahan describes waking up
from a delirious sleep, his energy almost totally spent:

The ghosts reach from the darkness and pull me
down. I'm falling. It's come.
"No!" I yell out. "Can't! Won't!" Can't let go. Tears
stream down my face and mix with the sea swilling
around my body. Will die, and soon. . . . Find the answer.
Want to . . . yes! That's it, want to live. Despite agony
and horror. Despite what lies ahead. I convulse, sobbing,
"I want to LIVE, to LIVE, to LIVE!"
Can't.
Must! Damn it, open your eyes. They blink, heavy
with fatigue. Try to focus.
Not good enough.
Quit your bitching! Do it! Grab ahold, arms. PUSH!
[He is trying to sit up.] Now again, PUSH! Good. Up a
bit. Won't drown now. [The bottom of the raft where he
has been lying face down is full of water.] Breath is
heavy. O.K., steady, boy. Head sways, eyes blur. A
wave comes in. Cool. Keep your own cool, too. Stop
that whining! Get that bag over you! [It keeps him
warm.] Do it! All right. Rest now. You're out of it, for
now. You're O.K. You hear me?

Yes.

O.K.

Now what? Next time it won't be so easy.

Shut up! You've got to come up with something. Got to get warm, got to rest, got to think. Maybe one chance left. Maybe not even that. It's [the "it" he is referring to here is ambiguous] got to work first time. If it doesn't, you WILL DIE! *Will die*, Will Die, will die. Yes. I must make this one [?] good.[34]

Lauren Elder[35] relates how she talked to herself as she walked down the mountain after a plane crash:

I moved backward over the side, feeling with my toes until they found a hold on the face of the rock. I repeated to myself what I had been taught: *Stay bunched up. Keep your hands and feet close together, test with your fingers and toes for firm holds.*

Monkeylike, I began to move down the cliff. One bad choice of footing and I would fall. I could feel it, the terror of coming loose from the wall, of falling free, of breaking on the rocks below. *Oh, God, don't think about it*, I told myself. *Concentrate on not reaching too far, not getting all spread out.*[36]

Note that in order to give oneself commands, there must be two "parts" to the self: a command giver ("I") and a command receiver ("me"). Wilfrid Noyce[37] discusses this tendency to talk to oneself during adversity:

The first stage, and it comes to many of us, is that we seem to become two people. It has been said that "it doesn't matter talking to yourself; it's when you start answering yourself back that you should get worried." But in fact the interesting sense of detachment and of "another person" begins to come just then. Lawrence found it in Arabia [Noyce quotes from T. E. Lawrence's *Seven Pillars of Wisdom*]: ". . . Such detachment came at times to a man exhausted by prolonged physical effort and isolation. His body plodded on mechanically, while his reasonable mind left him, and from without looked critically on him, wondering what that futile lumber [Lawrence's contemptuous reference to his weakened body, similar to Callahan's "lazy vagrant"] did and why. Sometimes these selves would converse in the void; and then madness was very near."

It [madness] is not always near, however. Lone seamen make a practice of conversing with themselves, asking when breakfast will be, what the time is, and so on. I remember the sensation as very clear, almost expected, on Everest in 1953. I was trying to speed my pace a little, with a load of over forty pounds, over the Geneva Spur without oxygen. I had one Sherpa with me. A week before, with oxygen to help, the thing had seemed a fairly Alpine climb. But now, at the stopping places every three steps, a regular conversation took place, the top half expressing itself scornfully [like Lawrence and Callahan] about the panting body below. And there seemed nothing odd about it."[38]

Callahan[39] speaks in a similar way about his experience adrift in the tiny life raft:

I see myself divide into three basic parts: Physical, emotional, and rational. [Recall Lindbergh's comment earlier that there are "three elements" to himself.] It's common for solo sailors to talk to themselves, to ask for a second opinion about how to deal with a problem. You try to think as another person, to get a new outlook and to talk yourself into positive action. When I am in danger, my emotional self feels fear and my physical self feels pain. This tendency is increasing as my voyage lengthens. The lines that stretch between my commanding rational self and my frightened emotional and vulnerable physical selves are getting tighter and tighter. My rational commander relies on hope, dreams and cynical jokes to relieve the tension in the rest of me.[40]

At the beginning of my voyage, there was little distinction between my rational mind and the rest of me.
My emotions were ruled by nearly instinctive training
and my body did not complain about having to work.
But the distinction between the parts of myself continues
to grow sharper as the two-edged sword of existence
cuts one or another of them more deeply each day. My
emotions have been stressed to the point of breaking. . . .
My body is now so beaten that it has trouble following
my mind's commands. It wants only to rest and find
relief from the pain. But rationally I have chosen not to
use my first aid kit because it is small and I may need it
more later if I am severely injured. Each decision like
this by my mind comes at increasing cost to the rest of
my crew. I must coerce my emotions to kill in order to
feed my body. I must coerce my arms and legs to perform in order to give myself a feeling of hope. I try to
comply with contradictory demands, but I know the
other parts of me have bent to my cold, hard rationalism
as best they can.[41]

Many survivors of solitary ordeals talk of this process of "splitting"
of the self, as did Lindbergh, for example, when describing how he
became aware of a new part of himself in the section on Confrontation
with "Others" in the previous chapter. It is clearly related also to the
process of detachment mentioned later in this chapter, where one
"part" of the self "separates" from the other(s).

Organizing One's Activities and Surroundings

Another means of gaining or maintaining self-control in an adverse situation—and thereby creating some autonomy and agency—is to create
organized and ritualized systems of behavior. Through such ritual one
becomes embedded in a set of behavioral requirements dictated by *oneself* rather than by the oppressive situation. Imposing order on one's
situation is one way of controlling it. For example, Admiral Byrd relates:

What disturbed me was the haphazard manner in
which the [supply] boxes had been stowed. . . . [In the

snow tunnel next to his hut] the [cans of] beans were hopelessly mixed with the canned meats, tomato juice, and boxes of odds and ends; and the roof was caving in. All this offended my growing sense of neatness. During my spare time I set about rearranging the whole set up.

I didn't try to rush the job. If the polar regions have taught me anything, it is patience. I rarely spent more than an hour on any one job, preferring to shift to something else. In that way I was able to show a little progress each day on all the important jobs, and at the same time keep from becoming bored with any one. This was a way of bringing variety into an existence which would be basically monotonous.[42]

It is almost as if an organized behavior pattern takes the place of the kinds of obligations required of one as a member of society. Making oneself a part of such a pattern makes one feel less "alone"—one has one's periodic obligations and rituals for companionship and to "belong" to. At the same time one has gained control and self-stimulation. Many people who live alone, such as isolated elderly people, frequently fill their lives with rituals to ward off loneliness.

Byrd describes other acts that he ritualizes:

After getting rid of my heavy clothes, I set about the afternoon ritual of lighting the gasoline pressure lamp. Anyhow, *I have made it a ritual.* [RDL] . . . I find that I crave light like a thirsting man craves water.[43]

Note that in the above excerpt Byrd again alludes to the solitary man's need for stimulation. He later describes another ritual:

. . . Each night I wash a different third of my body. I don't know how I came to decide upon that arbitrary division unless it was that I discovered my conscience could be placated by performing the ritual in install-ments.[44]

Byrd comments that being organized also adds another significant element—meaning—to his solitary existence:

From the beginning I had recognized that an orderly, harmonious routine was the only lasting defense against my special circumstances. The brain-cracking loneliness of solitary confinement is the loneliness of a futile routine. I tried to keep my days crowded; and yet, at the same time, I, the most unsystematic of mortals, endeavored to be systematic. At night, before blowing out the lantern, I form the habit of blocking out [i.e., scheduling] the morrow's work . . . half an hour to leveling [snow] drift, an hour to cutting bookshelves in the [ice] walls of the food tunnel, and two hours to renewing a broken bridge in the man-hauling sledge.

If the time was not sufficient, well and good; let the job be resumed another day. It was wonderful to be able to dole out time in this way. It brought me an extraordinary sense of *command over myself* and simultaneously freighted my simplest doings with *significance*. [RDL] Without that or an equivalent, the days would have been without purpose. . . .[45]

David Lewis[46] intimates that one of the things that helped him to survive his arduous sojourn through the waters of Antarctica was the fact that he became compulsively organized: "It was good that I was developing the old-maidishness so very necessary for seagoing—a meticulous fussiness. There must be a set place for everything."[47]

Christopher Burney, in solitary, organizes an elaborate daily schedule in which he eats (extremely slowly) at a certain time, then has a set time for pacing, a time for philosophical debates with himself, a time for his sewing project (making a waistcoat out of threads painstakingly unraveled from his blanket), and so on. Thus he organizes and fills his day.

Other forms of ritual, such as celebrating holidays and anniversaries and saying prayers, similarly help the individual to remain psychologically in control of himself by setting up his own demands on his behavior.

Dr. Alain Bombard, alone on a raft as described in *The Voyage of the Heretique*,[48] states after his watch and radio are accidentally broken:

This incident brought home to me how much the aimlessness of doing what I pleased, of not deciding in advance how to fill my day, could undermine me, and

> *I decided to work out a strict timetable of activity.* [RDL] I
> am convinced that in such circumstances it is essential for
> the castaway to remain master of events, rather than be
> content merely to react to them.[49]

Bombard virtually summarizes the point that organization produces control, as well as stating that one must manage to sense oneself as agent rather than object or victim in the situation.

Keeping Physically Active
Ritter suggests another coping device that enables the isolated survivor to maintain a sense of personal competence, instrumental agency, and autonomy in an oppressive situation—simply doing something physical:

> With iron consistency, as though my life depended
> on it, I take my walk every day. It is scarcely a walk any
> more, rather a daily crawl on all fours close to the walls
> of the hut. Round and round mechanically, in circles,
> ten times, twenty times. . . .[50]

Both Byrd and Burney also describe how important to their sanity and well-being physical movement is. Burney relies on exercise:

> When I could sit no longer, I did physical exercises,
> remembering a warning that one could never tell, even
> in prison, when fitness would be critical. But I performed
> them with a vigour much greater than the hope of
> escape which chiefly justified them, and there is doubt
> in my mind whether they did more good than harm.[51]

Byrd describes a ritual of walking and its benefits (including stimulation) as follows:

> . . . It is my practice to walk between an hour and two
> hours a day—when I have time. The walk gives me a
> change and it also provides another means of exercise. . . .
> The last half of the walk is the best of the day, the
> time when I am most nearly at peace with myself and
> circumstances. Thoughts of life and the nature of

things flow smoothly, so smoothly and so naturally as to create an illusion that one is swimming harmoniously in the broad current of the cosmos. During this hour I undergo a sort of intellectual levitation, although my thinking is usually on earthy, practical matters. . . .[52] [Note the oceanic metaphor and cosmic unity themes once again.]

Yet I could, with a little imagination, make every walk seem different. One day I would imagine that my path was the Esplanade, on the water side of Beacon Hill in Boston, where, in my mind's eye, I often walked with my wife. I would meet people I knew along the bank, and drink in the perfection of a Boston Spring.[53]

Papillon, wrongly imprisoned for theft and placed in solitary confinement in the penal colony in French Guiana, also tries to keep physically active:

The cell was nine feet high. Its ceiling was made of iron bars as thick as streetcar tracks, so close together that nothing of any size could get through. Above that was the actual roof of the building, about twenty-two feet above the ground. Above the cells and looking down on them was a walk a yard wide with an iron railing, where two guards paced back and forth from opposite ends, stopping when they met and turning to retrace their steps. There was a little light at the top, but at the bottom of the cell you could barely see even in broad daylight. I started immediately to walk, waiting for the whistle to signal the lowering of the bunks.[54]

Robinson Risner,[55] a Vietnam POW, describes remaining active out of a state of much more desperate urgency after being placed in a blacked-out isolation hovel:

It was not fear of the dark, for I had been in the dark before. But something strange was happening to me. I began trying to calm myself, saying, "Now you're acting foolish. Just go over and take a nap. Prove to yourself that being in a dark room is not going to bother you."

I walked over to the bunk, folded my shorts, put them on the leg stocks and laid down my head on them. The agitation continued to build and build. At the end of five minutes, I thought I was going crazy. I jumped up and began to run up and down the room. I ran and ran and ran. Sometimes I switched to push-ups and then sit-ups. It was a couple of hours past the nine-thirty gong when I finally stopped that night after hundreds of push-ups and as many as a thousand sit-ups.

It was as if I had an animal on my back. Absolute panic had set in. The fact that I could not control this thing driving me or get rid of it caused me to be even more panic-stricken. I could not understand it, and I could not get rid of it.

Sheer desolation permeated the miserable dark cell I lived in twenty-four hours a day. I was absolutely convinced I would never get to leave that cell until the war was over. And I had no idea when that would be. What I was going through would continue for as long as I could think. I was not scared of anything they would put me through because I felt they had already done their worst. But I was terrified because I could not get rid of the panic. I would go to sleep only after I was completely exhausted, then awaken during the night— at twelve, two, three—and immediately jump up and start running. The instant I awakened, the shock of it would hit me—there I was, in the same place where I had gone to sleep. It was always going to be that way— until the end of the war. . . .[56]

Because of having exercised methodically most of the time of imprisonment, I automatically kept track of how much I was doing. I knew approximately how long or how many steps it took me to run a mile. To combat my panic, I would run as much as twenty-five miles a day. My only salvation was exhaustion—the only time I could stop running.[57]

General William Dean,[58] a captive of the North Koreans during the Korean War, was deliberately prevented by his captors from keeping up the rigorous, self-imposed program of physical exercise that he considered important to maintaining his physical and mental health. So, while forced to sit rigidly upright in his cell under a bare bulb and the gaze of a guard, he quietly, systematically, and surreptitiously flexed and relaxed his finger muscles.

Maintaining Initiative

Survivors must also find some means to affect and alter their situation, to have an impact on it and make a difference. Edith Bone was determined to have an effect on her situation by whatever means she could muster:

> Having once realized into what hands I had fallen, I regarded the matter as a challenge, a challenge not only to myself but to that higher civilization of which I considered myself a product, however modest. My life in this prison I regarded as a battle I had to fight with these very inferior people. I had to convince them that the ideas that had been put into their heads by their superiors (though without much success, by the way), had no validity in the higher sphere of civilization from which I had come. There was also something else that helped. I do not think that I have ever quite grown up; I still like to play, and there was an element of sport in all this; the same urge which had prompted me to play tricks in school on the more stupid of my teachers prompted me to play tricks on the stupid thugs outside my door.
>
> My very first battle with the administration of the prison was a hairy business. I had no comb and no brush, my hair had grown long in close on two years of captivity and I was allowed neither side-combs, hair-clips, nor so much as a short end of string to tie my hair back, so that it hung into my eyes. I asked for a hair-cut and was told that women were not entitled to hair-cuts as they wore long hair. I remonstrated: "But I have always worn short hair," to no effect.

I did not argue the matter, but proceeded to tear off my hair thread by thread, leaving only a stub of about a handbreadth on my head. It took me three weeks to get it done and the result was much as if rats had gnawed my hair off. . . .

But when, another six months later, I started to shorten my hair a third time, the sergeant on duty outside my door came in and said: "The governor sends you word not to tear off your hair. The barber will come and cut it for you tomorrow."

. . . Encouraged by this victory, I began to campaign for a comb.[59]

Robinson Risner found a "passive" way of making an impact on his situation:

Even though he was using an interpreter, I looked [my interrogator] straight in the eyes. I had always used the eyes as a weapon, and most of the enemy I would look in the eyes until they dropped theirs. I had never lowered mine.[60]

Remaining Competent and Skillful

Edith Bone was also masterful at finding ways to exercise her mind in skillful ways in order to create things that she could use to enrich—a strange but apt word in her case to apply to solitary confinement—her life. She had first used balls of bread dough as a means of counting and keeping track of items she was cataloging mentally, but she eventually found this unsatisfactory:

The obvious thing was to substitute an abacus for the single pellets of bread which were forever getting lost. The only material at my disposal was the black convict bread I got and which I could not eat. I was, by the way, the only prisoner who got this bread—the others got so-called "white" bread, as I found later when I succeeded in widening my horizon. Not as if this other bread had been white in anything except the name, but it was certainly not as black as mine.

Although the black bread was uneatable, as sculptural material it was vastly superior to the "white." Being unkneaded, unleavened, and almost unbaked, it constituted a sticky mass which, after proper treatment, hardened into something very like one of the older type of brown plastics. . . .[61]

The problems that confronted me in this simple task inspired me with great respect for those who design and make the innumerable devices mankind uses in the struggle against the forces of nature by means of these forces themselves.

My abacus was comparatively simple and yet what a deal of pondering and contriving went into it. How to make the frame? How to make the beads? How to pierce them, with nothing to do it with? What to use for wires? The latter problem I solved by using straw out of my palliasse, and what a job it was to find suitable straws and elude the vigilance of the guards while searching for them! In the end I found that the sorghum stalks constituting the broom that was handed in every morning for a few minutes, made better "wires" for my abacus than ordinary straw. . . .

In addition to the abacus I made many other useful objects, such as sea-mats to protect my table from the dirty bottom of the mess-tin, which was invariably greasy dirty. I also made a tiny game of skittles and some little statuettes. . . .[62]

In the same Tolstoi story about a prisoner which I have already mentioned, the hero passes the time by taking an inventory of his knowledge on all sorts of subjects.

I had already tried something like this, before I thought of an abacus. What I had tried to do was to take an inventory of my vocabulary in the six languages I speak fluently. [This point obviously indicates the intellectual resources she brought with her to her ordeal.] But I failed because I always lost count so long as I had only my fingers to count on. Now, with my fine six-row abacus, I did better. Here, too, there were, of course, problems to be solved. How to avoid repetitions? The

answer was: strict alphabetical order. This brought a
fresh problem: what to do with the words one remembered after one had passed their proper place in the
alphabetical order. There was no answer to this one,
except to leave them out and later start afresh from A.
[Note how she stays strictly with her organized ritual
way of doing this.] This I did three times and found in
the end that I had enumerated twenty-seven thousand
three hundred and sixty-nine English words. That satisfied me, and I went on to German, French, and the rest.

There were many more inventories one could make
in addition to these general ones of vocabulary. How
many birds could I name? How many trees? How many
flowers? How many makes of cars? How many breeds
of dogs? How many English publishers? How many
states of the United States? (I got all forty-eight and
added Alaska for good measure.) [Bone was English.]
How many wines? How many characters in Dickens,
Balzac, Tolstoi, Stendhal, Dostoevski, Thackery, and
many others? I found, by the way, that Dickens, of whom
I had read less than I had of several other authors, must
be the greatest creator of characters, because I could
remember more than four hundred, even before I had
pencil and paper to help me, although I counted only
those of whom I could also remember in which novel
they appeared and what they were like.[63]

Having made an abacus using balls of bread dough sliding on
pieces of straw, she next wants to find a way to print poetry:

It was the bread that again helped me. By this time I
was an accomplished breadcrumb technologist and I
decided to make myself a printing set out of bread. It
must be admitted that, however little I thought of the
quality of my verses, I did feel I should like to see them
with my bodily eyes and not only carry them in my
memory.

I began to shape letters out of long very thin rolls of
breadcrumb specially processed for the purpose. When

a letter was formed I gave it a little bang with my fist so that it was flattened and all the joints pressed together.

The most difficult part was to make letters of the same size. This was difficult because, of course, I could not make them all at the same time. I had to wait until no one was about.

In the end I had four thousand letters and a compositor's case with twenty-six separate little pigeon-holes, and could lay out on my table not less than sixteen lines of verse, doggerel or poetry. This was great fun. It was also amusing for another reason: it startled the guards, who had probably never seen any prisoners doing anything of the sort. Altogether, they were very surprised at my constant activity. I was always doing things that were not "normal," that is, not within their experience.[64]

Edith Bone is perhaps the premier example in all of solitary ordeals of how much one can make of so little, of how "full" a life it is possible to have in the rigors of prolonged solitary confinement. She may be the most inspiring figure of all. In the following excerpt, she describes how a simple nail became the centerpiece of a vast weeks-long project, and how the nail in turn became a critical tool for further activities:

I decided I would try to contrive a spy-hole in my door through which I could look in through the regulation spy-hole which is a feature of every prison door. The door was made of two-inch solid oak, but of course its surface was not flush. It was built up of several beams and there were points where three of these joined; obviously these joints were weak spots, which could be attacked.

I had noticed long before that a nail, or rather the large head of a nail, projected from the door close to the floor. It stood to reason that it must be a large nail. I decided that the first thing to do was to pull it out and see whether it could be made into a bradawl. It only projected about an eighth of an inch, but that was enough to get a purchase on it with a cord, and then pull. This is not, of course, the most efficient way of pulling out nails, but I had no other. From this a second problem arose; I needed a cord, a strong cord. Where could I get one? The jailers were sensitive about the smallest piece of string, presumably because of their inexplicable, unreasonable and inconsistent fear of suicides among the prisoners.

I decided that the best possible cord could be made of threads pulled out of the coarse linen towels which we were given. . . .[65]

Fortunately for myself, I had always been a fanatical lover of knots, and possessed that most remarkable publication Astley's Book of Knots, which I had studied assiduously and which, in addition to knots, also contained a number of sinnets. I plaited a beautiful sinnet—a round one, the sort known as coach-whipping—out of thirty-two threads in groups of eight.

This cord was strong enough to carry even my own weight, so there was no fear of its breaking. I put a strangler knot (this, too, out of the Astley book) round the nail head, and, with my foot against the door, pulled for all I was worth; but the nail still resisted all my efforts. I realized that mere pulling was not enough. The nail would have to be loosened by joggling it up and down and right and left. For a long time I seemed to be making no headway, but I persevered until I felt a slight wobble. I loosened and pulled day after day, for many weeks [!], whenever I could be sure that none of the guards was loitering near my door, and in the end I got that nail out. This was triumph.

The nail was about an eighth of an inch thick and three inches long. I put an edge on the end of it instead of the existing point by the simple expedient of rubbing it on the concrete floor, which was exactly like a carborundum whetstone, especially with regard to the soles of one's shoes or boots. The result was a bradawl. With it I succeeded in boring a hole in my [cell] door at a point where three members of solid oak met. It was only a pinhole, of course, and it had to be very carefully concealed. It would not have done, for instance, for any wood-dust to have fallen outside, so I used my mouth as a pump and sucked out the little splinters of wood as my bradawl removed them.

By a dispensation of providence, the oak had been so blackened by age that it was exactly the color of my black convict bread. Thus, the little hole could be stopped up by a tiny plug which matched the wood so perfectly that my spy-hole was never discovered. The plug was a necessity, as otherwise my little pinpoint spy-hole would have showed up like a bright star whenever there was a light in the cell and none outside. I never took out the plug without taking care to block the light.

Until I was transferred to another prison . . . which was in May 1954, I had the constant use of this spy-hole and it gave me more information on the routine of the prison than my jailers intended.[66]

Bone was able to put the fruits of her long project to work in the interest of maintaining her vigilance, that other vital coping mechanism. Her spy hole also provided her with information and stimulation.

Sir Geoffrey Jackson[67] describes how mental competence and a satisfying kind of mental order are created out of the playing of solitaire:

I had for example made the curious discovery that my "patiences" [a type of solitaire with cards] were not really patiences at all; after my return home I was able to cross-check this impression against the expertise of my wife, not to mention several standard handbooks. It was quite clear that the three assorted "solitaires" I [thought I] had remembered, or evolved, were not at all games-of-chance which I had seen, watched and dredged up from subconscious memory. They were simply pattern-making activities with which—provided I concentrated and made no gross error of memory or judgement—I could not go wrong. I can only assume that their regular rehearsal satisfied my profound need to assure myself constantly that mine was still a universe of order, and of laws, and still to some measure

subject to my own free will. Certainly the occasions
were many when I withdrew contented into sleep,
tired out because I had refused to be satisfied till the
symmetry and order had been achieved which I expected
my functioning mind to produce from the initial confusion of the random cards.[68]

Later he describes another skill that he acquired, apparently at a
high level of mastery, under duress—a feat that should inspire the rest
of us:

All the occupational therapies which I have so far
described have, I notice in retrospect, been of a passive
and a receptive nature. Yet since the French prisoners
of the Napoleonic War and their wood-and-ivory
models—replicas in minutest detail of the ships-of-the-
line they had served in—the craftsmanship of the
captive has been famous, and undoubtedly has been so
since human time began, and with it the power of one
man over another. I was no exception, in at least intent
if not execution. . . .
. . . Certainly in my own disposition there has always
been something of the frustrated artisan; and within a
short time of my imprisonment I had invented for
myself manual tasks the outcome of which added to
my comfort, as their protraction supported my morale.
To my amazement I discovered in myself a quite
swiftly developing aptitude with the needle, which
began with relatively crude tasks but, with time, acquired
a considerable refinement, if always in a strictly utili-
tarian rather than an aesthetic capacity; I can now darn
a hole in a sheet to the degree almost of invisible mending,
though needle-point embroidery is still beyond me. . . .[69]
That I am not exaggerating my prowess when it
comes to invisible mending is even now open to ocular
proof. My cellular undervest, which served as everything from pillowcase to lampshade to towel, and
gradually progressed from white to drab brown, had
one of its meshes caught and torn. . . . With much

patience, a very fine needle, and a thread taken from the hem, I determined—and was finally able—to re-weave it, by copying it and reconstituting as exactly as I could the texture of the surrounding "cells." This garment, whiter than white again, can today be seen in the museum of that excellent firm, Messrs. Marks and Spencers ... in London.[70]

After describing how he ran up and down in his cell to exhaust himself so that he could sleep to escape his panic, Robinson Risner relates that he began to shift over to exercising his intellectual competence:

A couple of months later, around October, I began to get a little relief for an hour or two at noon by thinking of math problems that Ron [a fellow prisoner with whom he had previously shared a cell] and I had worked on. I had never liked mathematics before, perhaps because I did not understand it. But now it furnished me a welcome respite.

Ron had helped me review things like square root and fractions. And what was especially helpful, he had taught me to solve for unknowns. Because of the darkness I couldn't see well enough most of the time to write anything down, so I had to use relatively simple equations. But even then I could make up simple problems with as many as three unknowns and solve them in my mind.

For about a two-hour period during the day, there would be a reflection of the sun that was just right. A small rathole at the base of the brick wall let the sun shine on the end of the bunk. I would work a math problem on the end of my bunk with a piece of brick if the guard was not around.[71]

George Smith,[72] drifting alone in a life raft on the Coral Sea, describes some projects that occupied and stimulated his mind for a time:

Another project that was never completed (the work being interrupted by rescue), was a fishing spear I attempted to make from the tough, hollow bones of a booby bird. . . . I [first] tried to carve one out of the strips of bone from the life-raft case . . . but the bone was [hard] to cut. . . . I worked for hours and accomplished nothing.

With the stupid, self-conscious feeling a fellow gets when he has missed something that should have been perfectly obvious, I realized that the ideal material for this project was the bones of the birds I had been shooting. With this in mind, I enthusiastically saved the long, tough wing-bones, and the bill of the next bird that fell prey to my .45. By lucky coincidence, when the knuckles were cut from the outboard bones of the wings, the remaining section would telescope very neatly into the inboard bones. I hoped to fashion a long shaft by putting these together. Out of the bill, I hoped to make a spearhead. The lower jaw being very sharp, strong and V-shaped, was ideal for the purpose. . . .

Such simple activities as these served to keep my mind and hands busy. . . .[73]

Adrift on the high seas, and very much alone in a craft without wings, my thoughts naturally turned to building, and to the possible improvement of my environment.

Devoting much time to constructive thinking about the improvement of the emergency equipment carried by [World War II] Navy fliers . . . I vowed repeatedly that, if I should ever have the good fortune of returning to civilization, I would rig a life-raft with a waterproof, tent-like canopy which would protect the occupant from the elements. . . . I mentally designed a canopy that could be snapped or zipped to the edge of the raft and cover my head and neck. . . .[74]

There are, of course, any number of examples of POWs in Vietnam engaging in such exercises as designing their dream houses in their heads during their long captivity.

Defense Mechanisms

Various defense mechanisms are also relied on at different times in order to help the individual maintain his equilibrium, orientation, and sanity—to help preserve his conscious identity.

Escape

People undergoing prolonged, stressful ordeals also need to create escape or "time out" situations; they occasionally have to "get away" in some manner to avoid being worn down. The ego needs a rest from the continual stress of active coping and vigilance. Christopher Burney relied on fantasy on occasion:

> But at this point I abandoned calculation and sailed gaily off to a dreamland of camps of prisoners-of-war, where only English was spoken, where no one worked, and where daily arrived thousands of enormous parcels of food. Into the parcels I delved and romped in a heap of hams and plum puddings and bathed in condensed milk, until at length my rhythmic feet were quite disjointed from my spirit. . . .
>
> I was disturbed from my reverie one day by the sound of the trolley outside. "Soup," I told myself, not realizing that the morning had passed so quickly and congratulating myself on the fortunate and absorbing theme which has made time so harmless. This was in truth the secret of living in prison, and perhaps of all living: to dream of pleasant things when there were none real to be enjoyed, and to make the most of the few real pleasures.[75]

It is interesting to take this last bit of advice of Burney's, along with much of that of other survivors, outside of their ordeals and to reflect on how well they apply to "ordinary" life. All things being a matter of degree, I think they often apply passably well.

Burney also writes:

> Early in my imprisonment—I suppose it was the second Sunday, since my memory always worked strictly to the calendar—I found myself in a daydream walking back from the old church in Herefordshire where we used to be taken every Sunday in the holidays. The

fields had their August warmth and yellowness, the
hop-yards stood like orderly jungles waiting for the
pickers, there were blackberries in the hedges and
thirsty bullocks resting in their shade. And across the
stile and through the gate there was lunch.[76]

Papillon regularly hyperventilated during long months in a dark
solitary confinement in order to create pleasant escapist fantasies and
reveries:

> As I said, I'd been here over two months. It was clear
> to me that at the Reclusion escape was impossible. A
> deal, a "combination" [bribery], was out of the question.
> So I worked on splitting myself in two [note this theme
> again] and developed a foolproof method: in order to
> roam among the stars, to summon up various stages in
> my life or build my amazingly realistic castles in Spain,
> I first had to tire myself out. I would walk for hours
> without sitting down, never stopping, thinking about
> nothing in particular. Once I was truly exhausted, I
> stretched out on my bunk and wrapped the blanket
> around my head. This way, the little air there was in my
> cell was further cut off. My lungs became asphyxiated
> and my head started to burn. Suffocating with the heat
> and lack of air, I suddenly found myself in flight. Ah!
> What indescribable sensations! I spent nights of love
> that were more intense than real ones. I could sit down
> with my mother, dead these seventeen years. I could
> play with her dress while she stroked my curls, which
> she had left long to make me look like a girl. I caressed
> her slender fingers, her soft silky skin. . . .
> Hand in hand, we followed the river home. I was
> actually there, in the house of my childhood. I held my
> hands over my mother's eyes so that she had to play
> the piano without looking at the music. I was there; it
> wasn't my imagination. I was with her, standing on a
> chair behind the piano stool, and I pressed my small
> hands against her large eyes so she couldn't see. Her
> nimble fingers continued to skim over the piano until
> she had played "The Merry Widow" to the end.[77]

Papillon managed, however, to balance his introspective fantasies with outward problem solving (for example, the challenge of catching and killing poisonous centipedes in his dank cell to eat), so he did not totally live a fantasy life.

Frankl[78] also spoke of fantasy life in coping with the horrors of the concentration camps:

> [The] intensification of inner life helped the prisoner find a refuge from the emptiness, desolation and spiritual poverty of his existence, by letting him escape into the past. When given free rein, his imagination played with past events, often not important ones, but minor happenings and trifling things. . . . In my mind I took bus rides, unlocked the front door of my apartment, answered my telephone, switched on the electric lights. . . . As the inner life of the prisoner tended to become more intense, he also experienced the beauty of art and nature as never before.[79]

Byrd[80] escaped through reading; he felt that by doing so he was also warding off a tendency to become a brute and return to some ancient precivilized state.

> I am half through Somerset Maugham's *Of Human Bondage*, and I read a chapter as I ate. A meal eaten alone and in silence is no pleasure. So I fell into the habit of reading while I ate. In that way I can lose myself for a time. The days I don't read I feel like a barbarian brooding over a chunk of meat.[81]

Sir Francis Chichester's[82] "time out" from his taxing ordeal of sailing alone was only rarely fantasy or reminiscence. His early morning meal (when he frequently escaped through reading) and his morning snooze provided his escape:

> Breakfast was my best meal, partly, perhaps, because I felt more like eating after getting some sleep, but partly, too, because breakfast always seemed important as a ritual after coming through the night safely—candy for the kid. So deliberately I took more time over my

breakfasts. I was often up at dawn, and at it all day
until dark without a let-up, followed probably by three
or four dressings-up in deck clothes during the night.
So I sat for as long as I could over breakfast, and sometimes went back to my bunk for a snooze after it. My
bunk was the most comfortable place on the yacht, but
I had to give up the quarter berth which I liked best
because of leaks. My sleeping bag and everything else
got so sopping that I was driven out to another berth in
the cabin.[83]

Chichester also hints that meals as rituals provide both organization of time and continuity with his previous existence as a civilized
Englishman.

The "escape" from the present situation for Lindbergh didn't consist
of fantasizing as such, but rather of the frequent reminiscences about
the past that are scattered throughout his book. Those recollections, and
his mental "trips" outside his plane, were his "time out" experiences.

Rationalization

Then again, if one cannot rely on some kind of "time out" or escape mechanism, one can always fall back on a "things-could-be-worse" form of
defense mechanism. Note how Byrd rationalizes the permanent absence
of the sun as the antarctic night begins in his solitary deepfreeze:

If you hadn't lost the sun, I told myself, you would
have had something serious to think about, since that
would mean that the earth's axis was pointing the wrong
way, and the entire solar system was running amok.[84]

In other words, he convinces himself that, if you think losing the
sun is bad, consider that if it had appeared it would have meant that the
earth had turned upside down! The ability to imagine a situation worse
than the present one (and even stretching a point to do so) makes the
current one more tolerable. (We always seem capable of thinking of a
situation worse than our current one—although when we are not in an
ordeal we seem more capable of dwelling on ones that are better.) While
this may seem like the height of irrational thinking, it can provide some
comfort so long as it does not become a permanent, psychotic mode of

thought—and it is a coping mechanism used frequently by people under stress. The drowning Don O'Daniel gives another example of being able to think that he is better off than *somebody* as he struggles to stay afloat: "It's a good thing Chuck didn't come along—with those big boots—it's a good thing he didn't come along—he couldn't have made it."[85]

Keeping Occupied

A coping or defense mechanism related to escaping is simply keeping oneself *occupied* so that, as Ritter and Byrd suggested, one does not dwell excessively on oneself, one's isolation, and one's hardship.

Ritter in the Arctic provides an example of trying to become thoroughly occupied after her husband leaves:

> The next day I watch him disappear, a moving black speck in the distance, vanishing among the ice floes. By this time I have learned what I must do when I am alone—work, and go on working, to make the cold and the solitude tolerable. . . . I work the whole day, unthinking and without a wish, like a draft animal that must work to live. . . .[86]
>
> I sit in the hut and tire myself out with sewing. It makes no difference whether the work is finished today or tomorrow, but I know what I'm doing. I do not want to have my mind free for a moment to think, a moment in which to become aware of the nothingness outside.[87]

The degree to which Sir Francis Chichester[88] kept himself both occupied and organized during his single-handed circumnavigation is illustrated most concisely by a typical list of daily jobs to be done. In terms of what it says about remaining occupied, the list certainly speaks for itself:

> To make sure that things that needed doing got done, and were not overlooked in the next crisis, I used to keep a list of jobs in hand from day to day. I called this my "agenda." It may be of some interest to give my agenda for this period of the voyage. Here it is:
> Check water tank connections

Secure cockpit locker with hasp (actually I used cordage for this)

Fix preventer to galley drawers

Try self-steering vang without extra lead

Freshen nip of tiller lines to self-steering

Check engine water level

Stow burgee stick

Rig tiller tackle to cabin

Try more slack on self-steering oar

More solid cockpit repair to keep deck water out

Drylube tiller lines

Examine alternator belts

Dry out cockpit locker

Open counter ventilator on dry days

Devise hold-down for tins in settee lockers

Spray bolt cutters

Fix starboard deck net

Stop starboard deck ventilator

Main topping lift

Start mustard and cress [plants he was growing]

Rig tell-tale on self-steering

Clean Very [flare] pistol

Sort out pole uphauls, downhauls, outhauls, and lifts

More hooks in "cloaks"

Deal with remains of deck net

Fix knotted warp for stern drag

Study camera light meter

Free Lewinar jammed main sheet slide stop

Fix lanyards to winch handles

Refill meths containers and bottle

Tauten leech in genoa stays'l

Free head of mains'l caught outboard in backstay

Check fruit and water

Sow wheat germ

Fix pendant for jib halliard

Fix lanyard for jib snap shackle

Dry out flying boat sextant box

Dry out bag of winter woollies

On calm day, up mast to dud crosstree light

Devise means of keeping pillow in heeled bunk
Dry out seat locker by my bunk
Fix lanyard for bilge pump handle
Spray e.l. capstan
Service blast horn
Fit rope end for pole outboard in place of shackle
Fix lanyard for reefing handles
Repair mizzen stays'l anti-chafe patch
Calm day—paint possible leaks over forepeak
Fit larger pendants to jib halliards
Chafe preventers on shrouds
Repair outhaul foot of mizzen
Put up more cup hooks
Remove flying cleats used for trysail tackles
Deal with leak at foot of my berth
Rig storm jib sheets
Renew pin and bolt in self-steering vang as soon as
weather makes possible
Deal with twisted shackle, storm stays'l
Fix a waterproof torch
Consider fresh position for inspection lamp, foredeck
Examine crosstree leads at deck and fuse
Deal with stays'l halliard twisted round stays
Check off-course alarm
Strengthen inspection lamp
Fix tarred twine for anti-chafe tie backs
Inspect dead Harrier unit underwater
Drylube chafing ropes
Re-lash mizzen 3rd slide up
Check cabin compass
Repair bolt of the sheave in the fife rail, loose
Deck bolt of stern pulpit looks loose
Freshen nip of all signal halliards

This list is nowhere near a complete record of the work done on *Gipsy Moth*—it is rather a list of merely extra jobs. It omits all sail changing, radio work, adjustments to the self-steering gear, navigation, all regular work in the galley, and all the back-breaking tasks of tidying up after the capsize. Some of the jobs listed—the cockpit repair, for instance—took several days to get done. Nevertheless, incomplete as it is, my agenda may give some idea of the human effort needed for singlehanded ocean sailing.[89]

With that much work to do, who has time to feel lonely? The weighty tradition of seaborne activities keeps him company, and occupies his existence almost totally, recalling the similarly involving routines of astronauts on long flights in space. He may be solitary, but he is not alone.

Christopher Burney keeps occupied in solitary confinement by, among other projects, painstakingly unraveling his blanket and resewing it into a waistcoat (all done surreptitiously, of course). The following are further examples of Burney occupying himself:

> On the other hand, I found a new activity, which was more enervating but seemed more useful than prome-nading. My straw mattress was filled with oat-straw, and I found that many of the oats had been left over from the threshing. I decided to eat them and spent many hours collecting, husking and amassing them in a little pile. When this seemed to be a small mouthful (perhaps twice a day if I worked hard), I ate it with due ceremony, thinking a little smugly that God helped those who helped themselves. . . .[90]
>
> To shorten the morning lap of this daily marathon [of activities he had set up], after I had washed, I used a series of pastimes which I regarded as ridiculous but useful. I started by manicuring myself with a sliver of wood which I managed to peel from the stool. I had never done such a thing before, at least with any but the most perfunctory attention, but now I made a great show of it, partly because the more care I took with it, the longer it would last, and partly because I had senti-mental memories of being chided for my ill-kept hands and thought that the least I could do now was to make myself presentable as might be. . . .[91]

Burney is also striving to preserve his sense of dignity and to find stimulation in the small details of his restricted world.

He had previously decided not to eat all of his daily bread ration at once and had made his efforts at self-control into a sort of game to occupy his time:

> The first two hours were generally the most difficult, for the soup was a mere *amuse guele*, tickling the appetite and tempting me with the suggestion that if I were only to eat my bread as well I could feel comfortably full.
>
> Sometimes I had to resort to the most absurd self-trickery to avoid doing so. I hid the crust under a blanket, or even under the bed, and tried to convince myself that it was not really there. But this was apt to be dangerous: oneself is a treacherous antagonist at bluff; and more than once I found that I was not only eating the forbidden fruit but had convinced myself that it was the wise and proper thing to do.
>
> It was safer to find some line of thought or day-dream which I could follow through the first half of the afternoon, until the finger of sunlight on my wall told me that the end was near. Then, as a rule, and unless I was too interested in my own thoughts, I embarked on a musical programme to conclude the day. Being no singer, even to my own taste, I whistled every tune I could remember, the martial ones to make me triumphant over my enemies, the homely ones which made me think of food, and the emotional ones which occasionally, and to my own amusement, brought a conventional tear out of its duct. This was a long programme, which grew as my memory became sharper.[92]

Sir Geoffrey Jackson,[93] imprisoned and isolated by terrorists in South America, writes a wonderfully insightful statement in *Surviving the Long Night*, a book that is one of the most articulate to come out of a solitary ordeal experience:

> In retrospect I can rationalize what at the time I suspect I did intuitively to survive, which was to confront the loss of the dimension of time—and the effective extinction of any future tense—by the creation of landmarks in my

small eternity. Just as the traveller in a snowstorm survives the mortal danger of wandering in a circle by taking even the shortest of bearings from one visible tree to the next, so the captive must break up his "day" into stages from one to the other of which he can progress without vertigo, emotional, intellectual, even spiritual. In my case the stages were of the simplest, furnishing something to look forward to, and a space to fill up profitably meanwhile.

For this reason meals become very important to a captive. Plain hunger is their secondary aspect; only once or twice did I experience it, and then never by the intention of my captors. Far more significant is their function as a compass bearing in a wilderness of time. Many writers have left us with harrowing vignettes of captives circling or crouched at the bottom of their pit or oubliette, awaiting with almost languorous entreatment the flung crust or hambone. Far more than from the pain of an empty belly, their anguish sprang, I can vouch, from the fear of an empty mind and an empty space of time [recall Ritter's "fear of nothingness"].[94]

Note how Jackson uses the metaphor of navigation as he struggles to "keep his bearings" during his ordeal. It is also interesting to note here that the very kind of ritualistic attention to small detail that we term pathologically "obsessive-compulsive" in everyday life serves the individual coping with a solitary ordeal so well. The point is, of course, that the person in confinement has no choice but to attend to the details of those things immediately around her or him for stimulation, while the "free" person has the whole wide world by comparison from which to draw stimulation. The existentialists maintain that many people in everyday life seek to avoid the meaninglessness of their "free" existence by "filling up time" with empty details and rituals to occupy their minds and thus avoid confronting the emptiness of their lives. In both cases one could say that life is a solitary ordeal. However, in the survivor's case it is an ordeal forced upon him or her in which time-filling activities can be very appropriate; in the case of "ordinary" life the cowardly person, in merely occupying himself in order to avoid facing up to a meaningless life, actually makes his life into a larger kind of solitary ordeal through his tedious attention to compulsive rituals. Such people could perhaps be said to define themselves as existential victims.

One factor that helped Lindbergh (and Chichester as well) to cope with extreme and prolonged isolation was that *both had constantly to focus on tasks at hand* in order to keep plane and ship from disaster. These kept them more or less fully occupied. The situation was quite different in this respect for Byrd and Burney and especially Ritter—their survival did not depend on minute-by-minute attention to tasks that *had* to be done. Thus, they had more time to dwell excessively on themselves, possibly to lose themselves, and to experience the "terror of nothingness," especially if they were not prepared to dwell on themselves. For them it was critically important to manufacture tasks, routines, and daily plans of activities in order to keep themselves occupied, keep their minds organized, and maintain their sense of being instrumental agents. Otherwise, they might fall apart.

So successful, however, is Byrd at keeping himself occupied and his mind off his lonely state that he is able to write ingenuously after working on various tasks: "Then I had an hour to myself." [!][95]

Detachment

A frequent defense during an ordeal, especially at moments of crisis, is the detachment mentioned earlier, the (sometimes eerie) feeling that "this is not happening to me" or that one is somehow a removed *observer* of what is happening rather than the *object* of what is happening. Chichester[96] provides one example:

> The sight of the self-steering gear broken beyond repair acted like a catalyst. At first I turned cold inside and my feelings, my spirit, seemed to freeze and sink inside me. I had a strange feeling that my personality was split and that I was watching myself drop the sails efficiently and lift out the broken gear coolly. . . .[97]
>
> [And at another time] . . . One's thoughts at these moments of crisis are sometimes curiously detached. . . .[98] As [the ship] started rolling I said to myself, "Over she goes!" I was not frightened, but intensely alert and curious.[99]

By *not* dwelling on himself, he copes.

Frankl[100] also speaks of detachment in the concentration camp:

> Apart from . . . humor, another sensation seized us:
> curiosity. I have experienced this kind of curiosity before,
> as a fundamental reaction toward certain strange cir-
> cumstances. When my life was once endangered by a
> climbing accident, I felt only one sensation at the critical
> moment: curiosity, curiosity as to whether I should
> come out of it alive or with a fractured skull or some
> other injuries.
>
> Cold curiosity predominated even in Auschwitz,
> somehow detaching the mind from its surroundings,
> which came to be regarded with a kind of objectivity.
> At that time one cultivated this state of mind as a
> means of protection. We were anxious to know what
> would happen next; and what would be the consequence,
> for example, of our standing in the open air, in the chill
> of late autumn, stark naked, and still wet from the
> showers. In the next few days our curiosity evolved
> into surprise; surprise that we did not catch cold.[101]

The psychoanalyst Bruno Bettelheim,[102] describing how he coped with
the degrading brutality of a concentration camp, observed that "from
the beginning I became convinced that these dreadful and degrading
experiences were somehow not happening to 'me' as a subject [person],
but only to 'me' as object."[103]

Another moving example comes from Kuki Gallman's reminiscence
I Dreamed of Africa,[104] about her life in Kenya, as she suddenly has to deal
with the tragedy of a deadly snakebite to her son, Emanuele. She had
been anxious for years about her teen-age son's fascination with snakes
and his extensive snake collection, including many deadly ones. Note
the way that her detachment goes along with and helps enable a kind of
cold efficiency on her part. Her way of describing her detachment as akin
to becoming another person during the crisis is especially evocative.
She is towelling her hair when she is interrupted by a knock on her
door:

> "Mama. . . . There is a small problem."

"Emanuele? A snake?"

"Yes." . . .

I did not stop to think for a second. . . . That day . . . I kept coming in and out of myself, watching myself acting as from a great distance, and suddenly re-entering my body and the agony of my tormented soul.

Now I watched one part of me splitting from the other, and taking over.

The new Kuki grabbed yesterday's clothes from the laundry basket. Like an efficient, emotionless robot, she [sic] took the glasses without which she knew she could not see, and the hand-set radio. Before reaching the door in two strides she was already screaming [a call to the Flying Doctors] into the set. . . . The stones of the passage were cold under her running bare feet. She was there. . . .

With a feeling of overwhelming unreality, she crouched in front of him. From his open mouth, green saliva dribbled. . . . The skin was grey, the eyes staring and glassy. . . .

At that moment I again became his mother.

"*Mamma,*" he whispered hoarsely. . . . "I am dying, mamma." . . .

[A short time later] that other Kuki, with a face of stone, knelt. . . . Numberless times she blew into his mouth. . . . How long it went on I will never know. . . .

Slowly I lifted my head and looked up at the sky of Africa. . . .

From a great distance my voice said, "He was my son."[105]

Note in the preceding discussion of coping the recurring theme of the self having two "parts," one part that observes and acts, another part that is observed and acted upon. This theme appears both in giving oneself commands and in the phenomenon of becoming a detached observer. Up to a point, the two parts of the self are within the realm of the conscious. As solitary ordeals become prolonged, however, a new part—the unconscious—begins to come under observation.

Expressing Pent-Up Emotions

Sometimes the captive solitary soul, in a situation of intolerable suffering and unable at the moment to deal effectively with it in some of the ways described above, simply has to let out his or her frustration and anguish. Robinson Risner, for example, professional military man imprisoned and cruelly treated in Vietnam:

> Sometimes it would give me great relief to scream. When I thought I was going to die if there was not a change, I would hold something in my mouth and another rag over my face and just let myself holler.
>
> Other times it seemed to help to cry. I remembered having read that women live longer than men because they are able to get rid of suppressed emotions by crying. I needed any outlet possible. I cried a lot. Much of it was out of concern for the other guys in prison.[106]

Maintaining Motivation

Lindbergh provides several examples throughout his book of how he stimulates his mind and his senses by thinking of problems and danger. Later he begins to use these techniques to *goad* himself to keep going, rather than just to stimulate his mind to alertness. After finding himself daydreaming again, he says:

> But I'm not in Minnesota. I'm in the *Spirit of St. Louis*, over the ocean, headed for Europe and Paris. I *must* keep my mind from wandering. I'll take it in hand at once, and watch it each instant from now on. It must be kept on its proper heading as accurately as the compass. I'll review my plans for navigation. Then, I'll concentrate on some other subject.
>
> The first quarter of my flight is behind. There's a sense of real accomplishment in that fact. How satisfying it is to have 800 miles behind—No! That's the wrong tack. Sleep has crept up a notch. Anything that's satisfying is relaxing. I can't afford to relax. I must think about *problems*—concentrate on difficulties ahead. Actually, I

haven't quite reached the quarter mark. In another three hours, I'll leave Newfoundland behind and start out over nearly 2,000 miles of ocean. If the wind keeps on increasing and swinging tailward, I ought to average over 100 miles an hour through the night. A strong tail-wind would put me over Europe well ahead of sched-ule—No, I'm getting off course again—*concentrate on difficulties*. [RDL] Suppose the wind shifts north or south during the night. . . .[107]

I've got to find some way to keep alert. There's no alternative but death and failure. *No alternative but death and failure* [RDL], I keep repeating, using the thought as a whip on my lagging mind; trying to make my senses realize the importance of what I'm saying. . . .[108]

The knowledge of what would happen if I let those needles get out of control does for me what no amount of resolution can. That knowledge has more effect on my mind and muscles than any quantity of exercise or determination. It compresses the three elements of existence together into a single human being.

Danger, when it's imminent and real, cuts like a rapier through the draperies of sleep. The compass may creep off ten degrees without drawing my attention; but let the turn-indicator move an eighth of an inch or the air speed change five miles an hour, and I react in an instant.[109]

He continually and deliberately goads himself by thinking of diffi-culties and, more starkly, of the possibility of "death and failure." He is spurred on by the desire to avoid this alternative at all costs.

Later he also says:

How could I face my partners [the investors who funded his flight] and say that I failed to reach Paris because I was sleepy? No matter how inaccurate my navigation, it must be the best I can carry on. Honor alone demands that.[110]

Lindbergh, the loner, was nonetheless extremely sensitive to the judgments of others, perhaps especially his father, as if he were always trying to prove himself. Of this, more later.

Chichester[111] is also spurred on by the desire not to be seen by others as letting them down: "My chief anxiety now was not to embarrass [his wife] Sheila [waiting in Australia for his arrival]."[112]

Don O'Daniel motivates himself to keep struggling in several different ways. His examples speak for those of many survivors:

1. By imagining the grief of loved ones if he gives up and is drowned: "What will my folks think. . . . Mother will go crazy. . . . What will Rose think of this. . . ."[113]

2. By thinking about the things he will miss out on if he doesn't survive: "Rose Bowl . . . you won't get to see it. . . . I won't be able to collect it [a bet he made?]. . . . You are all through in school. . . . You have wasted your folks' money. . . . You won't pass your exam. . . ."[114] "You'll have a nice Christmas. . . . You can come home and be with us. . . . Come home for Christmas with us. . . . We'll have Christmas together."[115]

3. By imagining the awful consequences of not making it: "I hope you [talking to himself] never wash up on the beach. . . . I saw a guy that did once. . . . You know what he looked like . . . one leg was gone . . . crabs ate the eyes out of his head . . . he fell off the jetty . . . you might as well shake hands with yourself . . . this is the last time you'll have both of them."[116]

4. By insulting and goading himself: "This is the end of the line . . . you can't make it any farther . . . you can't go on . . . you're just a weakling . . . you can't make it . . . this is as far as you can go . . . you're just a weakling. . . ."[117]

Byrd describes maintaining his motivation during a particularly trying period of his exile. He thinks of his family and his scientific work:

> Great waves of fear, a fear I had never known before, swept through me and settled deep within. But it wasn't the fear of suffering or even of death itself. It was a terrible anxiety over the consequences to those at home if I failed to return. I had done a damnable thing in going to Advance Base, I told myself.[118]

Finally, there is an aspect of motivation that is of overriding importance in determining whether one lives or dies under adversity: having a goal, a purpose, which galvanizes a person's will to live into a formidable force for survival.

Lindbergh, of course, had two powerful conscious goals to motivate him: first, a wish to be the first to make the momentous nonstop trans-Atlantic flight, and second, a strong desire to demonstrate the potential of aviation. Byrd was motivated by an overwhelming need to make his expedition a success (that is why he decided to man the weather station alone when the only alternative was to abandon it), to hand in his little pile of weather data, and later by a strong wish not to jeopardize others by becoming helpless. Chichester was strongly motivated by the goal of circumnavigating the world alone; Ritter by wanting to prove to herself and to others that she could make it; and Burney by a strong, disciplined sense that he must not betray his cause or his comrades.

Sometimes even rather ordinary-seeming activities provide goals that contribute significantly to survival. Kenneth Cooke,[119] eventual sole survivor of a torpedoed ship in World War II, describes such a phenomenon. After taking to the life raft, he fashioned a primitive spear, and he describes how this simple device gave him a goal to live for:

> [After two weeks on the raft] I still had not managed to bag a fish with my spear, although they were as plentiful as ever around us. Yet I still had not given up hope, and most of my waking time was spent looking at the water with my spear handy, in case opportunity presented itself. *I feel to this day that the spear had much to do with the fact that I am alive.* Small though the effort required was, *the hope and constant look-out for a chance to stab a fish kept me going,* [RDL] and, by the mere act of giving me something to do and something to think about, did a lot to keep hope and life in my body.[120]

Even this brief coverage indicates a great variety of ways for maintaining motivation. There may, however, be much deeper and more far-reaching goals for the sake of which people may endure the unspeakable, and for which they may even seek it—namely, self-discovery, particularly of the unconscious.

Maintaining Psychological Equilibrium

Several forms of equilibrium are necessary for successful coping: knowing where you are, maintaining self-esteem, and keeping drives at moderate levels. Psychological equilibrium is also maintained by deliberate efforts aimed at preserving one's conscious sense of identity.

Don O'Daniel, for instance, in reliving his struggle against drowning, recalls asserting his ethnic identity:

> . . . you're an Irishman . . . as good as any of them. . . . They don't let down . . . you're Irish and you don't quit. . . .[121]
> . . . Aye, an' sure enough you're from Ireland. . . . You can make it. . . .[122]

Numerous examples of the assertion of one's group or cultural identity during adversity could be cited ("Do it for Michigan!" etc.).

Don O'Daniel also recalls a girl that he had felt unworthy of and attempts to build up his self-esteem at her expense:

> You've learned lots of things . . . that phoney girl . . . talking about Hollywood . . . crazy people . . . Seaside [Oregon, a fashionable resort] . . . she's stringing you along . . . she thinks she's big-time . . . Chuck's [his best friend] on to her. . . . That girl is just trying to pull the wool over somebody's eyes . . . you're better than she is.[123]

George Smith,[124] who ditched at sea in the Pacific in World War II and survived several weeks alone in a life raft, relates how he maintained his sense of who he was. His excerpt stands for many others:

> Besides devoting much time to thoughts of home, I was able to recall, step by step, all that happened during my life. . . .
> In my reminiscing, I recalled all the places I had been in my 25 years, the things I had done, people I had met, friends I had made, and how much those friends had meant to me. I recalled names and faces that otherwise had long since been forgotten; and I realized then that it was association with other human beings, not things that money can buy, that really makes this life on Earth pleasant and worthwhile.[125]

Lindbergh, Byrd, Chichester, and Ritter all maintained their identities through the performance of familiar tasks and through recollections of their past, loved ones, and the like. Lindbergh especially reminisced at great length about his own past experiences during his flight. For example, he finds in the stars a sense of orientation that goes beyond that of navigation—a link to his past and his identity:

> But those glowing lines and dots [of the instrument panel] seem so much less tangible, so much less secure, than the stars overhead. The stars have always been there. I watched them through the screen of my sleeping porch when I was a child; I flew under them night after night with the mail. I can trust the stars; they're always the same—familiar constellations following each other slowly through the heavens. . . . As long as I can hold onto them I'll be safe.[126]

Chichester reminisces as follows:

> I am drinking a toast to Sheila in the delicious Montrachet [wine] she brought out from England, and left on board for me. A long life, health and happiness, with grateful thanks for our happy thirty years together. A very remarkable, exceptional woman is Sheila. I did what is supposed to be un-British, shed a tear. Life seems such a slender thread in these circumstances here. . . .[127]

Geoffrey Jackson, who is English, finds a vital link to his heritage and identity after being given copies of Agatha Christie mysteries to read:

> From that moment I never lacked an escape-route back to my native land, an escape-route of far greater and more instant efficacy than the "space-warp" beloved of science-fiction writers. With the help of Dame Agatha, and a small effort of will, the infinite separation of the galaxies was instantly bridged, the opposed dimensions of captivity and freedom were

brought together at their time-gate, the propositions of Einstein and the Laws of Thermodynamics—with all but a few spatial and temporal formalities—effectively bypassed.[128]

Creating Meaning

Another observation of those who survive prolonged solitary ordeals is that they either find or create something meaningful in their suffering or they are able to maintain a sense of purpose and meaning despite their suffering. Many of the preceding coping mechanisms actually have a great deal to do with maintaining, finding, or creating some kind of meaning in the throes of an ordeal. Thus finding meaning may be the most overriding need of all. Gordon Allport states in the preface to Frankl's *Man's Search for Meaning:*

> To live is to suffer, to survive is to find meaning in the suffering. If there is a purpose in life at all, there must be a purpose in suffering and in dying. But no man can tell another what this purpose is. Each must find out for himself, and must accept the responsibility that his answer prescribes. If he succeeds he will continue to grow in spite of all indignities. Frankl is fond of quoting Nietzsche, "He who has a *why* to live can bear with almost any *how.*"[129]

And Frankl says:

> We who lived in concentration camps can remember the men who walked through the huts comforting others, giving away their last piece of bread. They may have been few in number, but they offer sufficient proof that everything can be taken from a man but one thing: the last of the human freedoms—to choose one's attitude in any given set of circumstances, to choose one's own way.
> ... it becomes clear that the sort of person the prisoner became was the result of an inner decision. . . .[130]
> ... It is this spiritual freedom—which cannot be taken away—that makes life meaningful and purposeful.[131]

Notes

1 Byrd, 1938.
2 Byrd, pp. 110–111.
3 Solzhenitsyn, 1973.
4 Solzhenitsyn, p. 110.
5 Burney, 1952.
6 Burney, pp. 90–91.
7 Bone, 1957.
8 Bone, p. 115.
9 Bone, p. 122.
10 Bone, p. 123.
11 Bone, pp. 122–125.
12 Byrd, p. 91.
13 Lindbergh, p. 201.
14 Lindbergh, pp. 226–227.
15 Saint-Exupéry, 1939.
16 Saint-Exupéry, p. 189.
17 Lindbergh, pp. 343–344.
18 Lindbergh, pp. 239–240.
19 Lindbergh, pp. 241–242.
20 Byrd, p. 104.
21 Bone, 1957.
22 Bone, pp. 106–107.
23 Bone, pp. 108–109.
24 Lindbergh, p. 234.
25 Lindbergh, p. 366.
26 Byrd, p. 130.
27 Lindbergh, pp. 323–324.
28 Lindbergh, pp. 326–327.
29 Lindbergh, pp. 491–492.
30 Janis, p. 8.
31 Janis, p. 16.
32 Callahan, Steven. *Adrift: 76 Days at Sea*. Boston: Houghton Mifflin, 1986.
33 Callahan, p. 113.
34 Callahan, p. 153.
35 Elder, 1978.
36 Elder, pp. 138–139.
37 Noyce, 1958.
38 Noyce, 1958, p. 221.
39 Callahan, 1986.
40 Callahan, pp. 55–56.
41 Callahan, p. 158.
42 Byrd, p. 76.
43 Byrd, p. 103.
44 Byrd, pp. 105–106.
45 Byrd, p. 93.
46 Lewis, 1975.

[47] Lewis, p. 42.
[48] Bombard, Alain. *Voyage of the Heretique.* New York: Simon & Schuster, 1954.
[49] Bombard, p. 131.
[50] Ritter, pp. 138–139.
[51] Burney, p. 25.
[52] Byrd, pp. 102–103.
[53] Byrd, p. 115.
[54] Charriere, Henri. *Papillon.* Leicester: Ulverscroft, 1970, p. 218.
[55] Risner, Robinson. *The Passing of the Night.* New York: Ballantine Books, 1973.
[56] Risner, pp. 164–165.
[57] Risner, p. 165.
[58] Dean, 1954.
[59] Bone, pp. 120–121.
[60] Risner, p. 129.
[61] Bone, p. 129.
[62] Bone, p. 130.
[63] Bone, pp. 129–132.
[64] Bone, pp. 132–133.
[65] Bone, pp. 133-134.
[66] Bone, pp. 135-136.
[67] Jackson, Geoffrey. *Surviving the Long Night.* New York: Vanguard, 1973.
[68] Jackson, pp. 128–129.
[69] Jackson, p. 136.
[70] Jackson, pp. 136–137.
[71] Risner, pp. 165-166.
[72] Smith, George. *Solo Cruise on the Coral Sea.* New York: Vantage Press, 1970.
[73] Smith, p. 54.
[74] Smith, pp. 54–55.
[75] Burney, pp. 60–61.
[76] Burney, p. 41.
[77] Charriere, pp. 225–226.
[78] Frankl, 1963.
[79] Frankl, 1963, pp. 61–62.
[80] Byrd, 1938.
[81] Byrd, p. 101.
[82] Chichester, 1967.
[83] Chichester, 1967, p. 81.
[84] Byrd, p. 89.
[85] Janis, p. 14.
[86] Ritter, p. 167.
[87] Ritter, p. 171.
[88] Chichester, 1967.
[89] Chichester, 1967, pp. 141–143.
[90] Burney, pp. 97–98.
[91] Burney, p. 24.
[92] Burney, p. 29.

93 Jackson, 1973.

94 Jackson, pp. 110–111.

95 Byrd, p. 102.

96 Chichester, 1967.

97 Chichester, 1967, p. 84.

98 Chichester, 1967, p. 76

99 Chichester, 1967, p. 125.

100 Frankl, 1963.

101 Frankl, 1963, pp. 24–25.

102 Bettelheim, Bruno. "Individual and Mass Behavior in Extreme Situations." *Journal of Abnormal and Social Psychology*, 38 (1943), pp. 417–452.

103 Bettelheim, p. 127.

104 Gallmann, Kuki. *I Dreamed of Africa.* New York: Penguin, 1991.

105 Gallmann, pp. 195–199.

106 Risner, p. 166.

107 Lindbergh, pp. 236–237.

108 Lindbergh, p. 355.

109 Lindbergh, p. 365.

110 Lindbergh, p. 343.

111 Chichester, 1967.

112 Chichester, 1967, p. 87.

113 Janis, p. 12.

114 Janis, p. 12.

115 Janis, p. 14.

116 Janis, p. 12.

117 Janis, p. 17.

118 Byrd, p. 179.

119 Cooke, Kenneth. *What Cares the Sea?* New York: McGraw-Hill, 1960.

120 Cooke, p. 83.

121 Janis, p. 10.

122 Janis, p. 15.

123 Janis, p. 10.

124 Smith, 1970.

125 Smith, p. 60.

126 Lindbergh, p. 303.

127 Chichester, 1967, p. 151.

128 Jackson, pp. 126–127.

129 Frankl, 1963, p. xii.

130 Frankl, 1963, pp. 103–105.

131 Frankl, 1963, p. 106.

CHAPTER SIX

The Solitary Quest: Lindbergh, Byrd, and Chichester

"Something hidden. Go and find it
Go and look behind the Ranges—
Something lost behind the Ranges. Lost
and waiting for you. Go!"
————*The Explorer*, Rudyard Kipling

What kind of person actively seeks out the kinds of solitary ordeals that encourage the emergence of unconscious images and create the possibility of "self-discovery"?

Lindbergh had known fear as a child (and suggests that it is things from a dimly realized place beyond consciousness that frightened him):

> Dragons, tigers, jungle animals? How ridiculous! But it's true that I used to be fearful in the dark. It was years before I got completely over it. As a child I could wander alone, tranquilly, through the most isolated places by the light of day. But at night my mind conjured up drowned bodies on the riverbank, and robbers behind every sumac clump. The reality of life was tame compared to my imagination's fantasies. It was *what I couldn't see* [RDL] that frightened me—the python slithering overhead, the face beyond the curtain. And most of all, the imaginary horrors that took no clear-cut form.[1]

Yet his characteristic reaction to fear of a "realm beyond," perhaps partly because of a need to prove himself to a demanding, somewhat distant father and partly because of a desire to explore the unknown, was to confront it head-on rather than to avoid it. His fear of falling and of heights, for instance, led him to take up parachute jumping.

> I believe parachute jumping had an effect on my dreams as well as on my sleep. At infrequent intervals through life I had dreamt of falling off some high roof or precipice. I'd felt terror and sickening fear as my body sank helplessly toward the ground. It wasn't like that in a real parachute jump I discovered. Real falling didn't bring horror to mind or sickness to your belly. Such sensations stayed behind with the plane, as though they were too cowardly to make the final plunge. Strangely enough, *I've never fallen in my dreams since I fell through the air.* [RDL] That factual experience seems to have removed completely some illogical, subconscious dread.[2]

The fact that something in Lindbergh's personality led him to *confront* the source of his fears is of more than passing interest, for it sets Lindbergh strikingly apart from the ordinary. The usual human reaction to things that provoke fear or anxiety (high places, for example) is to totally avoid them and to continue to do so throughout life, long after the original frightening event, such as a fall, has occurred. Avoidance habits are "neurotic" because they serve little adaptive purpose, limit one's behavior, consume time, and use up valuable energy. They continue to be practiced, however, because every time a fear-producing situation approaches, anxiety rises, leading one to avoid it, which in turn reduces the anxiety and thus continually reinforces the "neurotic" avoidance behavior. Virtually all of us victimize ourselves by habitually avoiding anxiety-provoking things, both outside and *inside* of ourselves. This pattern is so widespread in human behavior, in fact, that it has become a cornerstone of most theories of how the personality works—those of Freud, Jung, Sullivan, and Rogers, for example. All are based on the assumption that it is *fear of knowing something about oneself* that is the source of most human psychological problems, because those things about ourselves that we strive to avoid eventually come back to haunt us. It goes without saying that if we get far into an avoidance mode we are also avoiding our own potential.

How was it that Lindbergh was able to swim against this overwhelming tide and confront rather than always avoid his fears? Early in his flying career—after having mastered parachute jumping—Lindbergh describes an encounter with death when he had to jump from an out-of-control plane. The encounter evoked again his fascination with a realm beyond:

> After jumping . . . I looked up to see the plane less than a hundred feet away pointed directly at me.
>
> Usually the stroke of death either passes before you're aware of it, or your senses are occupied with the fight for life, or there's good reason to hope you'll escape. That time I saw it coming. I was helpless. No movement I could make would have effect. There didn't seem a chance for it to miss. I braced my body for the impact—propeller, wing, or whatever death's instrument might be. Every muscle, every nerve, was tensed for the tearing blow on flesh. Danger had swept all unessential detail from my mind—it was clear as a pane of glass. [Somehow the plane misses him] . . . You couldn't come much closer to death than that. And *yet I've known times when the nearness of death has seemed to crack the door—times when I've felt the presence of another realm beyond—a realm my mind has tried to penetrate since childhood. . . .*[3] [RDL]

What is the "realm beyond" with which he is so intrigued, and why does he seek to penetrate it?

Lindbergh, Byrd, and Chichester had strikingly similar backgrounds. They all grew up under the domination of strong-willed fathers, had warm, affectionate feelings for their mothers, attended rigorous private schools, and lived in rural areas at a time (the turn of the century) when new and exciting things (machines, technology, flight) were happening elsewhere. These factors may have combined to produce an intense feeling of personal constriction and limitation in these three men as youngsters. Chichester especially emphasized that his lot in childhood was intolerable and that he was desperate to get away. In addition, because of their relatively privileged social positions, Byrd, Lindbergh, and Chichester were exposed to the endless things that *could* be done, seen, experienced, and explored elsewhere. They were fascinated, perhaps, by the knowledge that here they sat, while out there (in some other realm) everything was happening.

The desire to prove oneself to a strong father, the urge to achieve success and recognition, and the feeling of constriction add up to a powerful awareness of *personal incompleteness* in these individuals. This feeling led each of them to become a seeker fascinated with adventure and the exploration of realms beyond—new places, new experiences—as an expression of the desire to get away and seek personal fulfillment. Thus Lindbergh yearned to fly, Chichester to roam the seas (he went away to sea as a teen-ager), and Byrd to explore distant places (he went to the Philippines at the age of twelve).

Lindbergh perceives his former feelings of incompleteness during his flight:

> I realize that values are changing both within and without my mind. For twenty-five years it's been surrounded by solid walls of bone, not perceiving the limitless expanse, the immortal existence that lies outside.[4]

Further, because Lindbergh, Byrd, and Chichester grew up as rather isolated individuals and had time for introspection, and because they lived in changing times that exposed them to many apparent opposites (rural agriculture versus urban technology; nature versus machines; the frontier age versus the modern age), they may have had from early life a beginning awareness of and openness to the fact that life has *two sides*. They had a tendency already to not be one-sidedly preoccupied with outer challenge and adventure. Richard Byrd as a youngster, for instance, was regarded by many who knew him as a paradoxical collection of opposites, being described variously as adventurous but introspective, soft and hard, sweet and determined.

Lindbergh in particular was given both to adventure and introspective dreaming as a child growing up in the early 1900s. In the following excerpt he exhibits a fascination with two "opposites"—nature and the machine—without any sense of incompatibility between the two:

> One day I was playing upstairs in our house on the riverbank. The sound of a distant engine drifted in through an open window. Automobiles had been going past on the road quite often that summer. I noticed it

> vaguely and went on sorting the stones my mother and
> I had collected from the creek bed. None of them com-
> pared to the heart-shaped agate I'd found at the edge of
> a pool the week before—purple crystals outlined by
> stripes of red and white. Suddenly I sat up straight and
> listened. No automobile engine made that noise. It was
> approaching too fast. It was on the wrong side of the
> house! Stones scattered over the floor. I ran to the window
> and climbed out onto the tarry roof. It was an airplane![5]

The preceding is characteristic of the fact that Lindbergh's nature
showed signs of being two-sided from very early in life. On the one
hand he was shy, solitary, and introspective, a thinker and dreamer; at
the same time he had strong extroverted, outward-looking tendencies—
he was a hunter at six years old, a mechanical tinkerer and child inventor,
a skilled eleven-year-old driver, a youthful daredevil on a motorcycle, a
barnstorming pilot, and a masterful practical joker among his friends
most of his life.

Lindbergh's long-standing openness to his own other side (i.e., his
unconscious) is also expressed later during his famous solo flight when
he confronts what he terms "phantoms":

> ... these emissaries from a spirit world are neither in-
> truders nor strangers. It's more like a gathering of family
> and friends after years of separation, as though I've
> known all of them before in some past reincarnation.[6]

The fact that Lindbergh, Byrd, and Chichester were raised in some
degree of social and psychological isolation from their peers (this is
very much true of Lindbergh and Chichester, apparently somewhat less
so of Byrd), and were raised to feel different and aloof, meant that they
would try to prove themselves *alone* (the title, incidentally, of Byrd's
book). They naturally became obsessed with affirming that they could
find their own way by themselves. It seems significant that these three
men, although chosen for this book because of their solitary ordeals, also
happen to represent perhaps the three greatest navigational geniuses of
the early air age. What greater affirmation to their fathers and to the
world could there possibly be than the mastery of solo navigation as a
way of demonstrating the modern concern that "I can find my own way"?

Before taking up single-handed sailing, Chichester flew solo from London to Australia in 1931 and located isolated ocean islands with innovative feats of celestial navigation from his cockpit that were astounding for their time. Lindbergh found Ireland almost dead-on after a thirty-three-hour flight with no external navigational aids. His landfall was exactly the one he had abstractly projected: Dingle Bay. Prior to his solo stay in Antarctica, Byrd navigated to the North Pole by air. (Some have since disputed this.) Chichester was Britain's foremost navigation expert before and during World War II. Byrd was in charge of U.S. Navy programs in aerial navigation after World War I. Lindbergh was an expert relied upon by the military and airlines for advice on navigational systems until shortly before his death.

All of these men were characterized by meticulous natures, tremendous drive and perseverance, great tolerance for pain and discomfort, and a willingness to take substantial risks in pursuit of goals fervently sought.

Chichester's careful nature is well demonstrated by the fact that, although he later became a pilot of consummate skill, it took him three times as long to qualify for his pilot's license as it did the average student pilot. This was not because he lacked in aptitude. He insisted on thoroughly mastering every aeronautical detail before moving on to the next phase of training.[7]

Certainly one trait that enabled Lindbergh to face fearful situations was his extraordinarily systematic nature and his careful observation of surroundings. Lindbergh provides an insight from his childhood into the meticulous side of his character, which may have contributed strongly to his ability to fly alone across the Atlantic:

> When I was eleven years old, I learned to drive my father's Ford car, and at twelve I chauffeured him around the country. That car had seemed terribly dangerous at first. You could get your arm broken cranking the engine. You could skid off an embankment. You might collide with someone at any intersection. The Minneapolis paper carried stories about auto accidents each day. But as my driving experience advanced from a hundred miles to a thousand, and from one thousand to several, my confidence increased. There were foils against danger —judgment and skill. *If you clasped your thumb and fingers*

> *on the same side of the crank handle, a backfiring engine wouldn't break your bones.*[8] [RDL]

Lindbergh learned very early in life that careful preparation—and attention to minute detail as illustrated in his description of the proper positioning of thumb and fingers in cranking a car—reduced danger, and therefore fear, to acceptable levels. This personal coping style, which emerges over and over again in his book, reflects the controlling ability of Lindbergh's intellect over his emotion. Yet he also could, if he chose, use his intellect to seek out his inner life.

As I will attempt to spell out, I think the reason for these powerful opposites has to do with features of Lindbergh's early life that led him to be fascinated by rather than fearful of the depths of his own character, and to have a counterbalancing fascination with the outer world as well.

A particular episode in Lindbergh's later childhood clearly links mental control and meticulous planning with his fears. Many years prior to his parachute jump, he developed a careful plan to systematically condition away his fear of heights. (Psychologists would call his self-generated approach "systematic desensitization.") He went to a nearby water tower in Little Falls and climbed up first six, later eight, then ten, twelve, etc. rungs of the tower ladder, at each level looking down, relaxing, and remaining there until he felt no more fear, then proceeding in this careful fashion. Soon he was climbing all over the precarious angled framework of the water tower. Having conquered an "irrational" fear of heights, he was then free later on to focus in on the more "rational" fear of falling. His parachute jump, then, was the culmination of a careful years-long strategy of self-disciplined training of mind over emotion.

I will here indulge in some psychological speculation: The fact that these three men apparently had somewhat stern and distant fathers and attractive, refined, doting mothers may have produced unresolved "Oedipal" feelings of rivalry with the fathers for their mothers' affection, and a strong competitive desire to prove themselves to their fathers and to achieve greatness in order to win the mothers' affection and approval. This might partly account for their great drive. The strong feelings of rivalry with the fathers might then have been suppressed by their highly self-controlled, compulsively meticulous behavior. A meticulous style that served to control and dissipate both fear *and* anger might then also have been of help in trying to prove themselves.

In Chichester's case, he apparently was given to violent tantrums when a young child. Perhaps, therefore, a prime mover behind the meticulous care and planning of his adventurous acts was the life-long need to control a violent temper.

These three men's compulsive (even fanatic) attention to detail in preparing to face danger can thus be viewed as a defense mechanism. Lindbergh, for example, controlled his childhood fears (and his hostility?) by developing extremely careful and vigilant control of his actions and by extraordinary attention to the most minute features of potentially dangerous situations, reasoned through with computerlike attention to all possible contingencies, as has already been illustrated. With fear mastered, he had the confidence to take risks, but at the same time his meticulous habits helped materially to reduce those risks. Emotionally, however, he was still challenging and flirting with danger, as if daring it to do him in. Recall his detailed rehearsal of what he would do if he had to crash-land in the North Atlantic ice (see page 116).

Note the striking combination of ingenuity, sense of orientation, great patience, and careful behavior in the following incidents in which each of the three men has either lost his way or lost an object. Also note the remarkable similarity in the patient methods used by all three in finding their bearings. One can see, both by the content of the following episodes and by the fact that each man regarded this kind of episode as important enough to include in his writings, the great similarity in the self-reliant, I-can-get-myself-out-of-this-myself personalities of these individuals.

First, Byrd, describing one of his daily walks near the isolated Advance Base hut in the Antarctic during the twenty-four-hour night, writes:

> Being in a particularly fine mood, I had decided to take a longer walk than usual. It was drifting a bit, and the Barrier was pretty dark, but that didn't bother me. After parading up and down for half an hour, I turned around to go back. The line of bamboo [trail-marking] sticks was nowhere in sight! In my abstraction, I had walked completely past and beyond it; and now, wondering which way to turn, I was overwhelmed by the realization that I had no idea of how far I had walked, nor the direction in which I was heading. On the chance that

my footsteps would show, I scanned the Barrier with a flashlight; but my boots had left no marks on the hard sastrugi [ridges of snow]. It was scary. The first impulse was to run. I quelled that, and soberly took stock of my predicament.

Since it was the one fact I had to work with, I again pulled the flashlight up out of my pants, where I carried it to keep it from freezing, and *scratched into the snow with the butt end an arrow in the direction whence I had come.* [RDL] I remembered also, from having glanced at the wind vane as I started, that the wind was in the south. It was then on my left cheek and was still on the same cheek, but that meant little. For the wind might have changed, and subconsciously I might have veered with it. I was lost, and I was sick inside.

In order to keep from wandering still farther from the shack, *I made a reference point. I broke off pieces of sastrugi with my heel and heaped them into a little beacon about eighteen inches high at the butt of the arrow.* [RDL] This took quite a little while. Straightening up and consulting the sky, *I discovered two stars which were in line with the direction in which I had been walking when I stopped.* [RDL] This was a lucky break, as the sky had been overcast until now and had only cleared in a couple of places. In the navigator's phrase, the stars gave me a range and the beacon a departure. So taking careful steps and with my eyes on the stars, I started forward; after 100 paces I stopped. I swung the flashlight all around and could see nothing but blank Barrier [vast plateau of ice].

Not daring to go farther for fear of losing the snow beacon, I started back, glancing over my shoulder at the two stars to hold my line. At the end of a hundred steps I failed to fetch the beacon. For an instant I was on the edge of panic. Then the flashlight beam picked it up about twenty feet or so on my left hand. That miserable pile of snow was nothing to rejoice over, but at least it kept me from feeling that I was stabbing blindfolded. On the next sortie, I swung the course 30° to the left. And as before, after a hundred steps, I saw nothing.

"You're lost now," I told myself. I was appalled. I realized that I should have to lengthen my radius from the
beacon; and in lengthening it, I might never be able to
find the way back to the one certainty. However, there
was no alternative unless I preferred to freeze to death,
and I could do that just as thoroughly 1,000 yards from
the hut as 500. So now I decided to take 30 steps more
in the same direction, after scraping a little heap of snow
together to mark the 100-pace point. On the 29th step, I
picked up the first of the [row of] bamboo sticks, not more
than 30 feet away. No shipwrecked mariner, sighting a
distant sail, could have been more overjoyed.[9]

(Note, incidentally, yet another use of the oceanic metaphor.)
Compare Byrd's strategy of setting down markers for finding his
way with Lindbergh's as he loses his clipboard out his plane's window
during an early test flight:

I take a pencil from my pocket and pick up the data
board—The nose rises—a wing drops—I reach for the
stick—a gust of air snatches the data board from my
hand and carries it through the open window! All the
figures I've collected this morning go fluttering down
toward a brush-covered hill below! I bank sharply and
watch the board, flashing as it catches the sun, land in
the branches of a thick bush about two hundred yards
from the edge of a clearing. Now it's only a white spot
among brownish-green leaves.

The clearing looks big enough to land on with one
of the [aircraft] company's Hisso-Standards. I circle
around for several minutes, locating in my mind the
exact position of the data board. When I'm sure I can
spot its bush again, I fly back to Camp Kearney and
land. . . .

The Hisso-Standard arrives in a half hour. The pilot
and some of the mechanics want to go with me to help
hunt for the board, but I decide it's wiser to take the
plane alone. The clearing where I must land is small,
and there's not enough wind to cut down landing

speed appreciably. The weight of even one more man might cause a crack-up.

When I arrive over the brush patch again, I find the data board still clearly visible. I stall down into the clearing and stop rolling with several yards to spare. Leaving the engine idling, with a stone under each wheel of the plane to keep it from creeping forward, I crawl in through thick and scratchy bushes to where I think the board should be. After hunting for several minutes without result, *I remove my coat, spread it on top of some branches, return to the clearing* [RDL] [making a reference point], and take off again in the Standard.

As soon as I'm in the air, I see my coat to be at least fifty yards from the data board. My sense of direction certainly went wrong that time. Maybe I should have brought a compass. I land again, but am still unsuccessful in my search; so I leave the coat in a new location and take off once more. This time, coat and data board are only twenty feet apart. I land, pick them both up, and head back to Camp Kearney.[10]

Compare the preceding episodes with a story from Chichester's early manhood experiences in New Zealand when he got lost in the woods. Note his remarkable ability to find his way in the absence of external guideposts—the ultimate in mental self-reliance and self-guidance:

I was trailing up a small creek trying to spot a [trail] blaze which would indicate where I had to leave the creek, but I could not find any blaze, and finally mistook a deer track for the right trail. I followed this for some time, but an hour or so later I had to admit that I was well and truly bushed.

Panic came in a big wave. It was a new overwhelming panic which paralyzed my brain. I wanted to tear wildly through the bush [compare Byrd]. I knew that I had to fight this panic, so I set my whole mind to fighting it, and finally I had control. Then I unpacked my swag and, feeling intensely alone and lonely, rolled up in my blanket and went to sleep. This was beside another stream, which ran over a rusty-coloured bottom, apparently full of new-chum [fool's] gold which glittered more than the real stuff. It was hard to believe that I was not lying beside immense wealth, though I reasoned that real gold would have worked through the gravel to rock bottom.

When I awoke at dawn I lay still, pondering, *until I had worked over all my movements.* [RDL] If I could get a direction, I ought to be able to hit off the valley from which I had started, even though it was merely a thin streak running into a vast area of solid forest. I had no compass and it was impossible to see farther than a few yards. I decided to try to get a bearing from the sun. The only hope for this was to climb to the top of a hill. This west-coast bush was a rain forest, created by the Westerlies sweeping in from the ocean and emptying their moisture as continuous rain for weeks on end as they lifted over the Alps. In places the forest was so dense that, without a slasher, it would take four hours to move a mile through it. From the ground I could not get the least sign of the sun through the dense growth overhead.

The surface of the hill that I knew I must climb was covered in moss a foot deep. My feet slipped on the roots under the moss, and I had to scramble over rotting tree trunks which lay all over the place. When I got to the top I climbed a tree with difficulty. But when I got near the top I could see that I was going to be no better off, because the leaves were too dense to see through, and the branches too frail to support my weight if I tried to get up higher. I climbed down, and started thinking again. I told myself that it was panic which usually killed someone who was lost, and I made up my mind that I ought to be able to find the stream where I had first gone wrong. *I plotted all my movements in my head, and decided where that stream should lie.* [RDL] I set off in that direction. If I didn't find the stream within a certain time, I determined to follow a creek downstream until I came to the coast. That might take

> me three weeks, but I was bound to arrive there in the
> end if I could get food.
> I set off, and within an hour located my lost stream.[11]

While the obsession with navigation provided another arena in which to be compulsively meticulous, it also expressed a fundamental streak in the character of these men: They were each on a solitary journey, going into the uncharted unknown, and they would have to find their own way.

They sought adventure and navigated the unknown not only to prove themselves, but to "find their way" and find themselves. What they were looking for in searching "realms beyond"—danger, new places, new experiences, the unknown, death, fear, and all things "opposed" to everyday life—was the "other side" of their own characters.

In all of the previous illustrations, we have also been demonstrating something of Lindbergh's, Chichester's, and Byrd's sense of self. Each was a loner, a seeker, a detached observer, a meticulous analyst of objects and events, not a contemplator of himself. Each was egoistic, to be sure, but in the very special sense of being an "I-egoist" rather than a "me-egoist." They sought not to draw attention to themselves as objects ("me"), but rather to relate to the world almost entirely as "I" (subject) and to see what they could discover and accomplish through solitary pursuits in the world. Note how frequently the word "I" is used in the Lindbergh excerpts and how seldom the word "me." He was supremely confident in what he knew, saw, and understood, and in his skills—"I know I can do it," rather than "Look at me and my achievement." This type of egoism is another key ingredient of the "right stuff," at least as exemplified by the character of these individuals.

One consequence of being an I-egoist was that Lindbergh (and the others) was hard to know. Rather than seeking fame or to display himself, he sought to accomplish things in the world. Therefore, as a personality he was less readily observable, less easily knowable. Lindbergh as an I-egoist functioned as an analytical *observer* of the world about him, examining with extraordinary perceptivity the interrelationships among events and things. He also had an exceptional sense of orientation, as the clipboard excerpt indicated. He observed the world, not himself.

In short, these men represented a form and an era of individualism that has become old-fashioned. They lived vigilantly in the present but always aimed for the future, sought self-knowledge through exploring the outer world, and tended to use the word "I." That type of individualism has begun to give way to a new form that lives only for now, is devoted to exploring the inner world, and uses the word "me."

The next two chapters examine coping from Jungian and humanistic perspectives.

Notes

[1] Lindbergh, pp. 338–339.
[2] Lindbergh, p. 261.
[3] Lindbergh, pp. 307–308.
[4] Lindbergh, p. 390.
[5] Lindbergh, pp. 244–245.
[6] Lindbergh, p. 390.
[7] Leslie, Anita. *Francis Chichester: A Biography.* New York: Walker, 1975.
[8] Lindbergh, p. 246.
[9] Byrd, pp. 116–118.
[10] Lindbergh, pp. 126–127.
[11] Chichester, 1964, pp. 43–45.

CHAPTER SEVEN

Coping from a Jungian Perspective

Solitary ordeals have frequently been studied by psychologists as instances of sensory deprivation, stress, coping mechanisms, and the like, but rarely outside of religious writings, first-person accounts of ordeals, and tracts from wilderness survival schools have ordeals been presented seriously as occasions of self-discovery. I first became interested in studying real-life survival stories as a way to make a course on the "Psychology of Adaptation, Coping, and Survival" more dramatic and more immediate. But as I read and studied more accounts of successful solitary copings, a theme of self-discovery, of discovering another part or side of the self, began to emerge. This theme was expressed in such a way that only Jung's model of the personality as made up of two sides seemed to fit.

In Jung's model the personality consists of a conscious aspect containing the persona, or social mask, and the conscious ego. The unconscious consists of a collective unconscious, containing a series of memories, or archetypes, inherited from antiquity, including the "anima," or female principle, in males, and the "animus," or male principle, in females. The unconscious also contains the shadow, or alter ego, consisting of a set of personality traits, needs, desires, and tendencies diametrically opposed to those of the conscious ego. Descriptions of solitary ordeals suggest that some people may have survived partly because they confronted their own unconscious shadow and other archetypes, gaining strength, guidance, and energy from them and setting in motion the "individuation process"—beginning to incorporate their two sides into a larger sense of the self that transcends the bipolar opposition between the conscious and the unconscious. The individuated person becomes both thinker and intuiter, both senser and feeler, both male and female, both good and bad, both an introvert and extrovert.

It is not news to report that isolated individuals under stress have hallucinations, nor is it original to interpret such hallucinations as expressions of unconscious material that has been released by fatigue and a lowering of psychic defenses. Hallucinations during isolated ordeals, however, seem to provide striking examples of Jung's particular construction of the unconscious as containing an other side or other self. For example, the language Lindbergh uses to describe how he sensed the presence of "others" during his solo flight seems explicitly to suggest many Jungian themes:

> While I'm staring at the instruments, during an unearthly age of time, both conscious and asleep, the fuselage behind me becomes filled with ghostly presences— vaguely outlined forms, transparent, moving, riding, weightless with me in the plane. I feel no surprise at their coming. There's no suddenness to their appearance. Without turning my head, I see them as clearly as though in my normal field of vision. There's no limit to my sight— my skull is one great eye, seeing everywhere at once.
>
> These phantoms speak with human voices—friendly, vapor-like shapes, without substance, able to vanish or appear at will, to pass in and out through the walls of the fuselage as though no walls were there. Now, many are crowded behind me. Now, only a few remain. First one and then another presses forward to my shoulder to speak above the engine's noise and then draws back among the group behind. At times, voices come out of the air itself, clear yet far away, traveling through distances that can't be measured by the scale of human miles; familiar voices, converging and advising on my flight, discussing problems of my navigation, reassuring me, giving me messages of importance unattainable in ordinary life.

> These spirits have no rigid bodies, yet they remain
> human in outline form—emanations from the experience
> of ages, inhabitants of a universe closed to mortal men.
> I'm on the border line of life and a greater realm be-
> yond, as though caught in the field of gravitation be-
> tween two planets, acted on by forces I can't control,
> forces too weak to be measured by any means at my
> command, yet representing powers incomparably
> stronger than I've ever known.[1]

Note the phrases "messages of importance unattainable in ordinary life," "emanations from the experience of ages," "inhabitants of a universe closed to mortal men." These are virtually definitions of what Jung termed "archetypes"—inherited memories from the Collective Unconscious. Lindbergh shows neither surprise nor fear at the appearance of these phantoms. Is he somehow better prepared than others might be for their appearance?

Some isolated individuals have experienced even more concrete images of human companions, with whom they actually converse and who not infrequently give them helpful advice or assistance. Dr. H. Lindemann reports that, while sailing single-handed, he imagined seeing a black man of whom he asked, and from whom he received, directions. Joshua Slocum, first man to sail alone around the world, describes coming on deck one night to confront a "foreign sailor [with a] threatening aspect" who had taken the wheel of his ship. The sailor identified himself as the pilot of Columbus's *Pinta*.

Robert Manry, who sailed the bathtub-sized *Tinkerbelle* across the Atlantic, confronted the ruler of a "kingdom of the sea . . . a crusty old Scotsman named MacGregor [accompanied by a] demonic choir . . . of gravel voiced killers." Later, Manry came upon a little elfin character who looked like "a cross between a leprechaun and Gunga Din." This figure told him that his trouble was that he had been sailing clockwise, and that if he wanted to get out of the sea kingdom he must sail counter-clockwise.

Two themes seem to stand out in the hallucinations characteristic of solitary survivors. One is the appearance of threatening shadowlike figures (Slocum's foreign sailor, Manry's evil MacGregor, Christiane Ritter's "dark form" [see Chapter Four]). The other is the appearance of archetypal, guiding figures (such as the phantoms who gave Lindbergh navigational advice, the "pilot of the *Pinta*" who "took the wheel" of

Slocum's ship, the "black man" who gave Lindemann directions, the Gunga Din-like figure confronted by Manry who gave the advice about sailing counterclockwise, and Simpson's *voice*).

If the conscious ego becomes worn down by prolonged stress, the "other person," or shadow-guide, can according to Jungian theory emerge from the dark realm beyond consciousness and temporarily take over the direction of adaptive behavior. When one (i.e., one's conscious ego) feels that he is in a detached, dreamlike state during some highly trying time, or if he has amnesia concerning how he covered miles of high-altitude technical rock climbing, it may be that he was *not* in charge, his unconscious shadow-guide was—first dimly perceived as a presence, then as a companion of some kind, later emerging as a guiding force. Considerable resourcefulness and strength for survival can thus be gained from one's "other side" during an ordeal. As a result, one may be a significantly changed person thereafter if one takes the next step of incorporating such other-side elements into a new, more balanced, and more complex personality.

People who may have become intrigued early in life by what lies on the other side of their natures may express this through the feeling that they have a "rendezvous with destiny," through an unfulfilled yearning for an unknown something out there, or through the belief that they are somehow destined to do something great and magnificent. They thus begin to seek a "quest." As Jung expressed it in *Modern Man in Search of a Soul*,[2] "the modern man has always been solitary." Thus these solitary explorers coping with ordeals and pondering their circumstances, and ultimately their own psyches, are in fact the archetypal modern man.

According to Jung, man not only seeks his own other side, he also seeks to return to personal and collective psychic roots and to immerse himself in something larger than his personal ego. Lindbergh seems to link this additional need to his yearning to experience "realms beyond." From his early life, Lindbergh dreamed of escaping to the sky from the limits of an earthbound existence:

> When I was a child on our Minnesota farm, I spent hours lying on my back in high timothy and redtop, hidden from passers-by, watching white cumulus clouds drift overhead, staring into the sky. It was a different world up there. You had to be flat on your back,

> screened in by grass stalks, to live in it. Those clouds,
> how far away were they? Nearer than the neighbor's
> house, untouchable as the moon—unless you had an
> airplane. How wonderful it would be, I'd thought, if I
> had an airplane—wings with which I could fly up to the
> clouds and explore their caves and canyons—wings
> like that hawk circling above me. Then I would ride on
> the wind and *be part of the sky*, [RDL] and acorns and
> bits of twigs would stop pressing into my skin. The
> question of danger didn't enter my dreams.[3]

"Ride on the wind and be part of the sky" suggests the wish to voyage to another realm, but it also suggests wanting to find a larger something to which to belong. (Elsewhere he mentions watching a parachutist who was "swaying with the wind, a part of it.") Part of the yearning here, then, is that of the lonely young boy who has been raised as a social isolate and loner to find something to become a part of. The yearning may also be that of modern man seeking to find and immerse himself once again in the *participation mystique* of the Collective Unconscious.

The desire earlier in life to be a part of something perhaps helped to set the stage for the desire to get out of the conscious self to realms beyond, and may have helped also to prepare Lindbergh to experience his in-flight "loss of self" experiences as harmony with the cosmos rather than destruction of identity. He was predisposed by early life desires of becoming part of the sky or wind to have feelings of cosmic unity under stress rather than becoming unglued by the experience. He had been seeking the feeling of harmony and oneness with the universe all along.

The following quotation from Byrd suggests the same interpretation:

> This [time alone at Advance Base] was a grand period;
> I was conscious only of a mind utterly at peace, a mind
> adrift the smooth, romantic tides of imagination, like a
> ship responding to the strength and purpose in the
> enveloping medium. A man's moments of serenity are
> few, but a few will sustain him a lifetime. I found my
> measure of inward peace then; the stately echoes lasted
> a long time. For the world then was like poetry—that
> poetry which is "emotion remembered in tranquility."

Perhaps this period was just the repeated pattern of my youth. [RDL] I sometimes think so. When I was growing up, I used to steal out of the house at night, and go walking in Glass's woods, which were a little way up the road from our place. In the heavy shadows of the Shenandoah Valley hills, the darkness was a little terrifying, as it always is to small boys; but, when I would pause and look up into the sky, a feeling that was midway between peace and exhilaration would seize me. . . .[4]

Byrd, sounding here very much like Lindbergh, makes it explicit that his childhood fascination with nature is the psychic precursor of his later feeling of cosmic unity at Advance Base. He also exemplifies a strikingly common phenomenon in the writings of solitary adventurers: the use of the oceanic metaphor (adrift—tides—ship) to describe their situations. The oceanic metaphor is peculiarly well suited to convey key aspects of the psychological quest of these adventurers, suggesting as it does the ideas of isolation (island, ship, etc.), the sought-after goal of an encompassing whole to which to belong (ocean, sea), and unity with the rhythms of nature (tides, adrift). It is also the ideal medium to underline the centrality of *navigation* (and the dominance of the navigator-guide archetype?) in the quest for "realms beyond."

The fact that Lindbergh, Byrd, Chichester, and others were seeking to discover their own psychic realms beyond and then harmonize the opposites within their own character is suggested repeatedly in their writings. Lindbergh hints that this integration is in fact happening during his solo flight when he feels he exists balanced between opposite poles within himself: "I'm on the borderline of life and a greater realm beyond, as though caught in the field of gravitation between two planets. . . ."[5]

The kinds of explorations Lindbergh, Byrd, and Chichester engaged in are perhaps also symbolically important. First, in exploring danger, new places, far horizons, fear, and death they actually sought their own other sides. Then they sought a balance between the two sides by also seeking a center—unity, wholeness, completion. Byrd, for instance, sought to go first to the North Pole and then to the South Pole—the balance points, the axis, the center of the world. Chichester first sought to fly, and then sailed, *around* the world—finishing where he had started—a circular act of completion and wholeness. (Chichester had earlier overcome cancer—another act of completion and wholeness.) Lindbergh sought to forge a connection between New York and Paris, on the opposite sides of the ocean (New York representing the male principle, Paris the female?)—another act of completion, of joining together of opposites. In later years, Lindbergh too was to fly around the world, more than once.

There may be an answer, then, from the Jungian point of view to the ancient question "Why do men climb mountains?" They are climbed because they have *summits,* which are center/balance points between opposites (earth and sky, worldly and spiritual) and are thus symbolic of the search for such balance within the self. The attainment of a summit is also an act symbolic of achieving personal *completion.* And finally, mountains, like endless numbers of other frontiers, have been tackled in order to find out what lies on the *other side* (the "realm beyond"). Consider

The compass as mandala or self-symbol.

space explorers who want to learn what is "out there"; deep sea divers wanting to know what is "down there"; spelunkers trying to discover what is "in there" in the dark recesses of caves; explorers who have sought long-lost gold mines and buried treasure, or been fascinated by the darkest depths of Africa, or sought the source of the Nile or the Mississippi "deep in the interior."

The reasons why Lindbergh, Byrd, and Chichester developed a genius for navigation and an obsession with finding their way must now be examined more deeply, for there were *two* uncharted unknowns into which they headed. One was the worldly, geographical realm beyond of their exploration, the other the personal realm beyond of their own psychic depths. They were embarked on a psychic navigation from the conscious sides of themselves and their isolated positions of incompleteness toward a more encompassing balance of their two sides within a larger wholeness. The word "encompassing" is more than appropriate, for the tool of their worldly navigation was the compass. Yet it is also the symbolic expression of their psychic navigation and of its ultimate goal, individuation and wholeness. For the compass, with its circular formation balanced on a center point and the four cardinal directions arrayed in balanced opposites, is what Jung terms a *mandala,* or self-symbol. And it is perhaps as perfect and simply elegant an example of a mandala as it is possible to find— the squared circle. It is the symbol of the quest of modern man in search of his soul, of the self become whole and complete, encompassing all of the opposites (good and evil, male and female, introverted and extroverted, thinking and feeling) that make up human nature in full. Mandalas are also termed "symbols of transformation," because they convey to us that we are prepared to become more whole.

Concerning mandala imagery, incidentally, consider again Robert Manry's hallucination: He first meets the violent, shadowlike MacGregor and his demonic choir, then the quiet, contemplative elfin/Gunga Din character who says that the way out is to sail counterclockwise. Manry first personifies what Jung would term the evil shadow complex in his unconscious—his own "other side"—and then meets a guidelike figure who invokes the mandalalike image of a circular clock face and indicates that the way out is to compensate for past activities by striking a balance between them. In other words, to Jung this second hallucination is a message from his unconscious telling him that he now has the opportunity to incorporate his unconscious into a larger and more complete conscious self.

The remaining question is, did the subjects of this character study indeed find their other sides through their solitary adventuring? Did opposite traits in fact emerge and then become integrated in their character?

Note how Chichester,[6] during one of his long solo voyages, begins to develop a set of maternal interests that balance his masculine adventuring interests:

> I found a handsome homing pigeon . . . on the foredeck. Pidgy . . . he was soon to be called. . . .[7]
>
> [I] contented myself with making his tent as snug as possible. I gave him a box full of muesli which was his favorite food (except for the raisins which he threw out, just as my son Giles does). . . .[8]
>
> June 15th. Pidge! Pidge! Pidge! He ruled my life then. Every morning I had to feed and water him as soon as I emerged . . . [then] I had to go around and clean up all of [his messes] . . . before getting to work on the ship. . . .[9]
>
> June 18th. I hit a head-on gale. . . .[10] I was getting very worried about Pidgy. He looked bare, wet and cold, and had whitish scabs around his eyes. I could not bear to see him looking so miserable. . . .[11]
>
> [After Pidgy drowns] I felt cut up as I held his soaking body; I felt responsible for him. . . . I squeezed his lungs . . . wrapped him in hot clothes . . . but it was no good.[12]

One is reminded by Chichester's caring for the pigeon after weeks alone of another famous isolated individual who did something very similar: Robert Stroud, the famous "Birdman of Alcatraz." Perhaps Stroud also managed to contact and to express his maternal side after years in isolation and to become a more complete, balanced individual. There is no question that Stroud, a convicted murderer, did undergo a major personality change.

In beginning to sum up Chichester's character, biographer Anita Leslie writes:

> Our only purpose in life [quoting Chichester], if we are able to say such a thing, is to put up the best performance we can—in anything—and only in doing so lies the satisfaction of living.

"In anything," he said, and he meant just that, "it is
the effort that counts, the perfections of individual performance." Success lay in pitting yourself and in not
failing through weakness or boredom. A worthwhile
aim must be found, but what is more worthwhile than
balancing [RDL] he had discovered in ways unlike those
of other men, he had needed color and danger to achieve
the exceptional. Fate had woven unusual stress into his
existence. He had *had* to try to do things differently, but
he was only beginning to realize the true value of
achievement—it was self-knowledge.[13]

Was Lindbergh at the young age of twenty-seven really on his way
to becoming an individuated person? The fact that he later in his life
delved fully into opposite, and to some incompatible, interests (the
maternal nurturing of the natural world through conservation and the
masculine problem solving of aircraft technology) suggests that he
might have been, although his seemingly pro-Nazi views during World
War II are problematic, to say the least. (Did they represent Lindbergh's
fuller experience of his own evil shadow complex?)

In these accounts the relative absence of clear anima (the archetypal
female) imagery indicates that the ordeals have not provoked the complete
individuation process. If these solitary figures had confronted more
female "others" in their hallucinations, this would have indicated a deeper
contact with their unconscious—i.e., confronting their female opposite
in their unconscious. Most of the people described apparently had not
yet confronted the anima and could not therefore incorporate it into
fully complete personalities. Another interpretation is that the anima
was present—in the form of the vessels (*Tinkerbelle, Gipsy Moth,* etc.)
used during the quests, or in the form of the sea.

Antoine de Saint-Exupéry, the French aviator and writer of *Wind,
Sand, and Stars,* after being rescued near death following a plane crash
and several days' wandering without food or water in the Libyan
desert, writes:

Once again I had found myself in the presence of
a great truth and had failed to recognize it. Consider
what had happened to me: I had thought myself lost,
had touched the very bottom of despair; and then,

when the spirit of renunciation had filled me, I had known peace. I know now that in such an hour a man feels that he has finally found himself and has become his own friend. An essential inner need has been satisfied, and against that satisfaction, that self-fulfillment, no external power can prevail.[14]

Knowing oneself and being complete is, in short, the ultimate coping mechanism. Wanting to know oneself and *become* complete keeps the human spark alive and accounts, I submit, for certain remarkable instances of successful coping and survival.

Saint-Exupéry concludes:

Truth is not that which can be demonstrated by the aid of logic. . . . If a particular religion, or culture, or scale of values, if one form of activity rather than another brings self-fulfillment to a man, *releases the prince asleep within him unknown to himself*, [RDL] then that scale of values, that culture, that form of activity, constitute his truth.[15]

Notes

[1] Lindbergh, p. 389.
[2] Jung, Carl Gustav. *Modern Man in Search of a Soul.* New York: Harcourt, Brace & World, 1933.
[3] Lindbergh, p. 244.
[4] Byrd, p. 144.
[5] Lindbergh, p. 389.
[6] Chichester, 1964.
[7] Chichester, 1964, p. 349.
[8] Chichester, 1964, p. 356.
[9] Chichester, 1964, p. 358.
[10] Chichester, 1964, p. 360.
[11] Chichester, 1964, p. 364.
[12] Chichester, 1964, p. 366.
[13] Leslie, pp. 172–173.
[14] Saint-Exupéry, p. 239.
[15] Saint-Exupéry, pp. 240–241.

CHAPTER EIGHT

The "Flow Experience": Coping Examined from a Humanistic Perspective

Many have argued that extreme ordeals of the kind described earlier are metaphors for life (cf. Viktor Frankl, 1963), with the difference that in ordeals life's fundamental issues stand out in higher relief. (I, of course, maintain that *solitary* ordeals are metaphors for modern solitary individualism.) Others (cf. Huizinga, 1970) have maintained that play is also a metaphor for life. While it may not be justified to conclude from the above that "extreme ordeals are a lot like play," that statement is in a sense what I propose to address in this chapter, in the particular form of detailing some striking similarities between the qualities of successful coping with adversity and the qualities of experiences that people find enjoyable.

Csikszentmihalyi's "flow experience" concept is the vehicle for linking the psychology of successful coping with the psychology of enjoyment. In his book *Beyond Boredom and Anxiety*,[1] Csikszentmihalyi describes the features of experiences that make them enjoyable. These include being able to (1) merge action and awareness, (2) center attention on a limited stimulus field, (3) lose oneself in one's activities, (4) control actions and the environment, (5) receive coherent demands for action, and (6) pursue activities that are self-rewarding. These traits might be reduced to three: getting "caught up" in what one is doing, controlling what is happening, and creating variety and stimulation so as to make activities novel and challenging enough to stay caught up in them. The concept of "flow" actually blends together many of the preceding coping mechanisms described in Chapter Five. Many play and recreational activities have these qualities; if the work experience has these qualities, then work too can be experienced as enjoyable.[2] Paradoxically, in that situation seemingly farthest removed from the enjoyable, the solitary prolonged survival ordeal, survivors also exhibit the flow experience. In fact, the description of the flow experience can be taken as one prescription for how to cope. One characteristic of individuals who manage to survive situations of prolonged hardship is that they arrange their situations and their activities so as to create the elements of flow experiences. Sir Geoffrey Jackson, writing about his many months as a captive of South American guerrillas, hints at this:

> Whether it is an original discovery I cannot say; but I
> have concluded that the captive requires two classes of
> routine, corresponding to two distinct human needs—
> the need to break up his day, and the need to fill up his
> day. I had already developed many such routines. . . . [3]

"Breaking up" one's day refers to the need for variety and stimulation; "filling up" one's day refers to occupying oneself. Both help create conditions for getting "caught up" in things to do. Establishing routines to achieve these ends provides the element of control over one's surroundings. Since the capability of getting caught up in doing something depends on a balance or match between environmental demands and individual capabilities,[4] a flow experience will not just "happen" when one is coping with an ordeal. Individuals may have to go to extraordinary lengths to create or find activities in which they can get caught up, that will provide control over their situation, and that will provide variety and stimulation. It is also true that some individuals who cope successfully are unusually capable of setting up flow experiences. (Edith Bone may be one such individual.) A key reason for their capability, to be addressed later in this chapter, is what might be termed a non-self-conscious or "instrumental" individualism, which enables some individuals to be highly capable observers of their surroundings and controllers of their actions.

They are able to get caught up in mental and/or physical activities precisely because they do not dwell on themselves.

Creating "Flow" in Solitary Ordeals

Christopher Burney[5] spent many months in solitary confinement as a prisoner of the Nazis during World War II. He gives the following examples of getting caught up in "flow." Forced to exist in highly limited circumstances, he creates flow by "making the most" of what was available. The following excerpt could fit well in the section on mental stimulation:

> If the reach of experience is suddenly confined, and we are left with only a little food for thought and feeling, we are apt to take the few objects that offer themselves and ask a whole catalogue of often absurd questions about them. Does it work? How? Who made it and of what? And, in parallel, when and where did I last see something like it and what else does it remind me of? [Note that this sets off a wide range of other associations in which to get caught up.] And if we are dissatisfied at the time, we repeat the series in the optative mood, making each imperfection in what we have at hand evoke a wish or an ideal. So we set in train a wonderful flow of combinations and associations in our minds, the length and complexity of which soon obscure its humble starting-point. . . . My bed, for example, could be measured and roughly classified with school beds or army beds, according to appearance and excepting the peculiarity of its being hinged to the wall. . . . Yet this bed retained a quality of bedness which summoned all my associations with all the beds I had ever known. . . . When I had done with the bed, which was too simple to intrigue me long, I felt the blankets, estimated their warmth, examined the precise mechanics of the window, the discomfort of the toilet (perversely, for its very presence was an unexpected luxury), computed the length and breadth, the orientation and elevation of the cell.[6]

Solzhenitsyn[7] relates the following ingenious example of mental self-stimulation in a fellow prisoner:

He resisted by striving to use his mind to calculate distances. In Lefortovo [prison] he counted steps, converted them into kilometers, remembered from a map how many kilometers it was from Moscow to the border, and then how many across all Europe, and how many across the Atlantic Ocean. He was sustained in this by the hope of returning to America. And in one year in Lefortovo solitary he got, so to speak, halfway across the Atlantic. Thereupon they took him to Sukhanovka. Here, realizing how few would survive to tell of it—he invented a method of measuring the cell. The numbers 10/22 were stamped on the bottom of his prison bowl, and he guessed that "10" was the diameter [in centimeters] of the bottom and "22" the diameter of the outside edge. Then he pulled a thread from a towel, made himself a tape measure, and measured everything with it.[8]

Papillon,[9] in solitary confinement in the penal colony in French Guiana, created out of a devastating prospect a mental activity in which he became caught up:

One year equals three hundred and sixty-five days; two years, seven hundred and thirty days, unless one's a leap year. I smiled at the thought. One day more wouldn't matter much. The hell it would not. One day more is twenty-four hours more. And twenty-four hours is a long time. And seven hundred and thirty days each made up into twenty-four hours is one hell of a lot more. How many hours does that make? Can I figure it in my head? No, I can't; it's impossible. Why, of course, it's possible. Let's see. A hundred days, that's twenty four hundred hours. Multiplied by seven—it's easy—it makes sixteen thousand eight hundred, plus seven hundred and twenty which makes, if I haven't made a mistake, seventeen thousand five hundred and twenty hours. My dear Mr. Papillon, you have seventeen thousand five hundred and twenty hours to kill in this cage with its smooth walls especially designed for wild animals. And how many minutes? Who gives a shit!

Hours is one thing, but minutes? To hell with minutes.
Why not seconds? What does it matter? What matters
is that I furnish these days, hours, and minutes with
something, all by myself, alone![10]

At the end of this mental exercise, Papillon recognizes that he must continue to create additional ones. And he does so, over many days and months.

Solitary confinement deprives one of one of the most precious features of a fulfilling life—freedom. Yet, paradoxically, a key feature of the flow experience, a state in which people *feel* so free, is "centering attention on a limited stimulus field," a major feature of confinement. Not only does a confined setting make it possible to center one's attention on a limited physical field, it can also "clear the decks" mentally (recall Bone's comments in this regard) and give one the opportunity to focus on a particular topic, such as Burney's bed or Papillon's mathematical calculations.

If flow represents the kind of state that many who seek "freedom" desire to experience, then perhaps Frankl's[11] contention that he found freedom in the concentration camp is not so incredible, since he was able to create and experience flow despite all of his confinement, hardship, and suffering.

Furthermore, some who seem to be good at creating "flow" in their lives seem to seek out Spartan situations rather than "enriched" ones. Charles Lindbergh,[12] for example, gave this enlightening account of his view of the cockpit of the *Spirit of St. Louis:*

My cockpit is small, and its walls are thin; but inside this cocoon I feel secure, despite the speculations of my mind. It makes an efficient, tidy home, one so easy to keep in order that its *very simplicity creates a sense of satisfaction and relief.* [RDL] It's a personal home, too—nobody has ever piloted the *Spirit of St. Louis,* but me. Flying in it is like living in a hermit's mountain cabin after being surrounded by the luxury and countless responsibilities of a city residence. Here, I'm conscious of all elements of weather, immersed in them, dependent on them. Here the earth spreads out beyond my window, its expanse and beauty offered at the cost of a glance. Here, are

no unnecessary extras, only the barest essentials [RDL] of
life and flight. There are no letters to get off in the next
mail, no telephone bells to ring, no loose odds and ends to
attend to in some adjoining room. The few furnishings
are within arm's length, and all in order.

A cabin that flies through the air, that's what I live in;
a cabin higher than the mountains, a cabin in the
clouds and sky. After much travail, I've climbed up to
it. Through months of planning, I've equipped it with
utmost care. Now, I can relax in its solitary vantage
point, and let the sun shine, and the westwind blow,
and the blizzard come with the night.[13]

Because flow is largely an active state that we make for ourselves, it
may be easier to create if, as Lindbergh indicates, one is not freighted
with too many "things" to distract and diffuse one's attention. This
environment, which he stresses is *his* space, he can control.

Lindbergh (like Burney and Papillon) makes the most of his confined
surroundings and soon is caught up in what there is to attend to. He
gets so caught up he almost seems to insinuate himself into the very
molecules of his plane, recalling Burney's close attention to his bed:

I become minutely conscious of details in my cockpit—
of the instruments, the levers, the angles of construction.
Each item takes on new values. I study weld marks on
the tubing (frozen ripples of steel through which pass
invisible hundred-weights of strain), a dot of radiolite
paint on the altimeter's face (whose only mission is to
show where the needle should ride when the *Spirit of
St. Louis* is 2,000 feet above the sea), the battery of fuel
valves (my plane and my life depend on the slender
stream of liquid flowing through them, like blood in
human veins)—all such things, which I never considered
much before, are now obvious and important. And
there's plenty of time to notice them. I may be flying a
complicated airplane, rushing through space, but in this
cabin I'm surrounded by simplicity and thoughts set
free of time.[14]

After many hours of involvement in flying his plane and in pursuing various lines of thought, Lindbergh toward the end of his flight relates the following statement of what it is like to get caught up, and of another feature of flow, the "loss of ego." He describes the flow experience precisely:

> It's been like a theater where the play carries you along in time and place until you forget you're only a spectator. You grow unaware of the walls around you, of the program clasped in your hand, even of your body, its breath, pulse, and being. You live with the actors and the setting, in a different age and place. It's not until the curtain drops that consciousness and body reunite.[15]

Others who have managed to survive some of the most horrible ordeals imaginable also talk of a flowlike loss of ego. Admiral Richard Byrd,[16] for example, describes an ordeal of isolation, cold, starvation, and living in a black void that is almost beyond comprehension. Yet he created for himself rituals, schedules, and activities in which to get caught up, and he was able one day to experience the following:

> The day was dying, the night being born—but with great peace. Here were the imponderable processes and forces of the cosmos, harmonious and soundless. Harmony, that was it! That was what came out of the silence—a gentle rhythm, the strain of a perfect chord, the music of the spheres perhaps.
> It was enough to catch that rhythm, momentarily to be myself a part of it. In that instant I could feel no doubt of man's oneness with the universe.[17]

The preceding excerpts seem to illustrate, and to be well summarized by, the following quote from Csikszentmihalyi:[18]

> The ability to control the environment by limiting the stimulus field, finding clear goals and norms, and developing appropriate skills—is one side of the flow experience. The other side, paradoxically, is a feeling which seems to make the sense of control irrelevant.

> Many of the people we interviewed, especially those
> who must enjoy whatever they are doing, mentioned
> that *at the height of their involvement with the activity they*
> *lose a sense of themselves as separate entities, and feel har-*
> *mony and even a merging of identity with the environment.*[19]
> [RDL]

Csikszentmihalyi's final sentence describes precisely what happens to many people who are dealing effectively with solitary ordeals, as we have previously discussed when considering the loss-of-ego reactions.

The final question concerns the kind of person who manages to create "flow experiences" under adversity and use them as coping devices. Since the flow experience involves the virtually total absence of self-awareness, might it be inferred that those who are not absorbed in self-contemplation would be in a better position to get caught up in what they are doing? Most of the list of characteristics of the flow experience imply that during flow the self exists non-dualistically simply as "I"—acting, controlling, attending, observing, but *not reflecting* on itself. The "me" (i.e., one's awareness of oneself) is absent when one is caught up. Even self-rewarding activities where one is rewarded by feedback are experienced non-dialectically rather than reflexively: In the moment of the act, the *doing* is the sheer pleasure, not the self-conscious awareness of "what it does for me."

The above point is essentially that made by Frankl[20] in his concept of *dereflection.* Although he addresses the concept primarily as a means to improve sexual encounters, he clearly implies application much beyond that when he says: "Instead of observing and watching [one]self, [one] should forget himself."[21] It is noteworthy that such insights of Frankl's originated in the confinement of a concentration camp.

Other traits that follow from non-self-conscious individualism include being a "seeker." Of course, that which is subject (the seeker) must, ultimately, have its object (the "sought"). Thus many non-self-conscious individualists still are "looking for something" and have goals toward which they strive. To take one example, Lindbergh all his life was fascinated by "realms beyond," leading him to become a trail-blazing aviator.

The ultimate goal that many an adventurer sought was, in the old cliché, to know her or him*self* (as object). If that was the ultimate goal, why then have I maintained that concern with self as object is maladaptive in coping? The answer is found, among other places, in hundreds of ancient myths that convey the deep human significance of the "quest" (cf. Odysseus). (And many quests were solitary ordeals par excellence, full of all kinds of arduous trials.) "Finding" the self requires a very long period of seeking by the self-as-subject. Jung's theory, for example, hinges precisely on that point: The Self is never truly known until (if at all) late in life. Such could also be said of Maslow's theory: One can only become "self-actualized" after all of one's other needs have been met. Perhaps, then, the problem so many people who are "caught up" in them*selves* have in coping with adversity is that in our inward-looking, narcissistic age *we have fostered a far too premature concern with the self-as-object*—as something to be searched for, "gotten in touch with"—leading to (among other things) the need to use *artificial* means (drugs) to create flowlike "highs." Do the same kinds of challenging experiences that non-narcissistic individuals convert into flow merely "hassle" the narcissistic, who rather than feeling challenged feel victimized? Maybe a far longer apprenticeship in questing, building, and being caught up in the world needs to precede getting caught up in oneself. Successful survivors do seem to teach us that lesson.

While it may be that individualists who are not very self-conscious can enter into flow experiences more readily, it might also be true that those who are too immersed in themselves may be most in *need* of flow experiences to compensate for that overinvolvement in self.

Ordeals, then, are more than metaphors for life. They are lessons *about* life. Jackson's observation about the need to break up and fill up one's day applies to more than the "captive," just as Frankl's work does. Lindbergh's enthusiasm for being in the sparest of surroundings, and the extent to which this spareness enables him to become caught up in flow, I think speaks volumes about the dependency of those who live as "me" on material things to occupy, distract, and stimulate them. The "I," on the other hand, can fill up whatever blank slate is set before it, and in fact yearns to do so. James Lester,[22] speculating about what drives people into arduous and risky adventures, observes: "whenever I think about reasons for such activities [specifically, mountain climbing] I always return to the notion of a desire to *pare life down to something essential*, [RDL] and thereby to experience living more wholly and more intensely. That requires a focusing of attention, and a wholeheartedness of purpose."[23]

The solitary ordeal as explored in this book also tells us about the solitary ordeal of everyday life—i.e., the fact that so many today find the simple fact of being *alone* a great ordeal. (For an eloquent statement on the virtues of solitariness, I recommend Anthony Storr's[24] book *Solitude*, the subtitle of which, incidentally, is *A Return to the Self*.) Perhaps the solitariness of ordinary modern life is a hardship because we dwell on ourselves so much that we can't get into a flow experience. In fact, we even say it that way: "I just don't know what to do *with myself.*" The challenge to create flow in spare and limited conditions is not just the condition of the captive, then, but of the ordinary "lonely" individual caught up in boring routine; indeed, such has been said by existentialists to be the modern human condition. The experiences of those who have undergone solitary ordeals remind us that any challenge can lead to a fulfilling experience, if we sense that we are subjects and instrumental agents in the world.

Here I must digress into a consideration of Erikson's[25] concept of identity, since what I have termed the "sense of self" is central and Erikson speaks to this issue. Since Erikson's "psychosocial" personality theory focuses on the relationship between the ego, or self, and society, it would seem to follow that significant changes in the surrounding cultural environment might alter somewhat the essential nature of ego identity formation. I propose that we have gone through (or are going through) a change in fundamental life-style orientation in American society that may be significant enough to have such an effect. A major feature of that change has been a shift from a life style dominated by production and work to a life style increasingly dominated by consumption and leisure. Concomitantly, there has been a shift from living and working for the future to seeking more self-expression and self-fulfillment in the here and now.[26]

One reason for my suggesting another look at Erikson's "Identity" concept is that his conception seems to resonate with the first life style far more than with the second. For instance, when Erikson[27] first used the concept of Identity, he termed it "Occupational Identity"—linking it firmly to work and a productive role for the individual. Furthermore, Identity was built upon Industry, the instrumental skills acquired in middle childhood. There was thus a strong *instrumental* flavor to his conception of how the individual formed an identity—one worked at it; one constructed an identity as an agent and non-victim. This instrumentality is also a hallmark of the preceding stages upon which Identity is built, and stands out in their very labels: *Initiative, Industry*. The individual, though influenced by society, was seen by Erikson as an instrumental force in the world and an instrumental force in the building of an identity, or sense of self, from early childhood. This instrumentality works against the tendency to think of the self as a passive victim of the world, and many successful survivors seem to have found ways to maintain this instrumental stance in relation to the world, as was discussed in Chapter Five.

Cultural support for the formation of such an instrumental identity seems to have declined. Not only has instrumentality declined in the surrounding culture in general (more consumption, more service, less direct involvement in production), the young also have been more completely separated (in most schools, for example) from those instrumental work and production activities that do exist in the adult world. Are "creativity" and "imagination" in the Initiative stage of early to middle childhood as instrumental as an earlier era's preparation of young children for future work roles through training in basic skills? Is today's "school-work" for the Industry-aged child as instrumental as chores and apprenticeship? There also seems to have been a recent trend in education (which reflects general life-style changes) toward favoring the expressive (creativity) over the instrumental (basic skills). Many successful survivors seem to have identified with the more instrumental life style.

The fact that living for the present seems to have somewhat supplanted living for the future has weakened the sense of historical continuity (as have mobility and further removal from tradition). Also, the increasing separation of age groups from each other has led increasingly to the experiencing of ages in the life cycle as *ways* of life (e.g., "childhood," "youth") rather than as rungs on the continuous ladder of life. These factors, coupled with the general life-style change toward living for the present, result in a heightened awareness of one's separateness and uniqueness in the world—one is less embedded in the continuous flow of history and the life cycle. This new kind of self-awareness, combined with the decline in instrumentality, has meant that concern with one's *existence* in the present has begun to take precedence over making something of oneself for the future. Looking *from* the self toward the future has given way to looking *for* the self in the present, an exercise that is doomed to failure. An "existential identity" has begun to replace the earlier instrumental identity. "Seeking," "finding," or "discovering" an identity has begun to replace "building" an identity—"be yourself" rather than "make something of yourself." In effect, self-as-instrumentality has begun to give way to self-as-object (or in economic terms, self-as-consumer has begun to replace self-as-producer). Rather than feeling like a builder and maker, the self has begun to feel it is on the *receiving* end of experience and the world.

What I am proposing is not simply that there has been an increase in identity uncertainty, which may actually be the case, but that there has been a change in the manner in which identity uncertainty is sought to be resolved. We can see the new identity style of seeking self-as-object at many points in current popular culture: in the "me" generation, and in the search for "my gut feelings"; in concern with my "body," my "head," my "parent/adult/child"; in the emphasis on self as "best friend," and in the self as *object* of contemplation, stimulation, and affection. We talk now of what technology does to us, rather than of how we build technology. In *Future Shock,* Alvin Toffler[28] describes the future as "coming at us" rather than as something we move toward. We are *result* rather than *cause;* victim rather than victor.

Perhaps still other trends and tendencies also bespeak this new identity style. For example, in an era of an instrumental self, building an identity is something that one either *succeeded* at or *failed* at. (Failure meant either identity diffusion or adopting a negative identity. A negative identity meant taking on the role of an instrumental rebel.) What replaces the success-failure dimension in an era of existential identity? If one senses that he or she is both unique and on the receiving end in life, perhaps the sense of failure is replaced by the sense of self-as-*victim.* Rather than being a failure in the world, one is now a victim of the world. (A negative identity here would mean taking on the role of "dropout.")

There does seem to be a "psychology of the victim" abroad today. In fact, some youths seem to *define* themselves as victims (consider the "punk" movement, for example), many drug abusers seem to be making themselves into victims, and there is of course the constant use of the term "hassle" among youth. There is also Charlie Brown, the archetypal victim of life and the world.

The rise of minorities and the handicapped in the public consciousness may also be due partly to the same "psychology of the victim." Rather than compassion motivating concern for the plights of minorities and handicapped people, could it be that they exquisitely symbolize the "self-as-victim-of-the-world"?

At the other pole, what replaces the sense of self-as-instrumental success? Could it be a sense of self-as-*beneficiary?* To what extent is becoming a beneficiary of the world the goal of contemporary identity seeking? There is much talk about receiving "unconditional strokes," and I note that Joseph Pearce[29] argues that a "natural plan" exists within us which we simply have to let unfold in order to be fulfilled. The fact that it is so commonplace today for some to view the child as the archetype for a healthy style of life, and to speak of discovering the "child" within them, also suggests a kind of "psychology of the beneficiary," since a child is generally cared and provided for by others.

For those for whom the self is primarily object ("me," consumer) there is a preexisting tendency even prior to an ordeal to regard oneself as on the receiving end of life and the world—to regard oneself as at least victim in potentia. Many who are hardly oppressed objectively (especially compared to one like Frankl) nonetheless feel "hassled" by life. In the profoundly real adversity of the concentration camp or other ordeal, would these people ever be able to free themselves from the orientation that "this is all happening to *me*" and go on actively to create flow? The self-as-subject or agent, however, cannot be victimized because it offers no target/object. Only an object in the world can be a victim of it. Here is one way of grasping the "secret" of Bruno Bettelheim, Viktor Frankl, Lindbergh, and thousands of other survivors of ordeals: Those who sense themselves primarily as subjects always have a built-in detachment from the victimization of themselves in the stance as *observer*. Bettelheim[30] in fact says that it was primarily through observing and analyzing his surroundings that he was able to cope. As subject he saw things in which he could get "caught up" intellectually. Frankl wrote, paradoxically, of the *freedom* he discovered in the concentration camp; perhaps it was the irreducible freedom of the self-as-subject. Those whose essence is that of the "non-victim" are the ones most capable of coping with ordeals by entering into the non-self-conscious state of the flow experience.

Notes

[1] San Francisco: Jossey-Bass, 1975.
[2] Csikszentmihalyi, 1975.
[3] Jackson, p. 110.
[4] Csikszentmihalyi, 1975.
[5] Burney, 1952.
[6] Burney, pp. 16–18.
[7] Solzhenitsyn, 1975.
[8] Solzhenitsyn, p. 182.
[9] Charriere, 1970.
[10] Charriere, p. 219.
[11] Frankl, 1963.
[12] Lindbergh, 1953.
[13] Lindbergh, pp. 227–228.
[14] Lindbergh, p. 228.
[15] Lindbergh, p. 466.
[16] Byrd, 1938.
[17] Byrd, p. 85.
[18] Csikszentmihalyi, 1975.
[19] Csikszentmihalyi, p. 194.
[20] Frankl, 1978.
[21] Frankl, 1978, p. 152.
[22] Lester, James. "Wrestling with the Self on Mt. Everest." *Journal of Humanistic Psychology*, 23, 2 (1983), pp. 31–41.
[23] Lester, p. 40.
[24] Storr, Anthony. *Solitude*. New York: The Free Press, 1988.
[25] Erikson, 1963.
[26] Logan, R.D., and O'Hearn, G.T. "Thought-Style and Life-Style: Some Hypothesized Relationships." *Science Education*, 66, 4 (1982).
[27] Erikson, 1963.
[28] Toffler, Alvin. *The Third Wave*. New York: Bantam, 1980.
[29] Pearce, Joseph. *The Magical Child*. New York: Bantam, 1977.
[30] Bettelheim, 1943.

CHAPTER NINE

Conclusion

I wanted, as much as possible in this book, to let the survivors speak for themselves. Since I have followed their lead, this has by no means been a comprehensive study. Many aspects of the effects of ordeals and means of coping with them have not been covered, I am sure. (I know, for example, that humor—dark humor, gallows humor—is an important coping mechanism, and that survivors mention relying on it a great deal, but I ran across very few good specific examples of the use of humor.) This book has been put together around opportunity targets discovered in the literature, with a loose conceptual framework. I have not attempted, for example, to look systematically at the differences in coping that occur across different kinds of solitary ordeals. I have been more interested in similarities; but, obviously, the solitary captive is not in the same situation as someone adrift on a life raft, and both of those situations are different from those of the beleaguered solo mountaineer, the isolated plane crash survivor, and the solitary adventurer. Furthermore, this work has been slanted toward "the good things that people manage to do when bad things happen to them." "Good" here has two meanings, one pertaining to effective coping, the other to the moral character of many survivors. In some cases people gained strength from the moral principles they had in the first place; in others, they became—many of them—better people as a result of their ordeals. Obviously, people also do bad things, in both of the same senses, during extreme situations.

These are inspiring, moving, uplifting, and dramatic tales, and they contain some insights (which I admit I have not fully exploited) into "human nature." The stories tend to validate, for example, the contention that we thrive in some sense on adversity and challenge—that surviving external adversity is something that we have evolved to be "good at." How well could the millions of years of evolution have prepared us for the introspection and self-reflection that has only in recent centuries come into the human experience?

These survival tales also serve as a reminder that human psychology, across a wide range of theories about the nature of human nature, is all about adapting and surviving. In that sense, survival situations are not unique, but only more extreme illustrations of human adaptability.

Another and powerful point is simply that we can endure a lot. It is absolutely extraordinary what some survivors have gone through, and we are right to admire them. But we ought to remember how "ordinary" some of these survivors were prior to their ordeals—ordinary enough to inspire the most provincial of us who read about them. Many of us could do as well if required to.

It is also striking that a solitary ordeal, depending on its nature, can be paradoxically freeing, both to the mind and (as Frankl would maintain) to the spirit. Even the most confining of situations do provide surprising scope for one to be mentally instrumental (excluding situations of chronic torture and/or excruciating pain). We really do need very little in order to survive, both in terms of material necessities and in the form of ready-made things to occupy and stimulate us; we can if required generate our own mental stimulation.

Another way to say this is that solitary ordeals can provide scope for the "flow experience"—the opportunity to generate mental activities in which one can get caught up. Bone, Burney, and Jackson seem to have been especially good at this (interestingly, they are all British, a people who have long thrived on "making do" and uncomplainingly carrying on through adversity). One can, at least in some instances, even have a surprisingly full life during an ordeal, Edith Bone being a prime example. We can do astonishingly much with extremely little—if we have the right (i.e., active) mental attitude. Odd that solitary sufferers have to be the ones to remind us about our overdependence on material things.

We do best in an ordeal at getting caught up in flow states if we dwell not on ourselves but on generating and getting engrossed in intellectually stimulating, problem-solving activities of various sorts that keep us engaged in the world, or, more importantly, that keep us engaged in activities themselves. (When the activity becomes the focus, the difference between the self and the world is literally nonexistent.) Thinking about oneself works against the creation of the flow experience and all of its benefits.

We humans are resourceful beyond belief. We have a lot of coping devices at our disposal, as I have tried to suggest in Chapter Five. We also have, if we can contact them, the resources of our own *unconscious* (whether as described by Freud in terms of repressed energy available to be mobilized in a crisis, or as described by Jung in terms of hidden wisdom into which we can tap), plus the numerous things we can generate consciously from our memories, skills, will power, and intellectual abilities. For example, we are all, to one degree or another, walking encyclopedias of life experiences. As psychoanalysts would also point out, we need not in the end fear our unconscious—it is another vast resource that can be called upon in extremity.

One of the more interesting phenomena in ordeals, as described by survivors themselves, is the "splitting" of the self in intense situations. Many actually use the word "splitting," referring sometimes to the detachment from themselves they feel during a moment of crisis; sometimes to the fact of talking to oneself and giving oneself orders; sometimes to the disembodied voice/element of spirit that seems to come from *outside*—the "something else that steps out of the background and takes command" (Lindbergh). Many survivors in their accounts distinguish all of the above aspects of the self from the "mind," which carries on independently, and of course from the body and/or from their emotions. The ordeal experience indicates that the "self" that we take for granted in our ordinary consciousness is in fact a complex, multidimensional, and mutable proposition.

Ordeals are also ideal (I realize the paradox in using this word) situations for self-discovery—for realizing what one is capable of, recalling one's own rich mental history, and uncovering the depth and breadth of one's own unconscious, personified perhaps in the form of the "others" that so commonly appear. The only rational explanation from within the field of psychology for the appearance of "others" during solitary ordeals is that they come from the unconscious—either representing Jungian archetypes or based on images of others (or perhaps composites of many others) from our own past. A "guiding figure," for example, or a disembodied authoritative voice could be based on the long-ago memory of a guiding parent. Interestingly, while these "others" are occasionally frightening, at least initially, they are far more often comforting by their presence, if not downright helpful to the beleaguered solitary soul. This makes the point even more directly that we need not fear our unconscious. It is largely our ignorance of it that makes it fearful to us.

Survivors therefore do get to know themselves much more fully when forced to rely on their own devices. And the prospect of still greater self-discovery can become an additional motive for keeping up the survival struggle.

Another powerful lesson taught by those who have suffered far more terribly than 99 percent of us is that we are not victims unless we choose to think of ourselves that way. It is Frankl's challenging thesis that we can choose how we react even to the cruelty of others and to the suffering it causes. If we have gotten into the habit of living life passively, then we may become more likely to think this way. Successful survivors, however, remain identified as instrumental subjects—and they all manage to remain active *in some way* in dealing with their predicament, always seeking through various means to do what they can to alter, affect, and redefine their situation, rather than allowing the situation to define them.

While Frankl would maintain that it is up to each one of us to create a meaningful life—in an ordeal as much as in "ordinary" life—it is also strikingly clear from the study of solitary ordeals that we also need *others!* This point is made very compellingly by the fact that so many individuals who are facing extreme adversity when utterly alone come to feel that they have companion(s)—whether sensing a compelling "presence" of some sort (Mawson, Ritter, Tiira), hearing an authoritative voice that gives commands (Elder, Simpson), vaguely feeling that "someone else" is close by assisting just beyond one's direct sight (Lindbergh), or actually seeing and even conversing directly with what appear to be other real human beings (Slocum, Manry).

Although it is not necessarily the recommended way to accomplish this, ordeals can also bring out our "better self"—they can enlarge our sense of who we are. By exposing us to extremes of the human condition, the ordeal enables one to build an identity based on a wider foundation of experience. Having experienced the extremes, survivors may find it easier to find the balancing midpoint between their masculinity and femininity, their anger and their fears, their goodness and their badness, their introversion and their extroversion. Ordeals also enable us to con-tact and incorporate the vast resources of our unconscious. Many ordeals can be, in the end, highly "positive" experiences.

Finally, I am struck by two metaphors. One is that of the solitary *adventurer*, a powerful metaphor for the modern individual seeking to find his or her way in the world. The other is that of the solitary involuntary *sufferer*, whose ordeal and the issues it raises stand as a powerful metaphor for the trials and tribulations of all solitary modern individuals. If these survivors can hack it, then surely the rest of us can too.

Bibliography

Best, Herbert. *Parachute to Survival*. New York: John Day Co., 1964.

Bettelheim, Bruno. "Individual and Mass Behavior in Extreme Situations." *Journal of Abnormal and Social Psychology* 38, 1943, pp. 417–452.

Bickel, Lennard. *Mawson's Will*. New York: Stein & Day, 1977.

Bombard, Alain. *Voyage of the Heretique*. New York: Simon & Schuster, 1954.

Bone, Edith. *7 Years' Solitary*. New York: Harcourt, Brace, Jovanovich, 1957.

Buhl, Hermann. *Lonely Challenge*. New York: E. P. Dutton, 1956.

Burney, Christopher. *Solitary Confinement*. London: Macmillan, 1952.

Byrd, Richard. *Alone*. New York: Putnam, 1938.

Callahan, Steven. *Adrift: 76 Days at Sea*. Boston: Houghton Mifflin, 1986.

Charriere, Henri. *Papillon*. Leicester: Ulverscroft, 1970.

Chichester, Sir Francis. *Gipsy Moth Circles the Globe*. New York: Coward-McCann, 1967.

———. *The Lonely Sea and the Sky*. London: Pan Books Ltd., 1964.

Cooke, Kenneth. *What Cares the Sea?* New York: McGraw-Hill, 1960.

Csikszentmihalyi, Mihalyi. *Flow Experience*. New York: Harper & Row, 1988.

———. *Beyond Boredom and Anxiety*. San Francisco: Jossey-Bass, 1975.

Dean, William F. *General Dean's Story*. New York: Viking Press, 1954.

Elder, Lauren. *And I Alone Survived*. New York: E. P. Dutton, 1978.

Erikson, Erik. *Childhood and Society*. New York: W. W. Norton, 1963.

Frankl, Viktor. *Man's Search for Meaning*. New York: Washington Square Press, 1963.

———. *The Unheard Cry for Meaning*. New York: Simon & Schuster, 1978.

Gallmann, Kuki. *I Dreamed of Africa*. New York: Penguin, 1991.

Greenwald, Michael. *Survivor*. San Diego: Blue Horizons Press, 1989.

Hamilton, Michelle. *A Mighty Tempest*. Texas: Word, Inc., 1992.

Hansell, Norris. *The Person-in-Distress*. New York: Human Sciences Press, 1976.

Hoyt, Edwin P. *The Last Explorer: The Adventures of Admiral Byrd*. New York: The John Day Company, 1968.

Huizinga, Johan. *Homo Ludens*. New York: Harper & Row, 1970.

Jackson, Geoffrey. *Surviving the Long Night*. New York: Vanguard, 1974.

Janis, Irving. *Stress and Frustration*. New York: Harcourt, Brace, Jovanovich, 1971. [Includes story of Don O'Daniel.]

Jung, Carl Gustav. *Modern Man in Search of a Soul*. New York: Harcourt, Brace & World, 1933.

Leslie, Anita. *Francis Chichester: A Biography*. New York: Walker, 1975.

Lester, James. "Wrestling with the Self on Mt. Everest." *Journal of Humanistic Psychology*, 23, 2 (1983): 31–41.

Lewis, David. *Ice Bird*. New York: W. W. Norton, 1975.

Lindbergh, Charles. *The Spirit of St. Louis*. New York: Scribner, 1953.

Logan, Richard D., and George T. O'Hearn. "Thought-Style and Life-Style." *Science Education* 66, 4 (1982).

Manry, Robert. *Tinkerbelle*. New York: Harper & Row, 1966.

Martin, Martha. *O Rugged Land of Gold*. Leicester: Ulverscroft, 1953.

Noyce, Wilfrid. *The Springs of Adventure*. New York: World Publishing Co., 1958.

———. *They Survived*. New York: E. P. Dutton, 1963.

Pearce, Joseph. *The Magical Child*. New York: Bantam, 1977.

Read, Pears P. *Alive: The Story of the Andes Plane Crash Survivors*. New York: Lippincott, 1974.

Reno, Janet. *Ishmael Alone Survived*. Lewisburg: Bucknell University Press, 1990.

Riesman, David. *The Lonely Crowd*. New Haven: Yale, 1950.

Risner, Robinson. *The Passing of the Night*. New York: Ballantine Books, 1973.

Ritter, Christiane. *A Woman in the Polar Night*. New York: E. P. Dutton, 1954.

Saint-Exupéry, Antoine de. *Wind, Sand, and Stars*. New York: Cornwall, 1939.

Sayre, Woodrow W. *Four against Everest*. New Jersey: Prentice-Hall, 1964.

Simpson, Joe. *Touching the Void*. New York: Harper & Row, 1988.

Smith, George. *Solo Cruise on the Coral Sea*. New York: Vantage Press, 1970.

Solzhenitsyn, Alexander. *The Gulag Archipelago*. New York: Harper & Row, 1973.

Stoker, H. G. "The Fourth Man." In *On the Run: Escaping Tales*, edited by H. C. Armstrong. London: Rich & Cowan, 1934.

Storr, Anthony. *Solitude*. New York: The Free Press, 1988.

Tiira, Ensio. *Raft of Despair*. London: Hutchinson, 1954. New York: E. P. Dutton, 1954.

Toffler, Alvin. *The Third Wave*. New York: Bantam, 1980.

White, Robert. "Motivation Reconsidered: The Concept of Competence." *Psychological Review* 66 (1959): 297–333.